"Connecting to the presence within absence of the deceased can be the saving grace for the bereaved, and yet a comprehensive text on this critical topic has been lacking. Brimming with theoretical and clinical wisdom, this book offers a unique and powerful combination of sociocultural, religious, and intrapsychic perspectives to broaden our understanding of the value of connecting to the presence of the deceased and how it may be therapeutically cultivated to console grievers."

— **Wendy Lichtenthal, PhD,** *assistant attending psychologist and director of the Bereavement Clinic at the Memorial Sloan Kettering Cancer Center Evelyn H. Lauder Breast Center*

"This book is destined to become a landmark contribution to the field of thanatology. Human beings have always found ways to stay connected to their deceased loved ones—what Burke and Rynearson term 'presence within absence,' and what others have called maintaining continuing bonds and after-death communications. *The Restorative Nature of Ongoing Connections with the Deceased: Exploring Presence within Absence* offers us a contemporary view of this enduring human phenomenon. It covers perspectives from all the major world religions, and it provides in-depth discussions of the clinical and research implications of the presence-within-absence phenomenon. I believe that this volume is on the cutting-edge of an important future direction in thanatology. As such, it ought to be read by anyone interested in role of the presence-within-absence experience in the healing process of grief recovery."

— **John R. Jordan, PhD,** *clinical psychologist in private practice in Pawtucket, Rhode Island, and coauthor of* Attachment-Informed Grief Therapy: The Clinician's Guide to Foundations and Applications

The Restorative Nature of Ongoing Connections with the Deceased

The Restorative Nature of Ongoing Connections with the Deceased is a guide to stimulating thought and discussion about ongoing attachments between bereaved individuals and their deceased loved ones.

Chapters promote broad, inclusive training and dialogue for working with clients who establish and/or maintain a restorative connection with their deceased loved one as well as those who find aspects of such connections to be psychologically or spiritually problematic or troublesome.

Bereavement professionals will come away from this book with a better understanding and a deeper skillset for helping clients to develop continuing bonds.

Laurie A. Burke, PhD, is a licensed clinical psychologist who specializes in traumatic loss, complicated grief, and spiritual crisis following loss. She developed the Inventory of Complicated Spiritual Grief 2.0.

Edward (Ted) Rynearson, MD, is a clinical psychiatrist and researcher in Seattle, Washington, and author of two books, *Retelling Violent Death* and *Violent Death: Resilience and Intervention Beyond the Crisis.*

The Series in Death, Dying, and Bereavement

Series Editors: Robert A. Neimeyer, PhD
Portland Institute for Loss and Transition, Oregon, USA

Darcy L. Harris, PhD
Western University Canada, Ontario, Canada

Volumes published in the Series in Death, Dying, and Bereavement are representative of the multidisciplinary nature of the intersecting fields of death studies, suicidology, end-of-life care, and grief counseling. The series meets the needs of clinicians, researchers, paraprofessionals, pastoral counselors, and educators by providing cutting edge research, theory, and best practices on the most important topics in these fields—for today and for tomorrow.

Loss, Grief, and Attachment in Life Transitions
A Clinician's Guide to Secure Base Counseling
Jakob van Wielink, Leo Wilhelm, and Denise van Geelen-Merks

Non-Death Loss and Grief
Context and Clinical Implications
Edited by Darcy L. Harris

Superhero Grief
The Transformative Power of Loss
Edited by Jill A. Harrington and Robert A. Neimeyer

New Techniques of Grief Therapy
Bereavement and Beyond
Edited by Robert A. Neimeyer

Pediatric Palliative Care
A Model for Exemplary Practice
Betty Davies, Rose Steele, and Jennifer Baird

The Restorative Nature of Ongoing Connections with the Deceased
Exploring Presence Within Absence
Laurie A. Burke and Edward (Ted) Rynearson

For more information about this series, please visit https://www.routledge.com/ Series-in-Death-Dying-and-Bereavement/book-series/SE0620.

The Restorative Nature of Ongoing Connections with the Deceased

Exploring Presence within Absence

Edited by Laurie A. Burke and Edward (Ted) Rynearson

Routledge
Taylor & Francis Group

NEW YORK AND LONDON

First published 2022
by Routledge
605 Third Avenue, New York, NY 10158

and by Routledge
4 Park Square, Milton Park, Abingdon, Oxon, OX14 4RN

Routledge is an imprint of the Taylor & Francis Group, an informa business

Library of Congress Cataloging-in-Publication Data
Names: Burke, Laurie A., editor. | Rynearson, Edward K., editor.
Title: The restorative nature of ongoing connections with the deceased : exploring presence within absence / edited by Laurie A. Burke, Edward (Ted) Rynearson.
Description: New York, NY : Routledge, 2022. | Includes bibliographical references and index. |
Identifiers: LCCN 2021050376 (print) | LCCN 2021050377 (ebook) | ISBN 9780367554859 (hardback) | ISBN 9780367554835 (paperback) | ISBN 9781003105077 (ebook)
Subjects: LCSH: Bereavement--Psychological aspects. | Bereavement--Religious aspects. | Loss (Psychology) | Death--Psychological aspects.
Classification: LCC BF575.G7 R47 2022 (print) | LCC BF575.G7 (ebook) | DDC 155.9/37--dc23/eng/20211104
LC record available at https://lccn.loc.gov/2021050376
LC ebook record available at https://lccn.loc.gov/2021050377
Access the Support Material: Routledge.com/9780367554835

ISBN: 978-0-367-55485-9 (hbk)
ISBN: 978-0-367-55483-5 (pbk)
ISBN: 978-1-003-10507-7 (ebk)

DOI: 10.4324/9781003105077

Typeset in Times New Roman
by MPS Limited, Dehradun

The work and topic of this book are in dedication to all grievers everywhere but most specifically to the bereaved individuals who directly contributed to what the authors have learned and shared here. These include our patients and clients, research participants, parishioners, friends, family, and others whose experiences have taught us what we know about ongoing attachments between bereaved individuals and their deceased loved ones.

Contents

Tables

Abbreviations

CG	complicated grief
CNS	central nervous system
CPTSD	complex post-traumatic stress disorder
CSG	complicated spiritual grief
EMDR	eye movement desensitization and reprocessing
f-MRI	functional magnetic resonance imaging
ICSG 2.0	Inventory of Complicated Spiritual Grief 2.0
MHP	mental health professional
PTSD	post-traumatic stress disorder
SED	sensory or quasi-sensory experiences of the deceased
TFCBT	trauma-focused cognitive behavioral therapy

Contributors

Jeffery Black, MDiv, CAS, MD, is a board-certified psychiatrist at the Defense Health Agency who has trained with native healers from South America and The Four Winds Society. He holds a Master's Degree in Divinity and a Clinical Ayurvedic Specialist Degree. His work focuses on grief, trauma, death, and dying.

Craig Van Dyke, MD, is professor and chair emeritus of the Department of Psychiatry, University of California San Francisco. During a 45-year career, his research encompassed human studies of abused drugs, cognition and neuroimaging, grief, and psychological responses following natural disasters with a particular focus on the importance of introspection.

Rabbi Ted Falcon, PhD, is a Reform rabbi with a doctorate in Professional Psychology who explores the frontiers of a universal spirituality. He founded meditative synagogues in Los Angeles and Seattle and has written extensively. He has worked with the Interfaith Amigos since 2001 and now with the Anokhi Institute.

Karina S. Kamp, PhD, is a psychologist at Familieinstitutionen Topshøj, Denmark. Her research, which is focused on sensory and quasi-sensory experiences of the deceased, has been conducted at the psychology department at Aarhus University, Denmark.

Donald M. Mackenzie, PhD, is a minister of the United Church of Christ. He has served churches in Princeton, NJ, Hanover, NH, and Seattle, WA. Together with Rabbi Ted Falcon and Imam Jamal Rahman he has since, September 11, 2001, been a part of the interfaith team known as the Interfaith Amigos.

Robert A. Neimeyer, PhD, directs the Portland Institute for Loss and Transition, actively practices as a trainer, consultant, and coach, and has published over 500 articles and 30 books, most on grieving as a meaning-making process. His most recent book is *New Techniques of Grief Therapy*.

Jamal Rahman, MA, is a popular author and teacher of Islam, Sufi spirituality, and interfaith relations. Along with his Interfaith Amigos, he has been featured in *The New York Times,* CBS News, BBC, and NPR. He is co-founder and Imam of Interfaith Community Sanctuary, and adjunct faculty at Seattle University.

John E. Ruark, MD, is a semi-retired clinical psychiatrist who spent 40 years on the adjunct clinical faculty at Stanford, retiring in 2015 as an associate professor. He is an emeritus fellow of the American College of Psychiatrists and has written and taught widely around end-of-life issues.

Edith Maria Steffen, PsychD, is an associate professor in psychology at the University of Plymouth, UK, and a registered counseling psychologist in private practice in Surrey, UK. Her research is focused on continuing bonds in bereavement, sensory and quasi-sensory experiences of the deceased, and meaning-oriented grief therapy.

Neena Verma, PhD, is an ICF-PCC coach, NTL professional member and TAOS associate. An Appreciative Inquiry expert, and Grief and Growth specialist, Neena works with those in grief and trauma. Apart from writing, editing, and serving on AI practitioner editorial board, Neena runs a library movement for underserved children.

Camille B. Wortman, PhD, is currently a professor emeritus of Psychology at Stony Brook University. Her area of expertise is in grief and bereavement, with a special emphasis on coping with the sudden, traumatic death of a loved one.

Series Editor's Foreword

Unlike any other experience, the death of a loved one hurls us into confrontation with the void that has been left by our loved one's absence. The profoundly simple phrase, *exploring presence within absence*, aptly describes the complex and often arduous journey of coming to terms with the absence of a loved one in myriad ways—everyday life, a future unknown, deep longing for reunion, and an inescapable need to find meaning in the midst of a very painful time. It has been said that the loss of a loved one rips the fabric of our lives; sometimes, all we can see is the shredded aftermath. The difficult and labor-intensive process of mending this fabric is the work of our grief, using threads from our shared times and memories that are all painstakingly woven together to create a new tapestry of our lives.

Laurie Burke and Ted Rynearson have put together a stellar volume of topics that approach various aspects of absence and the search for presence and the continuation of a connection with deceased loved ones. Readers will find a wealth of wisdom from the professional experiences and reflections of a diverse group of contributors. The volume starts with an historic account of the first human awareness of transcendence, followed by relevant descriptions of how different belief systems approach grief and address the desire to somehow turn the empty void of the physical absence of a deceased loved one into a meaningful presence that can continue with them on their journey of life. The common thread of connection is woven into each chapter, providing insight for those who work with bereaved individuals.

Although not explicitly discussed, this volume invites clinicians to appreciate grief as a journey into the unknown, being open to mysteries of human experiences that are perhaps not readily discussed in the mainstream culture, academic literature, or professional training programs. The contributors re-frame experiences such as hearing the voice of the deceased or feeling their touch on our skin as potential forms of healing connection, avoiding the diagnostic label that might mistakenly be applied to such experiences. Seeking to have an intangible connection through a spiritual medium may readily be dismissed by many as hocus-pocus, with shamanistic healers often perceived as taking advantage of people who are made vulnerable by their grief. Yet, contrary to this perception, many bereaved individuals have found these transpersonal experiences to be empowering and positive. Finally, the ability to "introduce" the loved one to a therapist who is deeply present and open holds the potential to invite the deceased loved one into the encounter, creating a welcome and healing space for grief to unfold, and for the mending process to begin.

I welcome this incredibly rich and insightful book, knowing that it will open the minds and hearts of readers, providing them with the opportunity to consider the various ways that we heal after loss by offering many opportunities to facilitate re-connection and the re-weaving of one's life, finding presence in the midst of a profound absence.

Darcy Harris
Series co-editor

Preface

This book is intended to stimulate thought and discussion about ongoing attachments between bereaved individuals and their deceased loved ones. There appear to be numerous ways in which grievers experience a continuing bond or *presence within absence* of the person who died, many of which include aspects of their belief system or occurrences and connections associated with an ethereal world (e.g., through religion, spirituality, mediums, shamanism, unsolicited "encounters" with the deceased). Largely, such connections with the deceased seem to be comforting and reassuring to the survivor, though this is not universally true. Rather than arriving at a definitive perspective, this book is designed to promote broad, inclusive training and dialogue among bereavement professionals to better equip them in understanding and assisting clients who desire to establish and maintain a restorative connection with their deceased loved one, and those who find aspects of such connections to be psychologically or spiritually problematic or troublesome.

Laurie A. Burke and Edward (Ted) Rynearson

Acknowledgments

As well as thanking Ted for his commitment and enthusiasm in collaborating together on this book, I want to thank him for his unique contribution as an author and co-editor. Although our writing and editorial styles may differ, his unwavering decision to join me in meeting each new challenge that came with creating this book was done with a positive attitude and respectful acceptance of our individual strengths. Thanks, Ted, for your patience and support through the long haul and for never giving up on our vision for this project.

Laura Jeffs, I will be forever indebted to you for all the ways in which your behind the scene efforts set the stage for this book project (and the conference that preceded it) to come to fruition and be successful. You are one in a million and I am grateful for your selfless contributions.

A big shout out to Laura Takacs who not only videotaped the panel interviews with grievers that comprise the final two chapters of this book but also navigated the process that made them available to me to transcribe. Thanks for always showing up in such meaningful ways.

Both Ted and I share a deep heartfelt sense of gratitude for the many hours that Terrance (Terry) King put into editing the videotaped panel interviews and making them available to us to be used in this book. The transcribed narratives alone (showcased in Chapters 16 and 17) are inadequate in capturing the lived experiences of grievers and the meaning that emerges as they describe their post-death encounters with their deceased loved ones. Terry's ability and willingness to prepare and provide links to the videos means that readers can hear and watch direct accounts from the grievers themselves, adding an invaluable resource to our book.

This book, and any of Ted's or my efforts, would be found wanting without the generous contribution of each author with whom we had the honor to include in this project. My goal in helping Ted select high-caliber authors was an effort to produce a manuscript that would promote broad, inclusive training, and dialogue on a topic that can be hard to describe and understand. My style of editing aimed to create a book that was meaningful, applicable, and easy for the reader to track, whether they were professional bereavement helpers or grievers themselves. No doubt, every editor has their own style and expectations, and surely I'm not alone in finding myself at times seeing more trees than forest, getting all caught up in the weeds (and even more annoyingly, the placement of commas) as I reviewed and re-reviewed the chapters of this book along with Ted. But working with a mature, patient, stellar group of authors made the process so much easier. To our authors, I've so enjoyed getting to know each of you better through this process. I have learned so much from you and am wholeheartedly excited to share with the public the book you've helped us create. Thank you, sincerely, for all your hard work and your gracious willingness to join us on this journey.

Finally, every square inch of this book was meant for grievers—all grievers, everywhere. You are at the heart of what I do and at the center of this book. I join each author represented here in showing gratitude for what we have learned from you about what it means and how it is that a survivor can remain connected with a loved one who is no longer alive. We've learned from you in a variety of settings—from the synagogue to the therapy room—as you have authentically, graciously, generously shared experiences that are not always easy to understand or discuss.

Most of all, I want to express immense gratitude to my own patients who have trusted me enough to voluntarily share specific details of their *presence-within-absence* experiences and allowed me to join them in their exploration as they attempt to make meaning along the way. Specifically, it is with such deep appreciation that I thank the seven bereaved women who participated in the two panels that make up the last two chapters of this book. Debbie, Elaine, Erica, Kristen, Lizzie, Rebecca, and Rebekah, I can't thank you enough for the substantial and highly meaningful gift you gave me and the readers of this book in terms of your time and willingness to help us understand your lived experiences of maintaining a continuing bond with your deceased loved one. I so enjoyed interviewing each of you for this project. Doing so not only increased my respect and admiration for all you've been through but also amplified my understanding of how much you each have to give to others who mourn. I find myself batting back the tears when I think of what an honor (and joy) it has been for me to walk alongside each of you on your bereavement journey. I will be forever grateful for knowing and learning from you. To all the grievers who long to stay connected to the one they lost, this is really your book.

Laurie A. Burke, PhD

The presence within absence of the deceased began for me as a personal experience immediately after my wife's suicide nearly 50 years ago. She and I *met* within a comforting, imaginal conversation within days of her death. At first, the conversation was a daily expression of my sadness and remorse over her dying and death. Later, there were themes of abandonment and anger. Following my personal expressions of grief were more resilient themes through retellings of our mutual concern and plans for our two pre-school children. Retellings with her continued at night with the traumatic reenactment of her dying counterbalanced with welcomed dreams of her return. These retellings during the day and her visitation in my dreams at night spontaneously diminished in the early weeks after her death but her presence within absence within me remains as implicit rather than frequent.

My dynamic interchange with her presence within absence played a normative and restorative purpose. Traditional models of grief of that time—that an imaginal preoccupation with the representation of the deceased was pathological (a product of repressed, unconscious ambivalence or an interruption in epigenetic stages)—did not consider our interchange as adaptive.

Through studies and presentations of grief treatment with child therapists, I began to appreciate the common presence of the deceased with grieving children. Their non-verbal drawings and play provided imaginal resuscitation and repair and an emerging restoration of their own autonomy beyond dying and death.

The retelling of presence within absence during childhood in an imaginal *third space* between life and death that is developmentally derived. This highly subjective third space between life and death may persist into adulthood and it is not uncommon for continued processing of the dying and death of a loved one to register at an imaginal level for adults as well.

To widen the frame, for thousands of years, shaman and clergy have assumed active roles within this third space after death through ritual gathering, memorialization, and journeying to restore a cosmic or divine restoration for the spirit or soul of the deceased. I wondered if shaman, clergy, and therapist found themselves in comparable healing roles with grief and the presence within absence, and if so, what might we learn from one another.

In May of 2019, Laurie Burke and I gathered representative clinicians and researchers from relevant practices (shaman, clergy, mental health workers) including patients (in-person and in videos) at a two-day meeting in Seattle for an exploratory consideration. Our clear objective was not a reductive analysis of presence within absence to rigorously define its etiology or predict its treated or untreated effects. Our collective understanding and practice(s) largely remain unverified and untested. Instead, we encouraged presenters to offer their understanding of imaginal connection and supportive and therapeutic practices to widen and deepen our collective understanding.

The meeting was well received by the audience and began the organizing of this book with the presenters. Each of the chapters has taken considerable thought and time volunteered by each author. Their willingness to contribute is a reflection of the excitement and stimulation we all felt at the time of the meeting.

Laurie and I are very grateful for their contribution to this volume and we hope we might gather again with new insights from an enlarged group of presenters.

Edward (Ted) Rynearson, MD

Introduction

Edward (Ted) Rynearson and Laurie A. Burke

The Ubiquity of Presence within Absence after Death

At the time of death, the life of the deceased may herald an event of absence as well as a state of continuance. The experience of *presence within absence* after death may be a determinative dilemma for the philosopher and scholar (Ratcliffe, 2019), but for many bereaved individuals it is a common and unmistakably real experience following the death of someone they love (Fuchs, 2018). The practical objective of this book is to present the presence within absence of the deceased during bereavement as common and normative, and often comforting and meaningful. To illustrate, consider the not uncommon response of a mother to the death of her child:

Sarah and Her Daughter

Though her daughter died years before, Sarah felt her proximity nearly every day. There seemed no boundary between her presence rooted in her absence. Her daughter's apparition bonded their relationship that had been ruptured by death and felt real. She had appeared twice while Sarah was wide awake, at the foot of her bed saying she loved her and was waiting in a time and space where they would be together again. Sadly, those were the only times she directly returned though she continued to reappear in comforting dreams where they held one another. There were many times Sarah tried to talk with her daughter—but she never replied.

Her presence wasn't always triggered by Sarah's active searching. Sudden and unanticipated visitations—a familiar cloud formation or sunset, a soaring bird, a butterfly landing on her shoulder, hearing their favorite song, or tasting their favorite food—carried an unforeseen meaning; instead of her searching for her daughter, Sarah felt a warming reassurance that her daughter was searching for her. This co-existence mutually pulled them toward their shared past rather than pushing Sarah away toward an incomprehensible future without her daughter. The presence of Sarah's daughter was more than an indeterminate object in Sarah's past world but

DOI: 10.4324/9781003105077-1

instead a condition of intelligibility for her world to continue. Worried she would be judged as deranged, Sarah was protective of these private interchanges and visitations. Keeping them to herself ensured their permanence.

This is not an uncommon story. Recent studies clarify the commonality of this phenomenon in community-based surveys following death (e.g., see Chapter 13). Usually comforting when it occurs, the imagined or sensed presence of the deceased by a griever should not be initially interpreted as a psychotic hallucination or delusion. To do so risks being defined as pathological, a sign to be treated instead of a relational focus to be meaningfully understood.

Reinforcing a sustained communication with the living and dying narrative of the deceased can be a stabilizing response in the early phase of accommodation after death, so natural that Sarah's experience reflects a timeless and universal epiphenomenon. An early response would be Sarah's opportunity to put words to her daughter's life and dying by retelling in her own voice a projected story of her daughter's living and dying with those she trusted.

Retelling in many forms (e.g., voiced, written, pictured, dramatized, performed, memorialized) was the basis of Sarah's readjustment to the interrupted attachment with her daughter. The revitalized retelling of her daughter's living and dying became a normative process. Months later, if Sarah remained highly distressed or disabled and sought professional consultation, retelling was, for her, rudimental to every healing practice she received. Repeated retellings provided an external frame and shared context for the presence in absence in which Sarah's stories of her daughter's dying and death could be revised into a comprehensible and bearable narrative, as they were modified enough to be integrated and carried forward into her own reworked identity without her daughter.

Restorative Potential of Presence within Absence

In their chapters and research citations that follow, each author develops a detailed focus on the socio-cultural and clinical prominence of presence within absence, highlighting divergent perspectives from oldest (e.g., paganism, monotheism, spiritual mediumship) to the more recent (e.g., psychotherapy, social media). The objective of this introductory chapter is to broadly outline the historical and descriptive unfolding of an integrated focus from ancient to present.

Prehistoric evidence honoring the immortality of the deceased has been documented in ancient burial practices—preparing for a journey beyond death including food, weapons, and valuable objects accompanying the physical remains of the deceased. This journey narrative was product of a reflective, human consciousness (simultaneously viewing self as subject and object) and an anticipation of death (the finite nature of self in time). Active focus on revising and reframing the journey has been the foundation of support and healing interventions for thousands of years. The passage or presence of the deceased between life and death in living terms likely was a conceptual absolute in preliterate times, restoring the enlivened deceased in a space, time, and action of immortality. Once immortalized, the presence within absence of the deceased would not register as a dilemma.

Over time, there have been at least three healing figures socially authorized as caregivers of bereavement and grief—the shaman, the clergy and, most recently, the psychotherapist. Each of these prototypical practitioners calls upon active focusing on the presence of the deceased while conforming to their absence.

Depending on the afterlife belief system of the patient, one or a combination of these ubiquitous practitioners and their techniques may be integrated in a contemporary healing of disabling grief. All three play a similar bridging function between the survivor and the deceased and may continue to play a role in grief treatment. There are enough similarities between the models to warrant an attitude of mutual respect and willingness to collaborate in management strategies and research.

Jerome Frank, a psychiatrist and researcher at John Hopkins University who devoted himself to the study of healing relationships of all kinds, learned from his extensive studies about what he called *curative factors* (Frank & Frank, 1991). Curative factors include:

- An emotionally charged and confidential relationship
- A healing setting
- A conceptual scheme
- A collaborative procedure

He learned that the presence of curative factors appears to be fundamental to every form of healing practice and that each of these factors is embedded in the healing practices of shaman, clergy, and therapist. Despite the ways in which their practices differ, shaman, clergy, and therapists each include a confiding and altruistic relationship, in a safe and secure place, a clear explanatory model of cause, and with prescribed, mutual enactments to restore health.

Shaman

In hunter-gatherer society, the shaman served as a guide in a collaborative journey to summon and incorporate the living soul relayed through the spirit of the deceased to reestablish an energic harmony through rituals of energy release.

Shamanic mythology differs from the religious idea of a journey toward a divine transcendence by clergy or exploration of past relationship by psychotherapist. As reflected in prehistoric burial practices, shamanic journeying of the soul was key for the prehistoric shaman. Perhaps more than journey, the shaman guides a transformative *quest* for soul retrieval and revitalization. The shamanic care seeker is given a clear model of supra-sensory determinacy (i.e., beyond the five somatic senses) through a collaborative ritual. Somatic senses confine the energy of grief to the memories of the past. A supra-sensory exchange through ritual allows restoration to occur by corresponding directly with spirit images needing energic retrieval and revision.

The bases of shamanic journeying are oral-mystical and prehistoric, where dying and death are migratory and transitional. Through incorporative connection, the shaman's intervention for grief operates at a level of high primal and relevant power. The energy of the honored spirits outside of time and space combines with the energy of the deceased, providing restorative energy to the interchange assisting the deceased across the threshold from the place of the living to the place of the presence within absence of the deceased to an energic wholeness and transcendence.

Shamanic techniques are formalized through ritualized ceremony within a sacred space, presence of linking objects with the spiritual world, and trance induction through chanting and drumming. The shaman and the supplicant join in a spiritual journey that includes the deceased incorporated within the shaman. Once connected through retrieval, shamanic practices become catalytic in re-equilibration of energies.

In shamanic tradition, each individual has two basic forms of energy surrounding the soul that can accumulate. The shamanic practitioner understands the healing release of heavy energy of grief *shadowing* the soul and makes room for the light energy of spirit. Shamanism does not endorse spirit as evil. When balanced, heavy and light spirits are natural and inevitable components of health. The soul is imbalanced for protection with grief and especially in traumatic grief after violent loss. An essential part of energic healing is engaging in processes to return the soul to wholeness not only from the loss of the deceased but also from the loss of a part of the soul itself. Thus, it is not surprising that the thematic substance and structure of retelling is revised by this guided quest. Fixated retellings of grief with intense compensatory fantasies of resurrection or remorse create a state of psychological readiness to imaginal presences, sensations, conversations, and conversions provided by the supra-sensory interchanges with the shaman.

Clergy

Later, in agricultural societies, the role of shaman was superseded by religious leaders playing a modified supernatural role through supplicating rituals to a divine figure overseeing a separate afterlife of transcendent safety and harmony for the presence or *soul* of the deceased.

Religious figures, such as priests and, later, clergy, who helped people make sense and meaning in their lives, expressed an evolving relationship between human beings and a power greater than themselves. An aspect of that relationship was the need to help people navigate the fear of death and the meaning of death and to look at the relationship of the material body to the spirit of a person. What happens to the spirit after death and what does that mean?

Although clergy often serve as an active intermediary during the person's dying, and even more active in organizing the memorial and burial service with the surviving family members and supporting congregation after death, their role remains ancillary. Unlike the shaman, who actively retrieves and incorporates the soul of the deceased, clergy remain firmly identified with the living survivors in a ritualized invocation (entreaty) for divine intercession. Likewise, intercession with the divine is less direct—established through memorial rituals with public ceremonies of lamentation, including observable objects of remembrance and sacrament rather than trance induction with imaginary retrieval and communication.

Invocational prayer and music are often introduced as a shared exercise with clergy and congregation and also can serve as a private and autonomous function, connecting the survivor with a divine resource of life-affirming meaning in addition to invoking the soul of the deceased. With these helpful supports, connection with a living image recedes but never disappears and can be summoned in the months and years that follow.

For some grievers, having a meaningful religious belief system may not include a belief in an afterlife. However, exploring the afterlife belief system shared between the patient and the deceased provides an important religious clinical insight into the potential processing of mental representation. Muslim and Christian traditions promise a continuity and reunion with the deceased, represented by, in some cases, the intercessional role of the clergy with the divine. If such a belief in the afterlife is operative, summoning the soulful representation of the deceased person as a therapeutic ally may be reassuring to the spiritually inclined griever searching for a life-affirming connection. A strong belief in the religious retelling tradition may also encourage an intertwining and meaningful story beyond dying and death.

Through their intercession with the divine, buttressed by religious sanctuary, vestments, sacramental objects, and ritual exercises, the clergy can direct a memorialized retelling, ensuring a divinely based rite of passage for the soul of the deceased. However, angry lamentation sometimes includes the denial of a divinely based belief system that would "allow something so horrible and evil to happen" or the belief that "God is trying to punish me in some way by taking my loved one." For instance, a divine meaning is hard to sustain in the retelling of a senseless homicide with violent dying, or a mutilating cancer treatment with natural dying. However, a spiritual sensibility can be found in the *Book of Job*, for example, as it attempts to understand the meaning of evil in human experience, and also in the *Book of Psalms* where we learn that all human emotions, even deep distress and anger, can be properly brought to God in prayer, has the potential to make a deeper healing possible. In many cases, spiritually inclined grievers can find a softening of pain and a transformation to a new way of understanding their bereavement experience with the help of a spiritual leader and/or support of their faith community.

Psychotherapist

Contemporary psychotherapies include the same four curative factors noted in shamanism and religion. However, what differentiates the psychotherapist from shaman or clergy is how the conceptual schemas and collaborative procedures are experienced. Generally speaking, psychotherapists focus on the survivor's narrative memory of the relationship with the deceased rather than a ritualized bridging with a supra-natural or supernatural presence. However, as this book highlights, creative techniques exist for the psychotherapist to assist the griever in connecting with the presence within absence of their deceased loved one (e.g., see Chapters 10, 11, and 17).

In some cases, the memory of the deceased may seem less provocative in a psychotherapy setting. Whereas, the *invocation* of the deceased through a shaman's mystical embodied merger or a clergy's divine intercession is based upon supernatural belief, the *evocation* of a private memory of the deceased is a recognized and culturally accepted in therapy. For example, generally speaking, in contemporary Western culture, even the most extreme realist or atheist recognizes a recalled memory as altogether natural. Thus, the psychotherapist serves as a figurative intermediary between the patient and their narrative memory of the deceased through dyadic retelling (i.e., between therapist and patient) that may include triadic retelling (e.g., joined through projective exercises with the image and voice of the deceased as a therapeutic ally).

For early psychological theorists, the importance of the relationship with internalized memory was central. Unconscious anger and ambivalence toward the internalized memory of the deceased was a basic postulate of grief for Freud and neo-Freudians (Hagman, 1995), to include developmental vulnerabilities of anxious attachment for British theorists (Klass, 1988), and later, observable stages of grief, which have now been empirically refuted (Holland & Neimeyer, 2010). Descriptive studies documenting the varied ways in which many grievers establish and maintain continuing bonds with their deceased loved one as a normative part of bereavement are plentiful (Klass & Steffen, 2018). In fact, one study noted the absence of sustained grief in the majority of spousal subjects who maintained a continuing bond with their loved one after death (Bonnano, 2002).

In the last decade, grief theory has become more capacious (Rubin, 1999). Grief often is described as an enforced change in identity for the griever or cultural *rite of passage* for the deceased (e.g., see Rynearson, Chapter 11) as opposed to a positive, hoped-for change in identity (e.g., following birth, baptism, adolescence, graduation, marriage, retirement). Death, and its accompanying grief, is now perceived as a passage or journey of psychological confusion and dissonance, often oscillating between divergent polarities, pulled by one's comforting premortem identity while, at the same time, pushed by the cultural demand for postmortem change. Thus, from a psychotherapy perspective, grief tends to be seen as an unavoidable, existential challenge, requiring healing from the pain of the loss, integration of the loss into the survivor's life, and development of a new life now lived primarily in the absence of the physical presence of the deceased.

Inviting the Presence of the Deceased

The shaman, clergy, and psychotherapist all introduce healing of grief as an imaginative exercise—a retelling of the narrative of the life and dying of the deceased as an expansive opportunity for healing and growth for the griever. Through a revised retelling, it is possible for the relational role of the griever experienced prior to the death to be deconstructed and then reconstructed into a more emotionally manageable narrative following the loss. The objective of the healing alliance may be a spiritual or divine restoration of the soul of the deceased and also a revision of the survivor's place in the retelling of their dying and death.

Perhaps the most comforting way to begin the healing process following loss is to invite the memory of the living presence of the deceased (e.g., a memorialization) before inviting the memory of their dying and death. For instance, the clinician might say "I didn't have the pleasure of knowing, Alicia. Could you introduce me to her? Maybe describe her personality or what you liked best about her." For the therapist, asking to view a photo of the deceased during the intake session often invigorates for the griever a commemorative connection of immediacy with the presence of their loved one when he or she was alive and happy, opening visual themes of hope and coherence as opposed to focusing first on the way in which they died or their permanently physical absence. Commemoration not only can be stabilizing for the griever but also amplified by a series of questions that might follow. For example:

• What beliefs do you and (name of the deceased) have about death and/or an afterlife?

- Are there ways in which you still feel connected with (name of deceased), real or imaginary, such as conversations, dreams, visitations?
- How would (name of deceased) feel about your being here and what would they recommend to help you?

These questions have a projective purpose—to enliven the *transitional* presence of the deceased into an active presence allied within a relationship expanding from dyadic (i.e., therapist and patient) to triadic (i.e., including the guiding presence of deceased). Imaginary communication with the deceased can lead toward a restored identity beyond the dying and death for both the griever and the deceased (Moules, 2010; Rynearson, 1987). Because they shared a significant, meaningful relationship, the voice of the deceased can reveal vulnerabilities and strengths of the survivor, allowing relevant insights that can enhance growth and facilitate acceptance.

When Presence within Absence Becomes a Fixation

In approximately 10–15% of survivors, grieving is intense, frequent, and sustained (Field, 2008) and is experienced as a fixation in time, space, and action and/or as an unalterable obsession or disabling imaginary interchange that cannot be surrendered (Malkinson, Rubin, & Witztum, 2006). In contemporary clinical models of *prolonged grief disorder* (PGD; Prigerson et al., 2009; also known as *complicated grief*; Shear et al., 2011), the fixation may have a compensatory purpose related to, for instance, the griever's attachment to the deceased. It can be challenging for the bereaved person to change a belief serving a compensatory function, particularly when compensating for a relationship marked by anxious attachment (Jacobs, 1993), where the very presence of the deceased was requisite for a sense of safety, hope, and security. Psychotherapeutic techniques of release from this fixation of the internal mental representation of anxious attachment (Field, 2008), can provide catharsis of sadness and anger (e.g., farewell exercises including empty chair conversations, directive letters, ritual burials, release of balloons) and assist in easing the terror of the trauma in cases of violent death loss (e.g., graded exposure; Saindon et al., 2014).

Fixation on the reenactment events of violent dying (e.g., following fatal accident, suicide, or homicide) often focus on the horror and helplessness of the deceased while dying, which may seem surreal to the griever and include traumatic replay. There can be no compensatory purpose in this fixation beyond its dysfunctional discharge (i.e., flashback) of overwhelming trauma and the intense repetition of failed rescue and prevention "because this never should have happened." Combined fixations of comforting reunion and traumatic reenactment are often present following violent dying, requiring careful staging of stabilization and imaginal exposure of both fixations (Rynearson, 2018).

The techniques of grief psychotherapy (e.g., emotional regulation, imaginal exposure, cognitive reframing) echo similar healing mechanisms embedded in shamanic and religious rituals (e.g., emotional *suspension*, spiritual *journey*, and meaningful *return*). This triad is basic to grief and trauma healing protocols (Rynearson, 2001) and follows a sequential ordering: stabilization, exposure, and transformation. Techniques to address these protocols can be applied and repeated at any time during the course of intervention; however, even manualized protocols for PGD therapy cannot be divided into discrete, epigenetic stages. The clinical needs of the griever are idiosyncratic and must take priority, and the healing of fixations must retain an artful stance in the collaborative search for meaning and security for the mourner.

The Neurobiology of Presence within Absence

It is important to reference the neurologic findings associated with bereavement and grief. The presence within absence of the deceased is more than just metaphorical—there is an irrefutable physiological determinant (O'Connor, 2019). Unfortunately, however, current empirical studies are limited to research centers and, thus, likely have little practical relevance to the individual griever. Their evidence is based on functional MRI (f-MRI) studies which are prohibitively complex and expensive for practitioners and have results that are suggestive rather than diagnostic. In one study, while viewing pictures of the deceased, f-MRI imagery showed activation deep in the griever's forebrain in the nucleus accumbens (O'Connor, 2019), an area responsible for pleasurable and rewarding experiences. In contrast, the remembrance of the life and dying of the deceased does not have a localized registration in the human brain (e.g., see Chapter 8). Thus, there is a qualitative difference between the registration of a pleasurable memory evoked by a picture of the deceased and their presence as a *phantom.*

To expand its physiologic registration, it is instructive to consider the clinical and research findings of phantom experience after amputation of a body part. Following amputation, there is a continual mental representation of the amputated limb that subsides but never disappears, not too dissimilar from the central nervous system's (CNS) localization of grief, where the continued activation of the deceased's representation registers as a phantom presence (Parkes, 1975; Ratcliffe, 2019). Like the amputation of a body part, the deceased's phantom representation may also include sensory perceptions (e.g., visions, voices, smells, tactile sensations) but primarily registers as narrative memory of the relationship while living and dying. The living and dying of the *dis-membered* person is *re-membered* through a reconnective retelling of the lost relationship.

Missing a lost part of the self (lost one) or a lost part of the body represent f-MRI changes that are roughly analogous. Relatively specific, localized changes in limbic and pre-frontal CNS regions appear associated with both grief and amputation. These findings suggest that phantom sensations are associated with similar CNS processes that underlie the experience of the body or attachment relationship when it was intact and that the corporeal or psychological awareness of both experiences is encoded in a thalamocortical network. There are nonspecific neuro-endocrine and neuro-chemical changes associated with grief, but no associated pharmacotherapy has been found to be effective in diminishing grief symptoms (Vance, 2018). Randomized, controlled studies of medication administration following loss document that there is no pill for grief. Despite these studies, treating physicians tend to over-prescribe antidepressant medications for grief symptoms that are misinterpreted as clinical depression (Johnson, 2017).

Restorative Healing

One way to conceptualize grieving is that the durable representation (e.g., spirit, soul, projection) of the deceased is *pushed* by neurobiological reflex, then retold as a story of living and dying which is *pulled* by psychological purpose, and sometimes becomes disabling when pulled into an unchanging fixation (i.e., PGD). This process may include, for instance, reenactment imagery with violent dying and/or reunion imagery with anxious attachment (Rynearson, 2001). Because the representation has a narrative structure, it follows that healing will target narrative revision of the fixated story of the living and dying of the deceased to enable the griever to hold the pain of loss in a more adaptive and manageable way over time.

Shaman, clergy, and therapists share similar objectives and techniques (e.g., emotional regulation, imaginal exposure, cognitive reframing) in their healing interventions after the death of a loved one. While each of these traditions has a different conceptual schema (e.g., energic release, divine intercession, narrative reconstruction), features from each can be combined to satisfy the conceptual needs of the mourner during the healing intervention. Having outlined the differences and similarities of these three prototypes, the reader might now better appreciate how this book's authors might respond if the presence within absence of Sarah's daughter was no longer comforting but had become a fixation. For instance, what if:

- During the first session, Sarah angrily sobbed, "I don't need therapy! I just need my daughter back!"
- Sarah was unable to regulate her anxiety and began hyperventilating, because, "Talking about my daughter's death makes me feel worse."

- Her daughter had died violently from suicide, homicide, or accident, and Sarah was obsessed with reenactment fantasies of her dying.
- Sarah felt that God had betrayed her, particularly with regard to her future as a mother—a future she could no longer trust.
- She complained that her husband could no longer tolerate her suffering.
- Sarah's sleep was interrupted by traumatic dreams of her daughter.
- She said life without her daughter felt meaningless and she was having suicidal thoughts so she "could be with her."
- Sarah believed she could reconnect with her daughter through a medium, and asked if that would help her?

These challenging protests and questions would reflect an intolerable fixation for Sarah in her attachment to the dying and death of her daughter. The healing of shaman, clergy, and psychotherapist, as process more than a protocol, could include her daughter's presence within absence through emotional regulation, imaginal exposure, and cognitive reframing, under different names and conceptual schemas; however, each tradition shares a restorative focus on the residual presence within absence to restore Sarah to a renewed commitment to life beyond her daughter's dying and absence.

References

Bonnano, G. (2002). Resilience to loss and chronic grief: A prospective study from preloss to 18-months postloss. *Journal of Personality and Social Psychology, 83*(6), 1150–1164.

Field, N.P. (2008). Whether to relinquish or maintain a bond with the deceased. In M.S. Stroebe, R.O. Hansson, H. Schut, & W. Stroebe (Eds.), *Handbook of bereavement research and practice: Advances in theory and intervention.* Washington, DC: American Psychological Association, pp. 113–132.

Field, N.P., Gao, B., & Paderna, L. (2005). Continuing bonds in bereavement: An attachment theory based perspective. *Death Studies, 29*(4), 277–299.

Frank, J.M., & Frank, J.B., (1991). *Persuasion and healing.* Baltimore, Maryland: John Hopkins University Press.

Fuchs, F. (2018). Presence in absence: The ambiguous phenomenology of grief. *Phenomenology and the Cognitive Sciences, 17*(1), 43–63.

Hagman, G. (1995). Mourning: A review and reconsideration. *International Journal of Psychoanalysis, 76,* 909–925.

Holland, J.M., & Neimeyer, R.A. (2010). An examination of stage theory of grief among individuals bereaved by natural and violent causes: A meaning-oriented contribution. *Omega: Journal of Death and Dying, 61*(2), 103–120.

Jacobs, S. (1993). *Pathologic grief: Maladaptation to loss.* Washington, DC: John Hopkins University Press.

Johnson, C. (2017). "Doing the right thing": Factors influencing GP prescribing of anti-depressants and prescribed doses. *BMC Family Practice, 18*(72), 1–13.

Klass, D. (1988). John Bowlby's model of grief and the problem of identifications. *Omega: Journal of Death and Dying, 18*(1), 13–32.

Klass, D., & Steffen, E. (2018). *Continuing bonds in bereavement.* New York: Routledge Press.

Malkinson, R., Rubin, S.S., & Witztum, E. (2006). Therapeutic issues and the relationship to the deceased: Working clinically with the two-track model of bereavement. *Death Studies, 30*(9), 797–815.

Moules, N. (2010). Internal connections and conversations: The internalized other interview in bereavement work. *Omega: Journal of Death and Dying, 62*(2), 187–199.

O'Connor, M. (2019). Grief: A brief history of research on how body and mind and brain adapt. *Psychosomatic Medicine, 81*(8), 731–738.

Parkes, C. (1975). Psycho-social transitions: Comparison to the reactions to loss of a limb and loss of a spouse. *British Journal of Psychiatry, 127*, 204–210.

Prigerson, H.G., Horowitz, M.J., Jacobs, S.C., Parkes, C.M., Aslan, M., Goodkin, K., … Maciejewski, P.K. (2009). Prolonged grief disorder: Psychometric validation of criteria proposed for DSM-V and ICD-11. *PLoS Medicine, 6*(8), 1–12. 10.1371/journal.pmed.1000121.

Ratcliffe, M.J. (2019). Grief and phantom limbs. *New Yearbook for Phenomenology and Phenomenological Philosophy, 17*, 1–24.

Ratcliffe, M.J. (2019). Towards a phenomenology of grief: Insights from Merleau-Ponty. *European Journal of Philosophy, 28*(1). 10.1111/ejop.12513.

Rubin, S. (1999). The two-track model of bereavement: Overview, retrospect, and prospect. *Death Studies, 23*(8), 681–714.

Rynearson, E. (1987). Psychotherapy of pathologic grief: Revisions and limitations. In S. Zisook (Ed.), *The psychiatric clinics of North America* (Vol. 10). Philadelphia: W.B. Saunders, pp. 487–499.

Rynearson, E. (2001). *Retelling violent death.* New York: Routledge Press.

Rynearson, E. (2018). *Manual of restorative retelling.* Free PDF Download. www.vdbs.org.

Saindon, C., Rheingold, A., Baddeley, J., Wallace, M., Brown, C., & Rynearson, E. (2014). Restorative retelling for violent loss: An open clinical trial. *Death Studies, 38*(4), 251–258, 10.1080/07481187.2013.783654.

Shear, M.K., Simon, N., Wall, M., Zisook, S., Neimeyer, R., Duan, N., … Keshaviah, A. (2011). Complicated grief and related bereavement issues for DSM-5. *Depression and Anxiety, 28*(2), 103–117. 10.1002/da.20780.

Vance, M. (2018). Pharmacotherapy of pathological grief responses. In E. Bui (Ed.), *Clinical handbook of bereavement and grief reactions.* Boston: Harvard Medical School, pp. 279–299.

Section I

Faith Tradition Perspectives

1 Faith Traditions: A Historical and Contemporary Framework

Donald M. Mackenzie

Introduction

In this introductory chapter, we will explore some of the important roots of spiritual wisdom spanning many of the traditions that provide purpose and meaning and which express care for the common good. Specifically, we will highlight Judaism, Christianity, Islam, Hinduism, Buddhism, and Shamanism. By moving from the primitive through the transition from goddess worship to the worship of the one God characterized in masculine terms, the chapter opens possibilities for ways to understand the relationship between religious experience and a therapeutic openness to the communication with those who have died. Such an openness is seen to be a feature of a spiritual sensibility that is inclusive, and which supports the essential interconnectedness of all being.

The Origins of Spiritual Wisdom

Imagine this: tens of thousands of years ago on a lonely hillside, we observe a primitive human being with arms outstretched, giving forth a sound so primal that we might not even recognize it. It is a sound of feeling and not thought. And it is sensual. What is happening here?

The British musicologist Wilfred Mellers (1976) suggests that such a moment marks the first music. This makes sense given that music is an externalization of feeling. We might also consider this moment as the first instance of a deep desire for a connection to the cosmos, an attempt to reconnect what has been separated at birth, a hope that something beyond the physical self exists. Thus, the moment can also be said to be the beginning of spirituality. This was long before words began to be used to give cognitive shape to the feelings that gave rise to music. But it represents the beginning of the evolution of trying to make sense of life, its purpose and meaning, trying to make sense of death, and trying to give some shape to the hope that there *is* meaning in *both* life and death.

As time goes by, the evolution produces almost an infinite number of variations, as different cultures and groups of people develop their own

DOI: 10.4324/9781003105077-3

sense of the particulars within these broad categories. Later themes include the relationship between the concerns of the self and the awareness of a larger and more inclusive way of understanding experience—spiritual wisdom. And within that, we find a recurring set of categories: cooperation and collaboration, forgiveness and acceptance, reconciliation and justice. Our ancient ancestor, as primitive as that person may seem, is in many ways not that different from those of us alive in the 21st century. We continue to yearn to understand what life is about, what death means and wonder if the universe—the container of both being and matter, spirit and substance—has the capacity for healing, for salvation for all creation. The word "God" comes into play to point to that entity that words cannot describe. Later in the Abrahamic traditions, for example, words such as "Father" and "Almighty," while reflecting the patriarchy in which these concepts were born, actually detract from the more inclusive hope expressed by that ancient person. Shamans arose to be connectors between the material world and the world of the spirit as well as storytellers of the healing powers of the universe. They also, depending on the particular tradition and moment in history, filled other roles such as worship leader. The shaman functioned as a guide to the deep desires that we saw expressed in that ancestor on that ancient hillside.

The Shift from a Feminine to a Masculine Understanding of God

A culture of matriarchy, which worshipped the goddess, represents some of the earliest evidence of religious practice (Stone, 1976). The feminine was worshipped because life appeared to be a feminine province, the obvious connection to the creation of human life at birth.

And while the masculine experience has been associated with strength, patriarchy as a domination system begins "with purely political motives aiming at goals that would allow the patrilineal Hebrews greater access to land and governmental control by destroying the ancient matrilineal system" (Stone 1976, p. 156). Another of the sources of the introduction of patriarchy is the masculine need to know a child is one's own. This need for control is a powerful aspect of unrestrained masculinity. Consider the difference between a feminine way of understanding experience and a masculine way of understanding experience and how they can function differently as they frame a spiritual sensibility. For example, a feminine sensibility enables an inclusive sense, does not require the use of violence to solve problems, exhibits an openness and support of human sexuality, and supports an openness to the new. Masculinity, on the other hand, is rooted in strength, domination, separateness, and superiority (Stone, 1976). Masculinity, in its need for power and control, can easily eclipse the vulnerability required to think and act on the theme of presence within absence.

The Evolution of the Idea of Heaven

The advent of the written word about 5,000 years ago was crucial because it meant that thoughts could be saved. In his work on consciousness as a mentality that requires making choices, Jaynes (1976) suggests that prior to being able to make choices, people heard voices (i.e., auditory hallucinations) when decisions were necessary. Stress would arise and one side of the brain would *speak* to the other, providing guidance. An example of this was that the sound of the voice heard as an auditory hallucination became associated over time with the voice of God. The evolution of the biology of the brain caused this to change. The shift from that mentality to our modern way of understanding experience, which includes the ability to make choices, took place over a period of at least 3,000 years. The change was not made by people choosing a new mentality. Instead, the development of the brain was driven by a complex set of forces both outside and within the ordinary lives of people. One of the consequences of this shift in understanding of how the brain worked was a general sense that God, whose voice was no longer being heard, had gone *somewhere*. The word "heaven" became a pointer to that mysterious new place for God to be. But this initiated a problem in the understanding of the meanings and purpose of life and death because God, then, was understood to be truly apart and separated from humanity. To be sure, there were moments when people understood God to be transcending human experience, but that sense of separation meant that people needed to reach for God, to educate God about human needs, and to obey God whose judgment should sometimes be feared. We will return to this issue shortly.

Religions Bring a Wide Variety of Understandings about Life and Death

The many worldviews represented by religions constitute different ways of making sense of life and death. It is generally understood that the five oldest surviving religious traditions today had roots in what scholars refer to as the Axial Age, roughly the 700 years prior to the birth and ministry of Jesus of Nazareth. They are Judaism (this Hebrew religion became post-exilic Judaism ca. 539 BCE, and ultimately, with the destruction of the second temple in Jerusalem by the Romans in 70 CE, became Rabbinic Judaism), Christianity and Islam (each with roots in the Abrahamic tradition of Judaism), Hinduism, and Buddhism. Each has evolved with many nuances and subtleties, but each also has had, ultimately, a focus on making sense of life and death. In different ways until now, each also has insisted on a condition of separateness and superiority to other traditions. Fortunately, interfaith dialogue, collaboration, and action are beginning to change that (Mackenzie, Falcon, & Rahman, 2009).

Of course, it is not easy to make sense of life because of the complications and variations contained in our experiences. But the experience of living on the planet is tangible, palpable, and actually yearning to be understood. There are many things we know about life. We tell stories to try to make sense of life. We sing songs to try to make sense of life. We seek to overcome loneliness and isolation by forming relationships with other people, relationships that, as they deepen, become precious. We write books, we travel, we listen, we compare our own lives to the lives of others, and we try our best to see ourselves in a larger picture of a healing and healed cosmos. Living is one thing. Death is another. Partly because we know very little about death. Thinking about death, from any perspective, requires more than scientific evidence or cognitive reasoning. It is, in fact, a great mystery. Most all spiritual traditions hold death as an essential element of life.

Perhaps one of the most important things to say about death is the ease with which we can avoid thinking about it—which is to say, we avoid bringing it from our subconscious awareness to our conscious awareness. That movement, when it occurs, is often prompted by some sort of catastrophe, some sort of loss, some sort of dramatic change to our ordinary activities of daily living. In fact, for most humans, an extraordinary amount of energy is expended toward not thinking about death. Not thinking about death, avoiding the topic of death, seems rooted in the great mystery of the meaning of death, a mystery that can produce fear. Such negative energy could be spent in more useful ways, for instance, as positive energy contributing to our own growth as well as to the improvement of the common good.

Egocentrism, Spiritual Wisdom, and God

Now, let us return to the belief that God actually exists apart from humanity much of the time. The silence of the voice of God as noted by Jaynes (1976) supports this belief. But verses in scripture suggest that God is Being, God is One, God is Love, and God is the source of all the features that we attribute to spiritual wisdom (e.g., Exodus 3:13ff; I John 4:7ff). Thus, it is important to consider the contrast between spiritual wisdom and the power and energy of our individual egos. As we think about what makes sense for life and for death, the ego as the holder of egocentrism can only give us a glimpse of a very narrow portion of human experience. Spiritual wisdom reveals a much broader band of human experience as it is framed by the awareness of the place of humanity in the cosmos. In fact, some of the scripture that we encounter is rooted in egocentrism and some in spiritual wisdom. Some tends toward a more exclusive sensibility and some toward an inclusive sensibility. Throughout the history of spirituality and religion, the urge toward inclusivity has been sporadic but powerful when it has surfaced. As we consider these variations in spiritual awareness in the context of trying to make sense of life and of death, there is a continuum with the extreme iteration of orthodoxy at one end. It represents the need to protect and control a set of beliefs within a spiritual tradition at all costs, often by employing separateness and superiority. At the other end is a more inclusive spiritual sensibility where separation and superiority do not exist. A mystical awareness can be identified at various points on such a continuum. A mystical awareness is a subjective awareness of connection with God, with being itself. One way to express this is to say that in creation the One becomes the many, which means that the vocation of living is to reach that awareness of connection back with the One.

Orthodoxy and Mysticism

In most traditions, orthodoxy has been dominant while the mystical, spiritual dimension has been a sub but important theme. As we now think about the theme of presence within absence and the therapeutic desire that many grievers have to communicate with those who have died, it is possible to see that some types of orthodoxy, in a way similar to patriarchy because of separateness and judgment, might actually be seen as a roadblock to achieving the wholeness and peace that might accompany such communication. Conversely, one of the aspects of religious traditions that has the possibility of playing a healing role in this theme of presence within absence is the belief that when the body dies the spirit or soul of the person lives on. In other words, some religions hold as a general tenet that after death people are *somewhere*. This is a belief that, for many people, makes sense of both life and death. This belief helps to answer questions such as, "Where did we come from?" "Why are we here?" "What are we to be doing while we are here?" and "What happens to us after we die?"

Ideally, religions are created to be conveyances for spiritual wisdom—that level of awareness that can eclipse ordinary egocentrism and helps to provide healing for self, for society, and for the planet we have been given to live on and protect. The evolution of religions is driven by spiritual desires to be sure, but also by cultural and social forces that help to support a need for community and, within that, a structured awareness of making sense of life, its purpose and meaning, and of death. Religions have the conviction that spiritual wisdom can, in fact, contribute to salvation, the healing of all of creation. Thankfully, in this extraordinary moment in history, a shift appears to be taking place toward new and more useful ways of understanding the role and place of religion in human experience.

References

Jaynes, J. (1976). *The origin of consciousness in the breakdown of the bicameral mind.* Boston: Houghton Mifflin.

Mackenzie, D., Falcon, T., & Rahman, J. (2009). *Getting to the heart of interfaith: The eye-opening, hope-filled friendship of a pastor, a rabbi and an imam.* Woodstock, Vermont: Skylight Paths Publishing.

Mellers, W. (1976). Music, Europe and communication. *The Malahat Review, 40,* 77–94.

Stone, M. (1976). *When God was a woman.* New York: Harcourt.

2 Buddhist and Attachment Perspectives on the End of Life

John E. Ruark

Introduction

About 2,500 years ago, a spoiled young aristocrat named Siddhartha Gautama had a series of encounters with illness, infirmity, and death that shook his complacent worldview to its core. This personal cataclysm eventually caused him at age 29 to abandon his comfortable life, including his wife and young son, in order to search for better answers to the problem of human suffering. After years of wandering the Gangetic plain in his quest, he awakened to some realizations about the ways our nature causes us to suffer and strategies for minimizing that suffering that has stood the test of millennia. These now form a cornerstone of belief and spiritual practice called Buddhism, which is practiced by approximately 10% of the global population.

Those of us who have been called or otherwise compelled to care for people dealing with serious illness, death, and bereavement are daily confronted with the very same awesome and painful realities about the human condition that sent young Siddhartha into his spiritual crisis. Since most of us probably lack the time and inclination to wander northern India for six years in search of answers, I am going to try to distill my best understanding of how the Buddha's insights can be brought to bear on the problems of suffering that those dealing with the end of life encounter every day. The ideas and practices that I present are the ones that have proven the most useful to me in confronting challenges in many years of work with those who are dying and grieving. Further, to my knowledge, no other author has specifically addressed the complex resonance between Buddhist principles and attachment theory, the branch of analytic thought that I have found most useful in making sense of our intimate connections to each other. I hope to enable readers to explore this resonance to help them work in their individual ways with the dynamic tension between attachment and letting go as they struggle to come to terms with death, loss, and grief. As well, this chapter explores three of the existentially most challenging aspects of end-of-life care: loss of the illusion of control, impermanence, and loss of cherished relationships.

DOI: 10.4324/9781003105077-4

Buddhist Principles

First, there are some caveats about religion and spirituality. Unlike the Abrahamic religions (i.e., Judaism, Christianity, and Islam) or the various animistic religions worldwide (e.g., Hinduism, Shinto, Shamanistic traditions), Buddhism does not demand a focus on beliefs regarding God or heaven per se. In fact, the Buddha himself said such dogmas could confuse the issue of suffering and its resolution. Rather, Buddhism is a philosophical and psychological system intended to help us better understand our own nature and the nature of the world in which we live. One corollary of this is that Buddhist principles can often comfortably coexist with other deeply held religious convictions (thus, this chapter is not intended to proselytize non-Buddhists away from their own spiritual paths). The primary article of faith in most sects of Buddhism is a belief in karma—that our actions or inactions and intentions have consequences for us in the world. Additionally, the core insight of the Buddha is that our suffering is created by our attachments, and that developing skillful ways to better manage the innate tendency of humans to form attachments is the most reliable pathway toward reduction of suffering.

This deceptively simple pair of ideas becomes a life's work to bring into practice, and much of that complexity arises around the definition of attachment. One good example of the kind of attachment that causes suffering is when we form an expectation about how things should be. The feeling we all get when reality demonstrates its annoying tendency to disappoint us by not performing according to our plans is called *dukkha* in Pali (the language in which the Buddha spoke), a word that can be translated as unsatisfactoriness. Depending on the importance of the issue at stake, the sensation of *dukkha* can range from mild irritation to the worst suffering imaginable. For example, when I am driving in my car, I have a sense for how fast I need to be going and how much space I prefer between my car and the others sharing the road. All too often, someone encroaches on that, say, by cutting me off or tailgating me or having the nerve to be blocking my way by preferring to go more slowly. The unpleasant feelings I have can range from irritation to rage depending on how egregious the violation of my sense of entitlement to have things the way I think they should be. In fact, I find driving to be my most reliable daily laboratory for practicing mindfulness, though I am embarrassed to report how often I lapse into reactivity, at least in my thoughts, and sometimes in my actions.

And, of course, we have other kinds of attachments that can bring us our greatest joy as well as our most poignant suffering, which are our attachments to the people we love. Here we have an interesting dynamic tension. On the one hand, we can, at least theoretically, avoid suffering by avoiding attachments. However, if we somehow manage to do that, life looks pretty bleak because we then are also excluded from what most of us experience as life's greatest joys, the rewards of loving and being loved. Therefore, to love is to sign on for suffering, and to fail to love is to avoid the very essence of the best of what life has to offer.

Interpersonal Neurobiological Perspectives

Our dilemma is further complicated by an unpleasant reality about the nature of our brains, as elucidated by the fascinating developing field of interpersonal neurobiology. In recent decades, there has been a scientific revolution in the field of brain science since functional brain imaging now enables us to watch human brains in action at relatively high resolution for the first time. This relieves neuroscientists from having to rely on rat and monkey brains as their best approximation of people. As a result, our knowledge of the human brain in sickness and health has been literally doubling every year, such that it is almost impossible to keep up with the new information. We will be looking into implications of some of this research later, but for now, the current, perhaps unfortunate truth about our brains is that the part that makes us human is literally designed to form attachments. What was our intelligent designer thinking? If you look at the size of the forebrain in mammals, you will see that it increases in direct proportion to the complexity of the problem each species faces in finding prey and avoiding predators, or in other words, predicting the future.

And the kinds of attachments that cause suffering are exactly that—predictions of the future and expectations about how that future should look. Therefore, no matter how hard we work at not forming attachments or expectations for others, we as humans are stuck, because the instant we let down our guard, our brain is going to start doing what it was created to do. And there we are again, flipping off other drivers on our way home from the meditation retreat. This is why mindfulness, which is the state of consciousness that enables us to be aware of and manage our attachments and reactions, is always characterized as a practice. We rarely get it completely right, and the instant we relax our efforts, we too often relapse into habitual patterns of reactivity that cause problems for ourselves and others. When it comes to freedom from the all-too-well-worn bad habits of obsessive thought, Aldous Huxley (2010), in his introduction to the radio broadcast of *Brave New World,* laid out our impossible task succinctly, "The price of liberty, and even of common humanity, is eternal vigilance."

The neurobiology of this process is dictated by a principle called Hebb's Axiom, which states that, "Neurons that fire together wire together" (Hebb, 1949). This simple concept has powerful consequences, because the more often we repeat a pattern of thought or action, the more hardwired it becomes. Fortunately, the reverse is true as well—if we stop repeating a pattern it decays and can be replaced by newer, more adaptive patterns if we diligently practice the new way of thinking and acting. For example, back when I was addicted to tennis, I always wanted to hit a topspin backhand, and I attended a famous tennis teacher's clinic to learn how. He got me up in front of the class, had me close my eyes, and take my customary backhand grip. He turned the racket in my hand to an unfamiliar position and asked me how it felt. I replied, "Crummy!" He said, "Get used to that crummy feeling, because you're going to hit a thousand balls with it this week." By the end of the week, I had a real topspin backhand, and another level of understanding of the old saying, "Fake it 'til you make it!"

A growing body of evidence shows that approximately one thousand repetitions over three to four months are required to replace an old neural network with a new one (Swart, 2015), which illustrates that this kind of change is not accomplished overnight, but it can be done. And, in fact, although the resolution and speed of a functional-MRI (f-MRI) scan are not developed enough yet to catch individual neural networks as they are firing, contemporary neuroscience research suggests that a thought, feeling, or action is actually a transient neural network. This group of around 10,000 neurons is often widely distributed in the brain and fire simultaneously, and, if they repeat enough times, actually register in consciousness (Siegel, 2007). Research looking at the neuroscience of mindfulness practice shows fascinating data on how meditation changes the way the brain is wired away from primitive reactivity and toward a more conscious higher level of functioning (Siegel, 2007). For example, before I started meditating over two decades ago, I would have challenging moments during psychotherapy where I would become emotionally activated when working with difficult patients. I would become confused or reactive, and all too often found that I would shoot from the hip and say things that I later regretted. After meditating for a few years, I discovered that when I began to feel confused or emotionally flooded during a session, if I centered my body in my chair and took a couple of mindful breaths, more often than not, I would calm down and have a better chance of responding skillfully in a challenging moment.

Meditation

To many people, the idea of sitting meditation is daunting and may evoke negative associations with religious cults or pretentious gurus. I try to demythologize it by describing meditation as a simple laboratory that eliminates as many outside distractions as possible from the task of observing what is going on in the mind and body. Siegel (2007) makes the point that meditation (along with yoga and tai chi) is an integrative activity in the brain, activating higher and lower centers as well as both sides of the brain, simultaneously. Similarly, studies cited by Goleman (2006) show that a ten-week mindfulness course enabled a fear reaction to

a subliminally perceived threat to be diverted from its usual terrified reaction in the right brain to the less reactive left brain and to avoid its
previously induced panic response, all within 250 milliseconds. Thus, the
more we meditate, the more robust our powers of self-observation and
self-intervention become, and the more likely we are to recognize dysfunctional reactivity as it is arising and to shunt our thoughts and actions
off onto more productive pathways instead.

A big part of what meditation practice teaches us is that we can tolerate
challenging physical and mental states without getting caught up in an
escalating panic. Further, once we return our focus to the breath, unpleasant inner states can be revealed as transient and insubstantial.
However, this important realization needs to be reinforced literally
thousands of times in order to become strong enough to call upon in
situations of extreme stress or emotional challenge. Meditation is a behavioral cornerstone upon which those contending with their own death
or that of a loved one can build their coping strategies for the overwhelming existential challenges often faced at the end of life or during
bereavement. In this way, mindful meditation provides the neuroscientific
basis for the phrase, *this, too, shall pass.*

Attachment Theory

We next turn to the key concepts of attachment theory. As a former
scientist, I find this body of thinking to be particularly convincing because it is substantially based on actual experimental evidence. John
Bowlby, Mary Ainsworth, and Mary Main have pioneered illuminating
experiments observing toddlers and older children confronted with a
series of challenges (called the Strange Situation experiments) that have
shed light on human attachment structures and mechanisms (e.g.,
Ainsworth & Bell, 1970). This body of research has led to a coherent
theory well summarized by Siegel (2012). To paraphrase Siegel: because
of the size of the human brain, Mother Nature faced a particular problem
in getting that large brain through each mother's limited birth canal,
which she solved by having us born far less developed than most other
species. As a result, human infants are by far the most dependent newborns of any species, requiring parental attention for close to two decades
before most offspring function fully independently. Thus, the intrapsychic apparatus of attachment was the evolutionary answer to fos-
tering the optimal degree of attention from parents to their relatively
undeveloped children. In fact, attachment is the very first developmental
task each newborn faces, which underlines attachment's importance to
healthy survival. To illustrate, high-speed cinematography of newborns
and their mothers show micro-expressions being traded back and forth at
rates far faster than we are capable of consciously registering, as the
brains of both participants actively wire to reinforce their connection to

each other. The success of this initial bonding is vital to the physical and psychological health of a baby, and many studies have shown the disastrous consequences of the failure of this primordial attachment (e.g., Siegel, 2012).

Object constancy, the evidence-based sense in children that their caregivers are effectively keeping track of them and their well-being, is established by being tested on a daily basis many thousands of times in early life. Those who lack it, whether by congenital defects (e.g., autism spectrum disorder) or parental neglect, are often doomed to struggle with relationship difficulties throughout life. Proximity-seeking behaviors such as clinging, protest, or yearning are universally present in normal infants and lead to appropriate parental reassurances of loving presence in normal development. And, likewise, across the lifespan, these primordial intrapsychic structures are at the heart of our reactions to significant losses and deaths, as our most basic sense of safety in a threatening world comes under terrifying challenge. These deep patterns of attachment also form the basis of the absence within presence that some grievers experience—an ongoing sense of rewarding connection to loved ones from whom we are parted through death.

The fascinating new field of interpersonal neurobiology (e.g., Cozolino, 2014) explores this realm in depth by stating that the intimate relationships that are the result of the attachment process create shared neural networks among the attached parties. One simple test of the function of such networking is the powerful contagion of a yawn among people who are bonded to each other in this way. These networks are quite durable as long as they are actively reinforced by attuned interactions. However, once interactions cease by virtue of absence or death, they tend to decay over time. They can be secondarily reinforced by reminiscing about the absent person, which is one reason bereaved individuals often find great comfort in thinking or speaking about their lost loved one, or by revisiting archival materials, such as photos or videos of the deceased person. Such networks form the basis of our ongoing sense of relationship to those we have lost through death. An intuitive grasp of this phenomenon might be reflected in the multi-cultural lore that the memory of an individual only remains as long as there is someone living to keep it alive. In grief counseling, it is quite possible and often comforting to use reminiscence, ritual, and courageous *leaning in* (Chödrön, 2001) to address the painful emotions of grief to reinforce these neural networks and maintain some vestige of relationship to lost loved ones. Conversely, avoidance of such practices can be a contributor to grief pathology.

The Importance of Professional Caregivers

So how might we help bereaved individuals by offering practical help in coping with the impossibly challenging work of abiding with dying and grieving? End-of-life experiences often evoke the deepest levels of re-activity and suffering for everyone involved, especially because it high-lights the loss of many of our most cherished attachments. The dying person is losing everything precious to them: their health, life, world, freedom from pain, cherished activities and functions, relationships, and all too often, their dignity. Additionally, every incompletely grieved or worked-through loss or trauma from earlier life is likely to be restimu-lated at some point in the course of a terminal illness. Professional caregivers often are there to support the dying and their loved ones and help them to maintain as much equanimity and grace as possible through these challenges. The families and support communities of the dying likewise will be confronted with endless similar variations of the chal-lenges faced by the dying person, especially with regard to grief. They, too, look to professional caregivers as their guides for making it through these harrowing times with as little unnecessary suffering and as much of a chance to offer support for their loved ones as they can.

Existential Realities

By definition, a guide has to lead the way through unknown territory. Although we may have traveled the harrowing path from diagnosis of a life-threatening illness through death and grief many times with our pa-tients, familiarity alone will not suffice to make us the best possible guides. For the sake of our own mental health, which will be reflected in our ability to continue to thrive while doing this work with heart, each of us needs to come to terms with illness, infirmity, and death for ourselves. If we have not done this serious emotional spadework, no matter how good our technique is or the level of our training or the depth of our knowledge, it will be prone to fail us when our own unresolved issues around loss or trauma get restimulated by what our patients and their families are facing. For example, my own early history is one of sig-nificant abuse at the hands of those who were responsible for caring for me. I have put in many hours of couch time in therapy trying to lay those demons to rest, but most of my biggest mistakes as a psychotherapist still surround that issue. Recently, a skilled and trusted supervisee of mine was presenting a case in which she got off-center in working with a pa-tient who had just summoned up the courage to talk about a shameful experience. In her rush to deal with her own anxiety about what he might reveal, she made a move that likely made it more difficult for him to tell his secret. Because of my own trauma history, I felt a sudden protec-tiveness of him and an intense need for her to see and acknowledge her error. In that critical moment, my old wounds were triggered and I lost my sense of self-awareness. Instead of responding to her as a trusted guide, I reacted from the place of my own woundedness. In retrospect, both the supervisee's and my own early experiences of being shamed by caregivers and other adults found enaction in my dynamic with my supervisee. As a result, I was not as gentle as she needed and deserved. In fact, I repeated her error. I actually represented the unkind parent, which meant that repair was needed to mend our professional relationship.

What this rather embarrassing-yet-all-too-common example illustrates is that even when we have put a lot of time and energy into facing our own issues, we will continue to get triggered when the sensitive areas of our trauma wounds get touched. If we lose the ability to practice mindfulness, our reactivity can be damaging for us and those who depend on us. Thus, mindfulness practice is a necessary vehicle for ongoing awareness of areas of challenge for each of us. But how might this be specifically important for end-of-life caregivers?

The Illusion of Control

The biggest emotional challenge faced as we confront death (or its early harbingers, the loss of cherished functions and relationships) is the inability to maintain our illusion of control. For many people, especially those who have been traumatized by loss, the world feels big and dangerous. However, it is a fantasy (however comforting) that we are in control of what happens to us and to those we love. A sense of control tends to feel extremely reassuring when Mother Nature is kind enough to leave us alone in the reverie that we have the power to keep ourselves and our loved ones safe. Unfortunately, life-threatening illness or accident or other forms of trauma often rudely interrupt that illusion, including for professional caregivers. The ability to notice when we are tempted to try to control the things we cannot, and to practice consciously letting go can allow us to be islands of equanimity when things get chaotic around us. If we stay calm and nonreactive, it is much easier for patients and families to remain calm themselves.

Impermanence

An equally formidable emotional challenge that death demands that we face is the notion of impermanence. The Buddha described impermanence as one of the basic characteristics of worldly existence, and science has done nothing to contradict him in two-and-a-half millennia. Everything in the world is constantly changing. If you adjust time or physical frame of reference, even the molecules in our bodies and our bodies themselves are changing. Americans are known for being materialistic. As a death-denying culture, our beloved possessions often are what allow us to hide behind an illusion of permanence. We can find temporary comfort in believing that our houses and furniture and gadgets are going to last forever, while intuitively knowing they will not.

For many of us, our aging bodies remind us constantly about this very issue, as pain-free life fades into distant memory and various cherished physical functions become steadily shakier. On good days, these little indignities can serve as teachers of how to face death with equanimity. On not-so-good days, we often react in protest, through personal pity parties and internal whining. But bringing consciousness to our own private encounters with mortality may be the best training ground for developing equanimity that can be lent to our patients and their families as they face more immediate and terrifying reminders of impermanence, such as looming loss. Routinely sharing feelings about our own fragility with sympathetic friends or colleagues can help our growth in this area. To illustrate, an anthropologist observing a tribe in the highlands of Papua New Guinea overheard a very wise statement spoken by an aboriginal sorcerer to his frustrated apprentice: "There are no obstructions, only instructions" (personal communication, March 23, 1980). A famous teacher of psychotherapy, John Firman (personal communication, January 13, 2005), put the same piece of wisdom into different words: "What's in the way *is* the way."

Loss of Cherished Relationship

A final more specific challenge experienced by professional and lay end-of-life caregivers is the loss of cherished relationship, both between our patients and their families and in our own lives. The Buddha said that nirvana (also defined as enlightenment or awakening) was more difficult, if not impossible, to be achieved by householders (as opposed to monastics) in part because the deep interdependence between family members made it impossible to maintain equanimity in the face of losing beloved persons. Interpersonal neurobiology shows that deep relationship between humans creates big changes in the brains of both partners, such that losing each other has devastating effects (Cozolino, 2014). The more deeply we love, the more intertwined our minds and brains become in relationship, and the greater the suffering we experience when inevitably one of us leaves the other. The fact that humans still choose to love in spite of an intuitive awareness of this truth about loss may be one of our most admirable and courageous traits. One way to practice equanimity with regard to this truth is to daily think about the loss of each of the people we love most dearly, to allow ourselves to sink into the terror and misery of that inevitability. This quick trip through our own ultimate nightmare can serve to sharpen our appreciation for those we love, lessen our tendency to take them for granted, and allow us to rehearse their impermanent state of presence. This exercise in trying on our most feared losses can help enable us to be more open-hearted and equanimous with patients and families who are facing such grim realities not by choice. Through this daily practice, we are reminded and can remind them that we are endowed with the mechanisms to get through the suffering of such losses and return more quickly to normal life if we allow ourselves to feel and express the misery we must endure when a loved one dies. One of the hardest realities about grief and mourning is that their successful navigation requires feeling and abiding with some of the most unpleasant emotions (e.g., sadness, anger, fear) that we will ever experience. Once we have found the courage to grasp this nettle, we are often surprised at how much vitality we can rediscover, and how the avenues into restorative connection to lost loved ones can reopen in our cherished memories, thanks to our deep attachment mechanisms.

Conclusion

Astute readers likely will have noted a similarity between the suggested techniques for attending to all three of the existentially most challenging aspects of end-of-life care: loss of the illusion of control, impermanence, and loss of cherished relationships. Like many other Buddhist techniques, this practice involves doing the opposite of what our primitive reactions advise us. This principle dovetails with how the nature of our mind causes us to suffer (e.g., through a false sense of control), such that around difficult issues it is often more skillful in the long run to do the opposite of our first instinct. Our initial impulses around painful topics are to avoid them. Many Buddhist teachers and authors discuss this tendency. Pema Chödrön (2001) calls it *leaning in* to painful issues. For many people, the metaphor of leaning in may seem more feasible, particularly to our less-brave side, than *diving in*, especially when current life stressors seem barely tolerable to think about, let alone embrace. Effective leaning in usually requires support for engaging in and staying with unpleasant emotional states until they are worked through by our intrinsic healing mechanisms and we become accepting of them.

Our journey has taken us from the depths of a 4,500-year-old ancient belief system to the cutting edge of modern neuroscience, as we explored the powerful resonance between humanity's longest-running experiment in observation of human consciousness to the exponentially increasing scientific examination of our brains and minds. We can take reassurance that these two widely disparate pathways dovetail in helping us to understand the power and mystery of how we attach to each other and how we can best support ourselves and others in navigating the hardest emotional challenges we face in the course of our lives, including death and grief.

References

Ainsworth, M., & Bell, S. (1970). Attachment, exploration, and separation: Illustrated by the behavior of one-year-olds in a strange situation. *Child Development, 41*(1), 49–67. 10.2307/1127388

Chödrön, P. (2001). *The places that scare you.* Boston: Shambhala.
Cozolino, L. (2014). *The neuroscience of human relationships.* New York: W. J. Norton.
Goleman, D. (2006). *Emotional intelligence.* New York: Bantam Books.
Hebb, T.O. (1949). *The organization of behavior.* New York: Wiley and Sons.
Huxley, A. (2010). *Brave new world* (11th ed.). New York: Vintage.
Siegel, D. (2007). *The mindful brain.* New York: W. J. Norton.
Siegel, D. (2012). *The developing mind.* New York: W. J. Norton.
Swart, T. (2015). *Neuroscience for leadership.* London: Palgrave.

3   A Shamanic Experience of Restoration: Journeying, Ritual, and Ceremony

Jeffery Black

Introduction

Shamanism, the oldest and most ubiquitous of healing practices, is no longer widely applied in Western or industry-based societies. Because its practice is based on oral and mystical traditions (originally common to tribal and hunter-gather societies) there is a notable lack of written theory or empirical verification of its effectiveness for review. Learning shamanic traditions and its practice are obtained through a mentoring relationship with a shamanic master rather than formalized training requirements, written studies, or examinations pursuant to licensure.

Unlike the *healing from without* of Western medicine and surgery (e.g., diagnostic tests, medications, extirpative procedures), the healing objective of shamanism is to create *healing from within.* In shamanic tradition, an autonomous identity (soul) requires the maintenance of an energic equilibrium between the spectrum of physical and mental energies, including supra-sensory cosmic energies (spirit), within and around us. When the energic integrity of the soul is disturbed, it may be restored through shamanic rituals that focus on internal states of consciousness, altered perceptions, and guided *journey* that may have particular value in healing energic disruption of grief-related fixations. This chapter's objective is to clarify the cosmology of shamanism as it pertains to the contemporary and useful application of working with bereaved adults, especially those whose grief experience includes a fixation on the *presence within absence* of the deceased.

Understanding Shamanism

As a board-certified psychiatrist, my professional training emphasized Western traditions of rationality, reductionism, and evidence-based medical and surgical interventions. The timeless and ubiquitous traditions of shamanic healing from within occurring energetically in the mind, body, and soul were disregarded by my profession. During my psychiatric training, an integrated biopsychosocial model was proposed

DOI: 10.4324/9781003105077-5

but not practiced and was, in my mind, incomplete without the addition of the spiritual component. Despite the imposed discordance, I became interested in understanding shamanic healing. The practices of shamanism are taught as an oral tradition and my teachers were energy healers from North and South America who were foundational for my own spiritual journey.

What drew me to the shamanic practices of energetic imbalance was its diverse and efficacious traditions of healing (Kirmayer, 2004). The shamanic practice of energetic transformation became an important adjunctive offering for my practice. Particularly when treating someone disabled by dying and death, the shamanic tradition of healing from within offers a timeless and useful model to consider. Grief or loss of any kind has a physiological response residing in the physical body (Van Der Kolk, 2014), as well as the psychological presence within absence of the deceased—the story of their living, dying, and death—that may absorb life-affirming energy untreated with medication or rational, reductionistic psychotherapies. My understanding and training in shamanic concepts of energetic transformation and journeying techniques remain additions in my efforts in healing the energic fixations of grief and reestablishing a harmonic balance of the perceptive presence within absence of the deceased.

Shamans are considered people of the percept more than the rational concept. With perceptual shifts, outer and inner worlds may be reframed in restorative combination. Energetic healing establishes connections with the energy of the universe (Spirit) as well as different states of consciousness (Villoldo, 2000). Perceptual shifts change the energy of the mind, body, and soul surrounding grief, reconstructing the image of presence within absence, and in so doing provide a revised perception of the acute pain of loss within a restored energic relationship.

Shamanic tools used in healing require a detachment from formal conceptualization and known rules of reductionistic thinking into the possibility of an experience beyond literal understanding (Villoldo, 2000). Kirmayer (2004) uses metaphor to understand the central core of healing as "transformations of the quality of experience" beyond Western healing modalities' dependency upon conceptualized reason for the illness (p. 34). Shamanic practices are more than symbol, ritual, and metaphor. They are deep and direct connections to Spirit.

Both Western medicine and shamanic healing share a goal of providing a framework for healing experiences (McClenon, 1993). The practitioner must have the intention of serving the patient's best interest and a goal to support the human spirit as well as restore the body, mind, and soul (Steinhorn, Din, & Johnson, 2017). A multimodal, integrative approach of shamanic practices supports the human spirit and provides an adjunctive healing that is nonverbal while utilizing the presence of non-ordinary reality and deep connection to Spirit.

After the traumatic loss of a loved one, the griever's perceptions of the deceased's presence within absence may become disabling and do not necessarily dissipate with the act of telling the story of the relationship with the deceased. With intensely traumatic and sudden loss, healing requires connection with the internalized presence in new ways (Van Der Kolk, 2014). The palpable act of remembering life more than the death itself becomes a conduit for change, and journeying through ritual transforms the story into an act of honoring.

The opening chapter of this book cites Jerome Frank's foundational principles of healing:

1   An emotionally charged and confiding relationship with a helping person
2   A healing setting
3   A conceptual scheme or myth providing a plausible explanation of symptoms
4   A collaborative ritual or procedure to restore health

As we will show, shamanic practices fit well with Frank's outline of therapeutic healing. And, although journeying might be considered under principle number four as a collaborative ritual, it is such an essential practice within shamanism that it will be considered separately here as an accessory principle of healing (Harner, 1980). These principles are observed in this shamanic intervention and will serve as clarifying reference points in this descriptive chapter. We will begin our inquiry with a case illustration to first illustrate the shamanic model and healing principles in action.

Case Study

John, a 30-year-old, married construction worker, was referred by his primary care physician a month after an acute illness left him with lingering depression and anxiety. In treatment over the next few months, John presented with rigid concepts about himself and his past, and, despite an initial response to medications and supportive psychotherapy, John felt stuck.

John usually saw his close friend, Tom, on a daily basis around the apartment complex; however, they had not met in over a week. Tom was not answering his phone and his voicemail was full. John felt a sense of urgency and dread as he found a way into Tom's apartment, where he discovered his lifeless body. Tom had hung himself. After cutting Tom down, John called 911 and held him until the police arrived.

John was initially numb and mindlessly focused on the practical aftermath—answering the questions of the police and medical examiner. But once separated from the scene and in his own space, John began vomiting, then shaking, and could not stop crying. He remembered rocking and making a guttural sound of pain as his supportive wife held him in a consoling embrace.

Over the next several days, questions about Tom's suicide became obsessions. He couldn't understand why Tom had killed himself, and could not interrupt the spiral of overthinking. Why? Why? Followed by the "if onlys" and the "what ifs." He both personalized the suicide and was enraged by it as he tried piecing together what had happened. In recurring nightmares, John re-experienced the visual reenactment of the hanging. His imagination began the process of filling in the gaps with remorseful self-blaming. His feeling of helplessness was overwhelming. He could not sleep or eat. Something was missing. In his grief, John was unable to process all that he had seen and all that had happened. His heart ached.

In many shamanic traditions, trauma creates an intense perception of loss, such that in that moment of finding Tom, a deep piece of John's identity or soul separated. His reenactment images of Tom's dying overpowered his conceptualization of his relationship with Tom. Thus, Tom's suicide continued as a senseless riddle. With no suicide note, no warning, no clues, John felt stuck and shaken.

In that first session after Tom's suicide, John remained immersed in the trauma of the reenactment story and felt that medication and talking were no longer helping. I offered an option that was based on the teachings of energy healers, described the process to him, and made an appointment within the next few days for a shamanic journey.

Together, John and I used journeying to retrieve the fragmented part of himself. I introduced a ceremonial, sacred space and called on the energies around us to guide and protect and to give wisdom for the journey. Music without words was played (accompanied by rhythmic drumming) and a rattle was used during the process of journeying. Prior to lying on a mat on the floor, John chose a healing stone or khuya (Wilcox, 2004) from a group of stones. This khuya was placed by John on an area in the center of his abdomen where he felt the most tension. As I used a rattle in rhythm with the drumming music, John breathed deeply and was instructed to breathe any thoughts, feelings, and emotions that no longer served him, from his body into the stone. This would allow him to release the energies that were potentially keeping him fixated on the traumatic aftermath of Tom's suicide. Once his breathing became steady and the energy flowed smoothly, I used the rattle to create a rhythm to journey to the lower world. The missing piece of John's soul was offered a safe

> *haven and returned to John. The message from the wisdom gleaned included the request that John tell stories of Tom's life.*
>
> *At the completion of the journey, the removal of the stone, and the closing of sacred space, John and I discussed the shamanic request. John remarked that he felt lighter and believed he could sit with his grief and the traumatic experience. Over the next week, he focused on his grief each day and included the living energy of Tom. He retold a fuller story of Tom's life and, by reaching out to their mutual friends and listening to their stories, understood that his grief was collective. His sleep improved and his despondency and anxiety lessened. The memory of the horrific event remained, but John focused on remembering Tom's life and not the traumatic ending. Journeying restored the lost fragments of John's soul that were taken by the loss. Once reunited, John's vitality and reengagement with life returned.*

Therapeutic Relationship

After Tom's suicide, John's distress was disabling. John's determination to obtain assistance in this difficult time and his confidence in the possibility of release of pain was based on his already developed trust in the therapeutic relationship that he and I had established. Unlike John, persons in non-Western cultures more readily accept a therapeutic relationship with a shaman whose therapeutic role, rituals, and worldview are consistent with their own (Walsh, 1991).

John willingly participated in the guided meditation, while I journeyed, with the objective of decreasing the repetitive nightmares and incessant intrusive thoughts. I applied energetic techniques to create a suprasensory experience that held the possibility of restoration and, most importantly, a reduction of his symptoms. His immediate distress needed to be addressed. It was my hope that lasting change might also follow.

A Healing Setting

Within shamanic traditions, rituals, ceremony, and journeying require a healing setting made sacred. Most experiences transpire in a space set aside for these practices; however, any setting can be made sacred by calling on the energies of the ancestors, the natural elements, the earth, and the sky. The known environment of my office and our established therapeutic relationship enabled John to engage in the experience of reducing the strong emotions surrounding his traumatic grief. We created a sacred space together, and the setting itself was less important than the intention and the energy surrounding the process.

Conceptual Scheme or Myth

In his work on shamanism, Eliade (1964) defines a shaman as one who uses ecstatic techniques and has a deep connection to a Supreme Being or Divine Consciousness. Shamans have an intimate connection with those they serve as well as an evolving connection with Spirit. They use non-ordinary states of consciousness to produce change and move freely between ordinary and non-ordinary reality. These altered states of consciousness afford the healer opportunity to move beyond the five senses into a suprasensory state (Harner, 1980). Shamans use ritual, ceremony, and journeying to create an active space to form energic connections with the deceased. They are deeply connected to a realm of images, symbols, entities, and energies. Through active intention, shamans assist those who are grieving to move beyond the created stories surrounding death and instead to build bridges with new ways of perceiving (Somé, 1993). The experiences are beyond the known memory and feelings of individual and collective moments.

Shamans are also map makers. The maps of non-ordinary realms (lower, middle, and upper worlds) become the tools to explore the progressively deeper parts of the self and the connection to the energy of all things. The practitioner uses these experiential gradations as guides to understand the energetic causes of disruption especially in grief, death, and soul loss (Greer, 2014).

Frank (1991) clarifies the *plausible worldview* in therapy as resting with the healing person and the transformation of meanings. The plausible worldview within shamanic cosmology and the accessibility of energy beyond the senses is poised between perceptual realms of the lower, middle, and upper world that not only represent different realms but require different states of consciousness (Walsh, 2001). These perceptual levels may represent different dimensions of experience and are perceptual maps. Within the shamanic cosmology, each world is independent, alive, and simultaneously exists. Practitioners can guide between and within these perceptual levels to reestablish an energic balance after traumatic and sudden dying (Walsh, 1991).

Shamanic healing practices are about balance and integration and require a sacred exchange of energy with Spirit. The Q'ero word *ayni* describes this sacred exchange. Ayni is the heart of shamanic healing practices and is defined as sacred reciprocity. It is the constant practice of a shamanic healer in any ritual, ceremony, or journey.

Energy in the Andean tradition of wisdom keepers and healers is both light and heavy, *sami* and *hucha* (Wilcox, 2004). Sami is the exquisitely beautiful living energy of the cosmos. It is the energy of health and vitality and a reminder of our true nature as spirit. Hucha is heavy and misplaced living energy that lodges itself in our bodies and is any thought, feeling, emotion, or perception that no longer serves the wellbeing of individuals or communities. This misplaced energy blocks the flow of life and creates dis-ease. This non-dual living energy is on a continuum. What is heavy for one person may be light for another. Working with sami and hucha creates ayni. Grief manifests both sami and hucha. The process of journeying offers a chance to restore ayni.

The traumatic experience of Tom's death created an imbalance in the continuum of energy between John and Tom. For John, Tom's dying felt "as if a part of me separated." It was, as Tick (2005) described, the "removal of the center of experience with the living body without snapping the connection" (p. 16). In his grief and anguish, John continued to recreate the story of Tom's dying and could not move beyond his own guilt and feelings of inadequacy. He felt he owed Tom something. Returning this energy, this soul piece, back to ayni was essential and lifegiving (Ingerman, 1991).

John's belief and understanding of shamanic cosmology was not necessary in the session; however, belief in the potential healing process of the relationship certainly was key. The consequential shift in John's energy and the subsequent reduction in symptoms cannot be explained by his immediate personal understanding of what occurred. After the initial description of the process, much of the session was spent in silence accompanied by music with drumming and rhythmic rattling. Any instructions during the journey included reminders to breathe and be fully present without being seized by the story of Tom's dying. The act of release through breathing gave John the experience of linking the traumatic event to a revised response beyond shock or horror. He gained some control over his response. Restoration occurred as the energy surrounding the witnessed traumatic death left John's body and mind, and the lost piece of his soul felt safe enough to return. If John believed anything prior to the experience, it was the hope that it would be helpful.

Collaborative Ritual or Procedure to Restore Health

Grief requires living consciously and deliberately. Shamanic rituals are active experiences that connect individuals and communities to states beyond the five senses and offer an opportunity to release those thoughts, feelings, and emotions that are no longer serving the individual or community. Using this tool, energy healers understand grief is best expressed in an offering of release so that beauty springs forth from the empty places. Rituals are necessary in healing because they can help alter the patient's subjective perspective (Frank, 1991). For many, death remains a time of self-absorption, fear, unpredictability, and pain. By creating connections through ritual, practitioners can aid the living and the dead in finding their way into the light.

Ritual is essential to shamanic restoration and is structured in four parts:

- After setting a clear intention, an invocation is offered and sacred space is opened.
- Participants engage in a dialogue with the invoked energies and call for assistance, protection, clarification, and wisdom.
- Repetitive actions represent the purpose and intention of the ritual.
- Rituals end with the closing of sacred space (Somé, 1993).

Through these rituals, those who grieve learn to hold their loss stories in new ways. The necessary remembering regains a sense of energic direction and shifts: from a story of traumatic loss to a story of the person, from the moment of death to moments of living, from the energy of affliction to the energy of expansion. The action in ritual can be something as simple as breathing while remembering, lighting a candle, gathering around a fire to say goodbye, attending a funeral, or traveling to the graveside. Attention makes the experience practical, while intention makes it supra-sensory. The actions taken are full of potential and become a conscious and deliberate creation beyond the known. In so doing, they deeply connect participants with Spirit (Somé, 1993).

Journeying

Journeying is the quintessential shamanic practice (Harner, 1980). The practitioner begins with a clear intention and makes use of sacred imagination within a ritualized space. The objective of the journey is to acquire perceptual transformation, even power, in order to heal (Walsh, 2001). Repetitive sounds and breathing create a transpersonal and supra-sensory connection with supra-sensory levels of energy and the practitioner explores these non-ordinary states of reality to gain insights and guidance for an individual and/or surrounding community (Villoldo, 2000). The objective of John's journey was to retrieve his soul fragment for safekeeping (Ingerman, 1991) and to bring the body, mind, and spirit back into ayni (Villoldo, 2005).

The traumatic moment of loss created an opportunity for a non-reductionistic intervention for John. In the journey, I accessed the lower world and engaged those energies in a more harmonic balance. The altered state of consciousness, experienced via rhythmic music and rattling, opened the threshold to the possibility of healing. John participated by breathing the full expression of the energies of the past images into the stone, created a redirection of energy to the stone, and then from his abdomen to his heart. In turn, it was my duty to return the wisdom, messages, and requests from the spiritual referents. We reframed the terrorizing imaginal death images and connected them to a new way of perceiving what happened. Given the task of describing Tom's life and no longer focusing solely on his manner of dying, restoration was possible, and John's traumatic grief was diminished by a healing from within. Grief could then continue to evolve, allowing for a reconnection with his living relationship with Tom (presence within absence).

For the next four months, I met with John for several supportive sessions before he terminated therapy and moved to a new city. If measured in symptom relief, the efficacy of John's experience of journeying was positive. His sleep, mood, and relationships improved. Most importantly, he did not have the intrusive reenactment of Tom's dying. John found that Tom's presence within absence was no longer encumbered by his own shock and horror from the death event and had crossed a threshold into a new way of experiencing life, loss, and death.

Summary

There is beauty in grieving that is natural and necessary. Experiences with presence within absence require those living with loss to remember and to reengage with the healing energy of grief. Moving beyond a reductionistic view that makes certain forms of grief pathological requires a full, integrative approach that draws upon the wisdom and knowledge of the biological, psychological, social, and spiritual dimensions of a full and vital life. To separate any of these at the expense of the others is to close the mind and limit the possibilities of wholeness. This creates suffering.

Today, stoic and individualized vs. communal grief expressions may be questioned because they are not efficacious in the broader goal of restoration and connection. The recent increase in awareness of different cultural grief practices has led to an influx of teachings, webinars, and seminars. This presents a solitary healing process as being *traditional* risking misappropriation. Instead, a more capacious healing honors all traditions with a deep appreciation for their transformation of potential myopic paradigms. The very act of incorporating a different ideology and methodology in an acceptable cultural form allows for an imaginal shift in the perceptions of grief leading to a broadening of metaphors and explanations of restoration. Novel, but ancient, approaches, especially ones such as shamanism, with ritual and journeying, create opportunities to experience loss differently and shift the connected stories and emotions beyond an unconscious implicit experience of the loved one's traumatic dying to the ongoing living of the survivor. Thus, the dance with grief becomes a restorative living with loss.

References

Eliade, M. (1964). *Shamanism: Archaic techniques of ecstasy*. Princeton, NJ: Princeton University Press.

Frank, Jerome (1991). *Persuasion and healing.* Baltimore, Maryland: John Hopkins University Press.

Greer, C. (2014). *Change your story, change your life: Using shamanic and Jungian tools to achieve personal transformation.* Scotland, UK: Findhorn Press.

Harner, M. (1980). *The way of the shaman.* San Francisco, California: Harper Collins.

Ingerman, S. (1991). *Soul retrieval: Mending the fragmented self.* San Francisco, California: Harper One.

Kirmayer, L. (2004). The cultural and diversity of healing: Meaning, metaphor, and mechanism. *British Medical Bulletin, 69,* 33–48.

Krippner, S. (2002). Conflicting perspectives on shamans and shamanism. *American Psychologist, 57*(11), 962.

McClenon, J. (1993). The experiential foundations of shamanic healing. *The Journal of Medicine and Philosophy: A Forum for Bioethics and Philosophy of Medicine, 18*(2), 107–207.

Somé, M.P. (1993). *Ritual: Power, healing, and community.* New York: Penguin Compass.

Steinhorn, D., Din, J., & Johnson, A. (2017). Healing, spirituality and integrative medicine. *Annals of Palliative Medicine, 6*(3), 237–247.

Tick, E. (2005). *War and the soul: Healing our nation's veterans from post-traumatic stress disorder.* Wheaton, Illinois: Quest Books.

Van Der Kolk, B. (2014). *The body keeps the score.* New York: Penguin Books.

Villoldo, A. (2000). *Shaman healer sage: How to heal yourself and others with the energy medicine of the Americas.* New York: Harmony Books.

Villoldo, A. (2005). *Mending the past and healing the future with soul retrieval.* Carlsbad, California: Hay House.

Walsh, R. (1991). Shamanic cosmology: A psychological examination of the shamanic universe. *ReVision, 13,* 86–100.

Walsh, R. (2001). Shamanic experience: A developmental analysis. *Journal of Humanistic Psychology, 41,* 31–52.

Wilcox, Joan P. (2004). *Masters of the living energy: The mystical world of the Q'ero of Peru.* Rochester, Vermont: Inner Traditions.

4　A Christian Way of Making Sense of Life and Death

Donald M. Mackenzie

Introduction

The Presbyterian *Book of Common Worship* contains a phrase by Henry van Dyke (1946), a Presbyterian minister who taught English at Princeton University, reads: "We thank thee for the unquenchable trust that life does not end with death" (p. 211). While this comes from a Presbyterian source, it is a generally held Christian conviction. It is a matter of faith but with no scientific evidence to support it. What does support it is the need for hope in the midst of a very troubled world. It points to things that Christian people (and others) believe. It is the hope that somehow, after we die, we are *somewhere*. But how does this work? The challenge of this chapter is to try to answer this and other questions: What do the traditions and teachings, cultural and spiritual practices of Christianity have to say about the theme of presence within absence? What pieces of the puzzle relating spiritual wisdom to the realities of life and death do they represent? The essence of this chapter is framed here on the basis of a spiritually inclusive sensibility, a religious belief in the essential inter-connectedness of all beings. It begins with a search for an evolving consciousness of eternal life through spiritual practices. This is where we encounter Jesus's statement that the kingdom of God is both coming and already with us (Luke 17:20–21). Where does the journey begin for those who believe? Where did it begin for me?

A Transforming Moment

In the summer of 1965 following my junior year in college, I had the extraordinarily good fortune to be accepted to a college work abroad program. My summer job for two months was as a lifeguard at the pool at the Nile Hilton Hotel in Cairo, Egypt. I was from the Midwest and had not even been to New York. The leap from St. Paul, Minnesota to Cairo was stretching, wonderful, and occasionally terrifying. To keep my balance, I tried to find parallels between my experience in Egypt and my home in Illinois and my college in Minnesota. I also kept trying to

DOI: 10.4324/9781003105077-6

understand the differences, the history of Egypt as well as the common ground of being alive on the planet. On the first of August that year, I left Cairo and flew to Beirut. I had written a letter to Douglas M. Hill who was the principal of Gerard Institute in Sidon, Lebanon, asking about visiting the school with the possibility of applying for a teaching position for the follow year after my college graduation. Mr. Hill met me at the airport and we drove up into the mountains above Beirut where the Hills and their four children were renting a vacation home. When we arrived, Mr. Hill suggested I take a walk around to get a feel for the landscape. I had already been struck by the difference between the desert of Egypt and the lush green landscape of Lebanon when we arrived in Beirut. I immediately thought of the Hebrew people crossing the Jordan into Canaan. I began to walk and saw a couple of young people standing by a car drinking from cans of Coke. Already it seemed different and, again, stretching, but more familiar than the Egypt I had just left and come to love. A few steps from there, I found myself standing on a promontory and, suddenly, I could see all of Beirut down below. As I lifted my gaze, I saw the Mediterranean, and the moment made it seem as if I could see the entire world, all of creation—that bigger picture that my adolescent soul longed to encounter. It was eternity, the goodness of God, and the reassurance of the essential and healing character of the universe. The moment was not only transforming, but it also seemed to fill an empty space in me. It also lifted me, briefly from my self-absorbed and preoccupied life. I was experiencing Oneness and my part in it. It was the commencement of my spiritual journey and has framed the character of my life.

At the beginning of any spiritual journey it is natural to feel incomplete. There is so much to know and do, so many things to learn and, for all of us, narrow passages of sorrow and difficulty as well as astonishing moments of joy. We search always for resources to cope with life's problems and for opportunities for growth and the experience of the preciousness of relationships. For a Christian, the spiritual journey with its accompanying spiritual practices such as prayer and meditation, are, because they release us from our ordinary self-centeredness, reflections of eternity. Within spiritual practices is a fullness of being unlike anything else. I learned this, not all at once, but at many places along the way of my pilgrimage. It was an evolution and, although I may have had a predisposition toward it, I needed many encounters to help me into it. One of those places was a reading of Carl Gustav Jung's collection of essays, *Memories, Dreams and Reflections* (Jaffe, 1965). In the essay entitled "Travels in North Africa," Jung describes an encounter in the desert with an Arab. The Arab, he says, is unselfconsciously the person he has always been. The European, in contrast, is defined rather by what he calls *le sentiment d'incomplimentitude*—the feeling of being incomplete. This characteristic is illustrated, he says, by rockets, progress, and the ever-increasing need for speed and accomplishments. Again, this feeling of being incomplete is a feature that rests at the beginning of any spiritual journey. But in each of our Abrahamic traditions we are taught that we are, in fact, complete. We have everything we need. In the iconic film, *The Wizard of Oz* (Vidor et al., 1939), the characters have embarked on a journey on the yellow brick road because they are each convinced that they are incomplete. The Scarecrow needs brains, the Tin Woodman needs a heart, the Lion needs courage, and Dorothy needs to find her way back home. Their trip to the Emerald City is a kind of spiritual journey wherein they finally discover that they each have what they most deeply felt they lacked. The beginning of a spiritual journey is one of the most precious moments in human experience.

Making Sense of Life and Death

The Variety of Christian Understandings of Life and Death

Each Christian person combines a personal story with patterns of belief to find a place on a continuum between strict orthodoxy and the mystical sensibility that is characterized by a spiritual inclusivity of all being. Being, the *I Am,* spoken by God to Moses in Exodus 3, is the response to the question from Moses asking for the name of God.

Orthodoxy

As Henry van Dyke (1946) suggested above, in Christianity there is a strong belief that those who have died are *somewhere.* I say "somewhere" cautiously because we actually have no idea what happens to the body and mind after the body dies. Orthodoxy, the need to be correct, provides a more literal answer. After we die, we go, if we have been good, to heaven, and if we have not been good, we go to hell. In some cases, the deciding factor could be the extent to which a person reads scripture literally. Either way, one must be very careful in describing the substance of a pattern of belief. Orthodoxy has evolved and developed through the centuries as a consequence of many different spiritual and cultural experiences. And while there are many particular versions of Christian orthodoxy, what really matters in this case is a bigger picture. Christian institutions committed to strict orthodoxy hold to three very important convictions: separateness, superiority, and correct belief. In fact, these three convictions are common to all religious traditions grounded in orthodoxy. What this leads to is an individual and systemic sense that because we are superior, we must remain separate and, more importantly, we are not vulnerable. We do not need to be vulnerable because we hold to the correct beliefs. The urge to be correct, to be controlling, may block aspects of experience that can widen horizons and lead toward a fuller sense of being, a sense that we are all connected, which, in turn, implies a certain level of vulnerability. Therefore, if the principle thoughts about death are limited to the images of heaven and hell, the road to a fuller understanding of a theme such as presence within absence might seem to end prematurely.

Mysticism

Mysticism, on the other hand, the idea that in creation the One becomes the many and the vocation of the many is to return to the One, offers a vision that makes spirituality and practicality able to cooperate—healing or salvation is the vocation of every living being. Mysticism is a way of being, not a system of beliefs. This way of being is more difficult for some and less difficult for others depending on the experience of spiritual awareness in life. But in mysticism there is no eternal damnation, *no hell.* With a mystical sensibility, ultimately, everyone will get *home.* With home as a metaphor for healing, home is the realized condition of oneness which originates in the Abrahamic traditions in Judaism and continues on in Christianity and Islam. The wholeness of being is pointed to, described, and supported by a mystical sensibility, a sensibility that resides within that larger conviction that all being is interconnected.

For example, I remember several years ago a concert in support of Farm Aid (1985, Champaign, Illinois), held in an attempt to help families keep their farms instead of having to sell out to industrial farming. The concert was organized by the country music star Willie Nelson. There was a huge crowd of 80,000, and it included people who would not ordinarily be friends. The concern for one of the core institutions of American democracy, the family farm, brought people together. And, of course, the music helped to penetrate the ordinary and daily concerns of egocentrism and preoccupations, and to reach that place of deep empathy and compassion that is such strong evidence of the reality of our interconnectedness. A wholeness of being can be reached via a mystical sensibility, and it includes the vulnerability and openness to the new that both lifts us and moves us and which can open us to the therapeutic and spiritual value of communicating with those who have died. While there are no churches that would call themselves *mystical* (that would be an objectification of something that is wholly subjective), there are churches that are rooted in a conviction that spiritual inclusivity is crucial to effective ministry. The road between orthodoxy and mysticism is a road of spiritual practices such as prayer and meditation, ways of experiencing our center in the context of the awareness of the interconnectedness of all being.

Spiritual Practices

Prayer is the most common of Christian practices, but it also is widely misunderstood. In fact, prayer is often understood to be a somewhat selfish exercise, asking God for things we want but do not have, or for protections and other conditions that we feel are needed. But that is not what prayer is all about. How does prayer help us to move in the direction of a release from the ordinary concerns of our egos and into a space of empathy for others and connection to God? Prayer is about opening the heart, about eclipsing the energy of the ego, if only briefly, to find our center in that bigger picture we call eternal life. God, Being, or the Universe does not need educating about our needs or wants and desires. That is why what is felt to be unanswered prayer can be so devastating to those assuming that an enlightened God will act on our behalf. Thus, a prayer that truly feels answered is a prayer that is less about getting our needs met and more about a renewed and clarified sense of our place in the cosmos and our connection to God. This is energizing and healing. It is, in fact, an experience or glimpse of eternal life. Meditation functions in a similar way. To find our spiritual center through the breathing and focus of meditation is also to eclipse the ordinary concerns of the ego (see also Chapters 2 and 5). While these two forms of spiritual practices may be among the most common, there are countless ways to move into that place of centeredness and momentary freedom from the ego. Each one gives us, once again, a glimpse of eternal life—the kingdom of God that is both now and coming.

The Energies That Move Us

In I Corinthians 13:13, the Apostle Paul wrote, "And now faith, hope and love abide, these three, and the greatest of these is love" (New Revised Standard Version of the Bible, 1989). Each of these sensibilities, faith, hope, and love play an important role in the reflections of eternity—that bigger picture where spiritual wisdom and a deep concern for the common good eclipse our ordinary lives.

Faith

An important part of the nature of faith comes from the meaning of the treaties of the ancient Near East. One king would conquer another and say to the conquered one, "You pay me money and I will protect you." This is the shape of reality and that reality is *enacted* (Freedman, 1992). It hinges on the question of what is real (Putnam, 1951). It involves a *seeing* of life from a particular perspective, the perspective of faith. It recalls the moment when Don Quixote says of the barmaid Aldonzo Lorenzo, "I know she is just a barmaid, but for me she is my lovely lady Dulcinea" (Putnam, 1951, p. 32). He sees her through eyes of love. There is a similar story in the Bible of Solomon's encounter with two prostitutes. He has asked God for an understanding mind to govern, and later, because of the encounter with these two women, he wisely includes all people, and perhaps especially those on the margins of society (1 Kings 3:9, 16–28). The shape of reality suggests that faith is a seeing, a seeing through eyes of hope and love. And while, for orthodoxy, faith is defined in terms of beliefs, in mysticism, faith is a way of being. As a follower of orthodoxy, one can find the adoption of beliefs to be relatively simple and frankly convenient. But the movement toward a way of being requires a path of spiritual practices that can, over time, transform an ordinary life into something extraordinary. The goal is to be present to the substance of the spiritual practices that, from time to time, give us that glimpse of the eternal life.

Hope

The energy of hope is truly astonishing. It gets us up in the morning and it calms us during the day and into the night. It is important to say that hope is not the same as optimism. Optimism is important and has its own energy. But hope has moral value, it hopes for something good. Hope engages our heart, mind, and soul. And hope moves us to act. But hope is also elusive and is sometimes hard to keep in sight. That is why Emily Dickinson's poem which begins, "Hope is the thing with feathers that perches in the soul and sings the tune without the words and never stops at all" (Todd & Higginson, 1890, p. 20) moves us and helps us to make sense of hope.

An anecdote from the life of my mother has helped me to understand this. My mother lived to be 102, and during her life she was, for the most part, completely lucid and had full access to all her cognitive faculties. At the age of 92, she was transferred from her assisted living apartment to the nursing home because of a fall and suspected TIA (transient ischemic attack or brief stroke). My sense was that she did not have long to live and so I began to call her every day. It turned out that she had been grossly overmedicated and once that was stabilized, she was back to her old self. I called her every day for ten years and, while some have thought it to be a great trial for me, the truth is that it was healing and therapeutic. My mother was a talented concert pianist with an intense personality. Her ambitions for me were sometimes difficult to bear but our ten years of conversations helped me to empathize with her condition and helped her to empathize with mine. One day when she was in her late 90s, she told me that on her way home from work that day she had had the opportunity to stop by and visit with her parents. My mother said she had been walking, and saw that her parents were sitting, as they so often did, on their porch swing. Mother went on to talk about the substance of their conversation. Mercifully, I did not say that her father had died in 1956 and her mother in 1968. Instead, I heard myself say that that must have been really wonderful. At the time, I simply understood that she had drifted into a memory and out of ordinary reality. Today, I would add that she had established a restorative connection with her parents. That was 2012, so they had been dead for a long time, but my mother had drifted away from the illusion of individualism and into a connection with the collective, the whole, a connection with oneness. These experiences helped me to see how hope was functioning in her life as she experienced the presence within absence of her deceased parents.

Love

In Christianity, love is the central tenet, the core of Jesus's teachings and ministry. The idea is complicated because of the variety of meanings that accompany the word love. For Jesus, the word means loving without conditions, unconditional love. It is an honoring of the Hebrew concept of *hesed,* which is translated *lovingkindness* and *steadfast love.* Unconditional love is especially difficult for humans to comprehend because we tend to fall in love *because* of conditions (e.g., physical attraction, personal characteristics, shared values, faithfulness). But like faith, unconditional love is a way of being and the consequence of spiritual practices. In my life, when I think of unconditional love, I think of my father. My father was a very kind and thoughtful person, a patient and careful soul. He was also accepting and forgiving, perhaps in the same way as the father in the story of the prodigal son (Luke 15:11–32). While Dad's career was in higher education, as dean and later president of several liberal arts colleges, he was also a skilled carpenter, painter, electrician, and plumber. In his retirement, he and my mother used to come to visit my family twice a year and often stayed for a week, sometimes two. During that time, he would repair all the things that needed his attention at our house. While I could do some of the repairs myself, I was never as careful as he, and I was busy with my work. It was always a blessing to have him come for a visit. After his death, I was faced with trying to hire someone to do those kinds of things, or, in some cases, try to fix things myself. One day, I was looking at a set of bifold doors that were not hung evenly. I looked at them and realized that there was an adjustable foot at the base of each door. I removed the door that was not right and adjusted it and put it back. Perfect! I stepped back from the doors and said, without even thinking about it, "Thanks, Dad!" In that moment, I, too, experienced the presence within absence of my deceased loved one—my Dad, his knowledge, his experience, his skills felt present and accessible to me.

Eternal Life

The following three examples are among the most common scriptures that point toward eternal life:

Who will separate us from the love of Christ? Will hardship, or distress, or persecution or famine, or nakedness or peril, or sword? No, in all these things we are more than conquerors, through him who loved us. For I am convinced that neither death, nor life, nor angels, nor rulers, nor things present, nor things to come, nor powers, nor height, nor depth, nor anything else in all creation, will be able to separate us from the love of God in Christ Jesus our Lord. (Romans 8:35, 37–39)

Very truly I tell you, anyone who hears my word and believes in him who sent me, has eternal life.... (John 5:24a)

Then I saw a new heaven and a new earth; for the first heaven and the first earth had passed away, and the sea was no more. And I saw the holy city, the new Jerusalem, coming down out of heaven from God prepared as a bride adorned for her husband. And I heard a loud voice from the throne saying, "See the home of God is among mortals. He will dwell with them as their God; they will be his peoples, and God himself will be with them; he will wipe every tear from their eyes, Death will be no more; mourning and pain will be no more, for the first things have passed away." (Revelation 21:1–4)

While the imagery is not necessarily something we would use today nor would we necessarily be as inclined to identify God as male, the truth underneath these texts is clear: God can make everything new, God intends healing for all of creation. These purposes are important features of a Christian's understanding of eternal life.

One particularly moving example of the way these truths have found their way into popular culture is an excerpt from the play *Our Town* (Holden, Scott, Wood, Lesser, & Wilder, 1940). The stage manager in the play puts it this way:

We all know that something is eternal. And it ain't houses, and it ain't names, and it ain't earth, and it ain't even the stars...everybody knows in their bones that something is eternal and that something has to do with human beings. All the greatest people ever lived have been telling us that for five thousand years and yet you'd be surprised how people are always losing hold of it. There's something way down deep that's eternal about every human being. (Beginning of Act III)

The stage manager representing ordinary people, people like you and me, places the sense of eternal life in the heart of people and shows why the words like faith, hope, and love ring true. These words suggest that we are on the lookout for things that point beyond this life to something good and something healing. They point to a sensibility that can embrace the idea of presence within absence.

The Death and Resurrection of Jesus

With the death and resurrection of Jesus, we are invited into key moments in the life of Jesus and an understanding of death in the Christian tradition. Especially within orthodoxy, the emphasis has been to defend the literal sense of resurrection, which is one road that has led Christians to the conviction that life does not end with death. But there is another road. Consider the idea that resurrection points to the reality that *God can always make everything new*. Remaining with a literal interpretation can eclipse the overarching importance of this story of resurrection, which makes unconditional love understandable and concrete. For me, one of the ways it became concrete is illustrated by a story about my great grandfather, Matthew Black, an Irish immigrant. In my desk drawer is a darning egg, used to darn the worn heels of socks. It was made by my great-grandfather, circa 1870. It has interlocking pieces of mahogany and spruce so perfectly fit together it is hard to imagine anything better suited for the purpose. I imagine him making it by candlelight because daylight would have had him outside with his farming chores. My great-grandfather was a widower, his wife died in childbirth with their fifth child, who also died. He raised four daughters by himself (one of his daughters was my grandmother), built his own house, and was also the local undertaker. He made coffins and likely made the coffin for his wife. These days especially, I take out the egg, hold it in my hand, and I thank my great-grandfather for his courage and resilience. That holding, sometimes really squeezing, is often accompanied by tears, tears of gratitude for the story of his life and for the great blessing of his legacy. Although I did not have the pleasure of knowing him personally, his life and legacy are present with me even in his absence.

Conclusion

My friend, Michael Sateia, a psychiatrist at the Dartmouth Medical School, who also teaches undergraduate neuroscience, so rightly identified the idea of presence within absence as the "inexplicable communication across space and time." Beginning with the notion of oneness and the vocation to make it real, he goes on to say, "When anyone dies, they are still a part of the oneness—we are all still complete in that sense. Their essence, which lives in the oneness is never and can never be lost. It therefore stands to reason that we would continue to communicate with those whose bodily manifestations have moved on" (personal communication, April 2019). And regarding time, he paraphrased Einstein by saying: "People like us, who believe in physics, know that the distinction between past, present, and future is only a stubbornly persistent illusion. So not only does the concept of isolating *individualism* get in the way, but our notion of time is, in many respects, deceiving" (personal communication, April 2019).

With those things in mind, let us return to the quote from the Presbyterian *Book of Common Worship*, "We thank thee for the unquenchable trust that life does not end with death" (van Dyke, 1946). I suggested that this means that after we die, we are *somewhere*. But to be as clear as possible, we must understand both the word *somewhere* and the word *life*. There is evidence in the traditions and teachings of Christianity, that the word *somewhere* points to a place, yes, but a place where the body, the mind, and the ego have been discarded (Luke 20:38; John 6:63). But what is left? The soul, that container-metaphor for the home of the spirit, the absolute essence of one's being remains. The spirit knows no separateness and no superiority. In death, the soul is *life* transformed. The ego, the arbiter of consciousness, is no longer needed because the soul needs neither protection nor guidance. These are convictions to be sure. They are not the result of scientific investigations. But they point to a Christian way of understanding experience that makes sense and can be both a therapeutic and spiritual tool as we try to understand and make use of the idea of presence within absence.

References

Freedman, D. (Ed). (1992). *The anchor bible dictionary* (Vol. 1 (A-C)), New York: Doubleday.

Holden, W., Scott, M., Wood, S., Lesser, S., & Wilder, T. (1940). Principal Artists Productions & United Artists Corporation. *Our town*. New York: United Artists.

Jaffe, A. (Ed). (1965). *Memories, dreams and reflections by C. G. Jung.* New York: Vintage Books.

New Revised Standard Version of the Bible. (1989). *Nashville*, Tennessee: Thomas Nelson, Inc.

Putnam, S. (Ed). (1951). *The portable Cervantes.* New York: The Viking Press.

Todd, M., & Higginson, T. (Eds). (1890). *The collected poems of Emily Dickinson.* New York: Avenel Books.

van Dyke, H. (Ed). (1946). *A general prayer in The book of common worship,* Philadelphia: The Publication Division of the Board of Christian Education of the Presbyterian Church in the United States of America.

Vidor, K., Fleming, V., Cukor, G., Thorpe, R., Taurog, N., & LeRoy, M. (1939). *The Wizard of Oz.* Metro-Goldwyn-Mayer (MGM).

5 Forming Paths of Continuing Connection from a Jewish Perspective

Rabbi Ted Falcon

Introduction

This chapter shares perspectives on communication between physical and non-physical realms in the context of Jewish tradition and from my own experience. We will consider the three levels of soul described in the Jewish wisdom literature, focusing on the separate self, the level of consciousness connecting the separate self to the Universal, and the higher self beyond the body. We will also consider a basic Jewish spiritual practice to ease the transition into death and support a consciousness open to continued connection beyond that transition. However, a disclaimer is needed from the beginning. Although I will be speaking from my understanding of the millennia of Jewish experience, it is important to remember that we are the people who have explored the meaning of life for thousands of years, and we are still exploring, still discovering, and often arguing about what we are finding. I often say that wherever there are two Jews, there are at least three opinions. I mention this because it is important to note that it is not possible to say what *the* Jewish view of the connection between the living and deceased is. Thus, in traditional rabbinic form, I will begin with a favorite story.

The Rabbi's Secret Book

The story is about a rabbi whose career was spent teaching. His classroom was always filled with young minds, some more eager than others, with whom that teacher met every day of the week except for Shabbat, the day of rest. Every day, as the rabbi entered the classroom, he would head to his little office off to the side of the main room. After entering, he would close the door. Some moments later he would emerge, and students over the years who were paying attention noticed that somehow his energy was different upon reentering their classroom. Over the years as the rabbi aged, he became less careful about closing the door completely when he secluded himself in his office each morning. And over those years, there were enterprising and daring students who would sneak up to peak into the office

DOI: 10.4324/9781003105077-7

room. What they saw was confirmed day after day and year after year. The rabbi sat down at the desk that pretty much took up the entire space of his little office. He would reach into the lower left-hand drawer of the desk. He would pull out a black book, set it before him, open it up, and read. After a few moments, he would nod his head, breathe deeply, gently close the book, and replace it in the drawer. The students who dared to peek into his office would scurry back to their seats. The little ritual was repeated every day before that teacher began his daily lessons.

There came a time when that teacher no longer had the energy to teach, and he quickly declined. Students from many years back attended that rabbi's funeral, after which many of them found themselves drawn to the classroom they had known so well. The most enterprising went directly to the little office, and one previous student, now an adult, sat down at the rabbi's chair. She reached down, her hand almost trembling with anticipation, to open that lower drawer on the left side of the desk. As she pulled out the black book, other students watching were holding their breath. What had the rabbi been studying each day before teaching? She opened the book to find every page blank, except one. On that page she found one sentence. One sentence in the entire book! One sentence that the rabbi had studied each and every day, year after year! She read that sentence aloud, "Remember the difference between the container and that which it contains."

Remembering Who We Are

The above story speaks about the essential nature of human being. In the biblical myth, before it was the name of a particular person, human beings were called "Adam." The text proclaims that Adam was created male and female, and they were called Adam. That word is Hebrew and begins with the letter "Alef," the first letter of the Hebrew alphabet. This is the only letter in the Hebrew alphabet that has no sound. It represents the *universal silence*—the essential *oneness of being* that is shared by all existence. "Dam" is the Hebrew word for blood and refers to the physical vehicle of a human being. Each of us is a physical container for that which is beyond physical, that which is universal. We are each a particular location for that which is beyond the limitations of location. We are each responsible for realizing this essential identity and appreciating how our individual separate identity, what we call our ego, is a limitation of this essence, and often inhibits our capacity to know our fuller identity. Perhaps this is the essential dilemma of being a human being, and it speaks directly to the issue of communication beyond the grave. In order to appreciate the dimensions of connection with those who are no longer manifesting through a physical body, we need to have some understanding of the fuller nature of our own true identity. Perhaps there is nothing more important than this inquiry into the nature of our being.

Jewish literature makes it clear that we are more than flesh and blood. There are many viewpoints within this tradition, but regardless of how the soul is conceived there is within each human being that which is greater than the physical manifestation. One of the verses taught as a focus for meditation proclaims, "Be still, and know, that I Am is God" (Psalm 46:11; translation by this author). "I Am," of course, is the Name of God proclaimed in the story of the burning bush (Exodus 3). Moses is portrayed as asking for the Name of God, and the response is clear: "Eheyeh asher Eheyeh," or "I Am as I Am" (Exodus 3:14).

This *I Am* is the essential nature of our identity. We are this universal I Am, manifesting in a particular place and a particular time. We infuse this I Am with the particularities of our separate identities and we often confuse this I Am with the more limited identity of our separate self. Yet this is the *who* that we are. What we call spiritual awakening is the realization of this greater identity. In that realization, we become more able to channel the peace, love, and compassion of that unlimited identity into our world. Without that realization, we too often promote a separateness that keeps us in conflict with each other. We are the *one* manifesting as the many, and when the many forget that we are *one*, we cause the kind of harm to person and to planet that we see manifesting in our time.

Birth, Life, and Death

Each religious tradition confronts this essential dilemma of human being in its own ways, just as each of us confronts this issue individually. When we consider the nature of death, we cannot help but wonder, "Where am I after this body dies?" When we lose someone dear to us, we cannot help but wonder, "Where is she or he now that they are no longer embodied?"

Perhaps it is helpful to remember that life and death are not opposites. Birth and death are opposites. The consequence of every birth will be death, and, in my understanding of my tradition, the consequence of every death will be birth. Life has no opposite. Life is that which flows through every birth and every death. Life is the very nature of this universe.

So, what about the individual? How are we to deal with the issue of maintaining connection between the living and the no longer living? I will share from my own experiences, the first of which was a total failure.

Personal Experiences

My father's mother was the first person in my family to die. I was in college and traveled home for the funeral and the shiva, the seven-day Jewish tradition of sitting with the mourners that follows the funeral. I had not thought about trying to contact my maternal grandmother until a few years later when my uncle, who was a very rationally oriented rabbi, gave me a book detailing contact with people after their death.

I remember him saying that if he believed such a connection was possible, which he did not, that book would convince him. In this remembering, I am struck by the challenges we have to overcoming our beliefs even in the face of compelling contradictory evidence.

The book was filled with examples of spirits of the deceased responding to contact from loved ones. The deceased tended to communicate their presence by causing lightbulbs and other glass objects near the one trying to reach them to shatter. I remember deciding that I would try that. I lay on my bed and began imagining connecting with Grandma Rose and asking for a sign that she was hearing me. But I only did that for a few moments before it suddenly occurred to me that I would not know what to do should a lightbulb burst. I remember leaping out of bed and never trying that again. My first experiment with contacting someone who had died had fizzled because of my own fear. I was not ready for the implications of such an experiment should it be successful.

Later, when I was 30, my father had a heart attack. Within the space of a few days, he died. That was many years after my first experiment, and my own understanding of life had greatly expanded. My father's death was sudden and unexpected, and I was left with an awareness of how much I would have wished to express to him had there been time. Obviously, this is hardly an unusual experience. But I decided to write a letter to him in order to begin to communicate what I had wished I had said to him personally. I also started writing responses to what I had written, as if he were speaking. At first, it was clear that I was making up his responses. But then there were moments when the words *he* was writing held surprises for me. I was reading aspects of his relationship with me that I had not known. Two years before his death, my parents divorced, and, as the writing progressed, I was hearing information about his experience that I had not heard before. I continued that process for some time and through it experienced a deep healing of our relationship.

On a lighter note, one of my father's particular talents was finding excellent parking spaces in crowded lots. He would head for the most parked up areas and would almost always find a perfect parking space. A few weeks after his death, I found that I was having that same experience—parking spots in crowded lots popped up seemingly out of nowhere. I remember that delightful process continuing for at least three months, and every time it occurred, I felt my dad manifesting as my *parking angel.* I felt a sweet connection each time that happened and thanked him aloud. That process faded, just as the journal writing did. But each brought a clearer sense of connection with my father and a sense of maintaining an extremely meaningful relationship. Certainly, this communication with one no longer embodied brought significant moments of healing between my father and me, and I also went on to discover other ways in which my connection with deceased loved ones could be experienced.

For instance, many years later, I had been in phone contact with a friend who had moved to another state and was very ill. I was standing in the shower one day and was suddenly aware of a *touch* from him and a clear message: "Goodbye, my friend." His wife called a few minutes later and I shared my experience right before she informed me of his passing.

To illustrate further, in July of 2001, my mother died. She had been an extremely athletic person, oddly paired with the rest of our family who did not naturally tend toward physical activity. Her favorite form of exercise, besides walking, was swimming. Prior to her death, she had asked that her ashes be scattered in the lake in which she had vacationed for many years in New Hampshire. After her death, my sister and I traveled up to that lake, borrowed a rowboat, and made our way into the middle of Lake Contoocook. We positioned ourselves with the wind at our backs so the ashes would not be blown back at us and gently poured them into the water. The current was clearly moving in the same direction as the wind. We watched as the ashes drifted downward. We watched them coalesce. And we saw them gather and move off below the rowboat and against the current. In those few minutes, we both felt a touch of gratitude and of love that marked a moment of precious communication with our beloved mother.

Much like the story of the Rabbi whose book simply stated, "Remember the difference between the container and that which it contains," for me, stories of such connection convey possibilities more clearly than conceptualization. I am struck by these precious moments of connection and understand that their reality is conveyed through the experience itself, not in something that must be proven. The *proof* is in the living.

Energies That Transcend Physical Death

The energies that a person carries also seem to transcend death. How often we find that when an artist dies, their art, which might not have been appreciated during their lifetime, suddenly becomes more appealing. It seems that something becomes more generally available that had been, prior to their death, encased in a particular body. Over the years, I have also noticed that the death of a very angry person can also free that anger to be experienced by those in mourning. The passing of a very loving and kind person can bring the blessing of that kindness to those experiencing that loss.

One way to understand this is to consider the three levels of soul identified in the Jewish spiritual tradition. The *nefesh* refers to the level of soul manifesting as the separate self, the individual ego identity with which we ordinarily experience ourselves and our world. It is our nefesh that carries our name and the identities, the beliefs, the conditionings, the prejudices, and the patterns with which we operate in the world. The nefesh is the soul bound to conditions experienced in the body, the mind, and the emotions.

The nefesh level of soul knows through contrast: there is no sweet without sour, there is no up without down, there is no easy without difficult.

The *ruach* is the heart-center soul, the place where the upper and the lower realms connect (these names are transliterations of the Hebrew, and the "ch" represents a guttural, like the first sound in "Chanukkah"). The ruach is the inner place of balance and is the soul level that is not bound to conditions in the world. From this vantage point, we can know unconditional love, unconditional peace, unconditional compassion. At this level, we are free from experiencing ourselves as victims of circumstance. Because the nefesh is unable to experience anything unconditionally, the ruach can provide the nefesh with what it most needs—unconditional acceptance.

The third level of soul is the *neshamah*, usually understood to be a level of soul that cannot be contained within the body and represents a consciousness that is beyond one's physical presence yet connects to the ruach through dreams, intuition, flashes of creativity, and spontaneous awakenings. The neshamah is the Greater I Am that is the source and the truth of our being. The neshamah knows radical inclusivity and the connection to all that is.

When a person dies, the nefesh loses its home and often does not understand what has happened. In the house of mourning, following the funeral, it is customary to drape the mirrors. When I was growing up, I remember being told that this inhibited mourners from attending to how they looked. Later on, I learned that this tradition came from the belief that the nefesh of the deceased, in its early state of confusion, might be present in the house and would be greatly disturbed to look in the mirror and fail to see any reflection of itself.

The nefesh may persist for a while after death, but ultimately needs to release itself, for it is a bundle of thoughts, beliefs, and personal experiences that do not endure for long without a physical vehicle. In the early days following death, the persistence of nefesh may be sensed by those who had been close to the person. As the nefesh releases its complex of conditionings, it is the ruach that may be sensed. Often, the communication experienced by those living reflects the greater kindness, forgiveness, and compassion from the deceased, reflecting the ruach identity.

The Spiritual Dimension

Awakening to the way consciousness arises within us is a spiritual process. Spirituality is not a *what*, but a *who*, opening us to the deeper nature of our own being. The more exclusive our sense of identity, the more separate we experience ourselves from others and from our environment. Our separateness drives us to strive more for personal satisfaction than for greater community well-being. As we open beyond the narrow confines of our separate sense of self, we can feel greater connection to those around us and to our world. From a more inclusive perspective, the continuing connection between the living and the deceased becomes more normal.

All authentic spiritual paths provide support for meditation, encouraging our awakening to greater inclusivity and connection. In many ways, meditation is practice for dying, since it offers a process through which we can release the stranglehold of ego and awaken to the more inclusive levels of soul within us. Through practice, the nefesh learns that letting go of itself, far from being dangerous or threatening, is the healthiest thing we can do for that part of our being. Awakening to being present beyond our nefesh not only encourages us to release the fear of death but also helps us understand the levels from which we can better connect with others, whether they are themselves embodied or not.

At the moment of death, Jewish tradition teaches us to recite the words of the central Jewish affirmation of faith. That affirmation is called the "Sh'ma." Its first word, which means, "Listen!" The recitation is in the original Hebrew: *Sh'ma Yisrael, Adonai Eloheinu, Adonai Echad* (Deuteronomy 6:4). While translation is always challenging, this is an affirmation of radical oneness. It begins, "Listen, Israel," where Israel is not referring to a country or even to a particular people, but to all who strive for the eternal dimensions of life. "Adonai Eloheinu," pairs the Absolute One with the one manifesting within each individual being, perhaps best rendered, "The Eternal Being awakens within each of us as our own being." And the final two words, "Adonai Echad," affirm that "The Eternal Being is One."

The Sh'ma is taught as the essential Hebrew mantra, to be repeated in consciousness always, to be shared in prayer morning and night, and to be recited at the moment death approaches. A proclamation of oneness from which none can ever be lost. An affirmation of our ultimate connection to an ever-flowing universal life. This oneness practice supports our connection to the more inclusive aspects of soul and opens us to appreciate connections that transcend the limitations of body, of place, and of time. A meditative practice naturally supports the deeper appreciation of our situation as containers for that, which is greater than our separate physical selves. This, in turn, allows us to open more easily to healthy and supportive connections beyond the boundaries of physical existence.

Life and death present us with the deepest mysteries of this remarkable journey. We may never know with certainty, while still embodied, the nature of our consciousness prior to our birth and following our death. For untold centuries, we humans have sought a certainty that eludes us. Because of this, we seek to learn from those who have probed these mysteries before us, and to appreciate and benefit from our own experiences.

Summary

As I continue to learn from my own Jewish tradition, there is always more to life. There is more to appreciate, there is more to love, and there is more to live. Sometimes this *moreness* arises beyond the usual evidence of our bodily senses. Sometimes, from such conscious connections, we realize a greater fullness and vitality in the lives we are now living. In our focus on the continuing connection following death, we open to dimensions of our existence that transcend the limitations of our physical being. We are the more that invites enduring connection, providing possibilities for support and ongoing relationship with our deceased loved ones.

6 Connecting through the Heart with the Deceased: A Muslim View

Imam Jamal Rahman

Introduction

How little we humans know about the mystery of birth and death! Where we came from? And where will we go after we die? This sense of mystery is encapsulated in a story of the 8th- century spiritual teacher, Hasan of Basra. While speaking to his followers one evening, the master walked up to a child who was holding a candle and asked, "This flame, where does it come from?" Whereupon the child blew out the flame and said to the teacher, "You tell me, where did it go?" (as cited in Shah, 1990, p. 247). That flame is a metaphor for the divine spark in every human being, but we have no idea where it comes from when we are conceived or where it goes when we die.

Muslims find spiritual answers in the Qur'an, which describes us humans as wondrous creations of Divinity. Molded from water and clay, imbued with innate goodness, and infused with the spirit of God, we humans can rise higher than the angels in the order of creation, if only we would recognize our divine nature and express it with gratitude and responsibility (17:61; 30:30; 32:9; 95:4). Our Holy Book teaches that we are meant to spend our time on earth evolving into the fullness of our being by serving God's creation and acting, in the words of the 13th-century sage and poet Rumi, as a "lamp, lifeboat or ladder to others" (as cited in Breton & Largent, 1998, p. 329).

Whether our allotted time is long or short, there comes a time when "every soul will taste death" (Qur'an, 29:57). At that time, the soul separates from the body and is received with tenderness by God, who places it in a state of deep tranquility and creates a barrier that prevents the soul from returning to the body on earth. This, in the Arabic language of the Qur'an, is called *barzakh* (23:100), a state of quietude in which the soul awaits reunion with its body on the Day of Judgment at the end of time.

It is within this frame of reference that Muslims are advised to view the natural rhythm of life and death, even as our hearts mourn the loss of our loved ones and long to connect with them after they die. We weep because they are physically gone forever, and we will simply miss them. Often,

DOI: 10.4324/9781003105077-8

there is the additional pain of *unfinished business* and things we wanted to share with them, not to mention concern for their well-being on the other side of life. What can we do to help a dear one's soul on its onward, mysterious journey? Are there ways to connect with the dead that will bring us comfort and solace?

Many sages and mystics of Islam have found a way. Through a lifetime process of self-purification and meditation, they have moved from a knowledge of the tongue to a knowledge of the heart and have learned to fathom the mysteries of the invisible world. Relying heavily on their teachings, this chapter describes a meditative process that is designed to help the reader connect with departed loved ones using three basic steps: (1) bringing knowledge of the heart to bear on the topic of the afterlife, (2) honoring and remembering the deceased, and (3) using insights and practices of the heart to connect with the deceased on the other side of the veil.

Step 1: Re-educating and Reassuring the Heart

The human heart, mentioned 132 times in the Qur'an, occupies a very special place in Islamic spirituality. Spiritual teachers rhapsodize over a verse, called Hadith Qudsi, revealed to the Prophet Muhammad in a dream in which God says:

> I cannot be contained in the space of the earth.
> I cannot be contained in the space of the heavens.
> But I can be contained in the space of the pure, loving heart.
> (as cited in Helminski, 1999, p. 85)

Thus, Divinity resides not only outside of us but also in the innermost chambers of the human heart. How astonishing that the space of the heart is actually boundless and infinite!

The Qur'an, too, tells us that God—omnipresent and manifest in all of creation—also dwells personally within each one of us (57:3). The closeness of God is tantalizing, "We are closer to you than your jugular vein" (Qur'an, 50:16). But sadly, our hearts are not always cognizant of their divine nature. Many religious people, and Muslims are no exception, pay more attention to the rules and regulations of their belief systems than to the knowledge and wisdom of their own hearts. For the practical matters of daily life, rules and regulations serve well enough. But for matters of life and death, we are at a loss if we have not taught our hearts to look more carefully at the sources of our beliefs, our hopes, and our fears.

Of all the resources available to Muslim believers—the Qur'an, the Hadith (sayings of the Prophet Muhammad), the advice of Islamic elders, jurists, and sages, and our own store of knowledge—none is more important than the purified heart, which "never falsified what it saw" (Qur'an, 53:11). No matter what an authority or expert may say, counseled the Prophet, "always consult your own heart" (as cited in Badi, 2019, p. 132). Human authorities may differ in their interpretations of the Qur'an and the Hadith, and one may go shopping for an expert opinion that matches one's own, but the purified heart knows its own truth. Therefore, let us look at the truth about Islamic beliefs and legends that distress us so greatly when we think about our own mortality or contemplate the deaths of our loved ones.

The "Hadith" of Munkar and Nakir

In my ministry, I have counseled a large number of Muslims (and even some non-Muslims) who believe that newly deceased individuals are visited by two angels, named Munkar and Nakir, who pose three questions as a test: Who is your lord? What is your religion? and, Do you accept Muhammad as your prophet? If they fail the test, they are tortured in their grave. Their mourners themselves are also tortured, wondering if their loved ones are truly being punished (Chittick, 1987).

Research by scholars Browne (1893) and Aksoy 2017 hypothesizes that the Hadith's author, the 9th-century Al-Tirmidhi, who visited Mesopotamia when Islam was being introduced to the region, based the angels Munkar and Nakir on the Mesopotamian Divinities, Rashnu and Nergal, to whom they bear an uncanny resemblance. In any case, this so-called Hadith has no merit for two important reasons. First, there is no mention of these angels or their terrifying mission in the Qur'an. Instead, the Holy Book teaches, in numerous passages, that what will get us into heaven is not our religion, but our faith in God and our righteous deeds (e.g., 2:62; 49:13; 19:76; 19:96). The critical criterion is righteous deeds, and anyone, whether Muslim or not, is assured of heaven according to that criterion. Second, and even more important, the Qur'an repeatedly describes Allah as boundlessly compassionate and infinitely merciful. (In fact, the invocation, "In the name of God, Boundlessly Compassionate, and Infinitely Merciful" opens each of the 114 chapters of the Qur'an, except one.) In our hearts, can we really believe that Allah, God of all of humanity, is tribal and sadistic?

Judgment Day

Fear of Judgment Day, described so vividly in the Qur'an, is another source of great anxiety that we need to rethink. On that phenomenal day, says the Qur'an, "piercing is your sight" (50:22) and it will be a time of "laying bare of truth" (69:1). Our bodies will rise from the grave and in the presence of angels and Divinity all of our good and evil deeds will stare us in our faces. Startlingly, our bodies will testify against us about any wrongs we have done. Rumi surmises that our hands might say, "'I stole money,' our lips, 'I said meanness,' our feet, 'I went where I shouldn't,' and our genitals, 'Me too!'" (as cited in Barks, 2006, p. 115). Spiritual teachers, drawing upon heart knowledge, have explained that the idea of Judgment Day is about gaining clarity and self-awareness as we attempt to follow the right path or allow ourselves to stray, so that we may be more mindful of the continuing work we need to do to evolve into perfection in the celestial realms. Rather than being terrified of Judgment Day, the oral transmission from our sages suggests that we approach the Divine with a trusting heart and a playful plea, "Please plead and advocate on my behalf with Yourself!" or "Please do what is worthy of You, and not of me!"

Heaven and Hell

The Qur'an describes heaven in alluring and sensual detail: "gardens under which rivers flow" (2:25), where abound "wide-eyed *houris*" (or beautiful virgins) (44:54), and "immortal youths" (56:17). But no matter how appealing heaven may seem, measured by our earthly knowledge, spiritual teachers remind us that what our souls really long for is proximity to God. "That is the supreme felicity" (Qur'an, 9:72).

Hell, on the other hand, is described as an abode of "garments of fire" (Qur'an, 22:19), where all around are "burning winds and boiling water" (56:42). Again, spiritual teachers see the fires of hell not as a place of punishment but as a source of purification. Those who have not done their inner work will get a second chance to cleanse and purify themselves before continuing their journey into mysterious realms. This insight is validated in a Hadith in which the Prophet and his companions, while discussing the fires of hell, watched a woman desperately searching for her child. When she found the child, the mother cradled and suckled the child with such love and care that the companions wept. Said the Prophet, "Do you imagine that this woman would ever throw her child into the fire?" "Impossible!" replied the companions. Whereupon the Prophet declared, "Even more than this woman loves her child, does God love His servants" (as cited in Al-Suhrawardy, 1905, p. 94).

The fictional comic foil in Islam, the Mulla, used by spiritual teachers to convey profound truths through humor, also weighs in on the subject of hell. It tells the story of a man who once had a dream in which his wife sent him to hell to bring back fire for her cooking. Upon arrival, he was told by the angel in charge, "There is no literal fire here. People who arrive in hell have an inner fire of rage and hate, the blaze burns from within" (as cited in Fadiman & Frager, 1997, p. 75).

Spiritual Understanding of the Journey of the Soul

To achieve a measure of inner peace, we often want to know what happens to our loved ones in their mysterious onward journey in the afterlife. "With God are keys to the Unseen that are beyond the reach of a created being's perception: none knows them but He," says the Qur'an (6:59). However, there are some tantalizing clues that our journey continues deeper into those invisible realms. The Prophet Muhammad said, "The grave is the first stage of our journey into Eternity" (as cited in Al-Suhrawardy, 1905, p. 18). The Qur'an teaches that God, who is the "Creator, Evolver, the Bestower of Forms" (59:24) and the "Lord of the Ways of Ascent," will "change your forms and create you again in forms that you know not" (56:61). Thus, it seems that we will be incarnated again and again in our journey to union with God. These incarnations will occur not on earth but in those heavenly realms. Such revelations have inspired mystics like Rumi to exclaim, "When was I ever less by dying?!" (as cited in Houston, 1987, p. 210).

Step 2: Honoring and Remembering our Departed Loved Ones

Remembrance

When a Muslim hears that someone has died, it is traditional to recite the Qur'anic verse, "To God we belong and to God is our return" (2:156). If indeed the soul returns to God, and God indeed is in your heart, then, say spiritual adepts, the soul of the deceased is also in your heart. But how can we make connection with our deceased loved one? A Hadith gives us a clue. In a dream, the Prophet Muhammad heard Prophet Moses asking God, "Are you far away that I should call out to You, or are you near that I should whisper to You?" God replied, "I am with the person who remembers Me" (as cited in Nurbaksh, 1981, p. 26). It follows from this Hadith that if we remember our departed loved ones, we connect with their souls. By regularly keeping their souls in our remembrance through regular prayers and rituals, we create a bond that nurtures and comforts all parties.

Righteous Deeds

Another way to unite with our deceased loved ones is to do what the Qur'an calls *righteous deeds* in their name. "Truly the most highly regarded of you in the sight of God is the one who does the most good" (49:13). But the dead are no longer in any position to do good deeds. Their money and titles are left behind, their families and friends can accompany their bodies only to the grave site; and, beyond that, what will propel their souls forward into the lofty realms is the record of their good deeds. The Qur'an tells the touching story of a soul in *barzakh* (where souls await Judgment Day), who implores, "My Lord, send me back, so that I may do righteous deeds in the life I have left behind." "By no means!" God replies (23:99–100). Since the partition between worlds is already in place, it is up to us here on earth to perform good deeds in our loved ones' place. Yet how do we know that the merits of our good works will reach them? The following Hadith is helpful. "On the authority of Abu Hurraiyah, the Messenger of God said, 'When one dies, one's record of deeds is sealed. However, for the following three deeds, one continues to earn God's reward even after one's death: an endowment for charitable work; leaving behind scholarly works that benefit subsequent generations; and virtuous children who pray for their parents'" (as cited in Kidwai, 2018, p. 47). In fact, Islamic literature is replete with stories of the Prophet advising grieving relatives to dig wells and plant trees in the name of the deceased (e.g., Krafess, 2010).

Step 3: Connecting with Our Departed Loved Ones

Does Islamic tradition have anything to say about connecting with our loved ones on the other side of death? In a beautiful passage, the Qur'an describes sleep as a miniature experience of death. When we fall asleep, our soul travels into the invisible realms and is received lovingly by God, who then returns it to us "for a term appointed" when we awake. The revelation ends with the verse, "Verily in this are signs for those who reflect" (39:42). The noted Islamic scholar Jane I. Smith has reflected that, "The sleep state is more than an analogy for death. It is often understood to be a time when the living and the dead share a common circumstance, a time when the departed may communicate to the living information otherwise inaccessible to them, as well as make their own wishes known" (1980, p. 224).

Not surprisingly, Islamic mystics advise those who want to connect with the dead to spend the day in charitable acts, invite only pure thoughts to enter the mind, and offer heartfelt prayers before sleep with the request to meet up with their loved one. Spiritual teachers remind us that our yearning to connect has to come from the depths of our heart, from a place of increased necessity. Rumi provided an example of this by asking, "Have you not noticed that only when a baby is born does the mother's chest become filled with milk?" (as cited in Helminski & Helminski, 1996, p. 31). There is an increased necessity for the milk to manifest. Friends and clients who have purified themselves and prayed with increased necessity often report with great joy and comfort that they have received insights and messages in their dreams that seemingly came from their deceased loved ones.

To illustrate this more clearly, there are recorded examples of the Prophet Muhammad connecting with the dead at their gravesites. In one such instance, he entered into a meditative state and saw a vision of a martyred companion, Abdullah, from whom he brought back a message for Abdullah's grieving son (Ahmad, 1990). Another time, following the Battle of Badr (a significant battle that allowed the new religion to turn from defensiveness to stability and expansion), the Prophet talked to the dead enemies in their graves. His startled companion, Omar, blurted, "O Messenger of God! Why do you speak to lifeless bodies?" The Prophet replied, "By the One who has sent me with the truth! You do not hear my words better than they do except that they cannot respond" (as cited in Dar Al-Ifta Al Misriyyah, n.d.).[1] With this knowledge in mind, the Prophet taught his followers that upon entering a graveyard, they should say, "Peace be upon you, O people of the graves" (Al-Suhrawardy, 1905, p. 82).

There are countless anecdotal examples of Muslim devotees who pray at the gravesites of saints and sages and sometimes are able to connect and converse with their teachers in a vision. The spirits of the dead saints do not come to them, but the uncovered veils offer a visual and auditory connection. Modern-day Sufis say that this spiritual encounter is akin to a Skype or Zoom conversation.

Spiritual Practices

In my ministry, I have counseled distressed Muslim and non-Muslim clients who sought solace for their loss and yearned to connect with the deceased. Invariably, I offer the Sufi practice called *expression and re-solution*, passed on to me by my ancestors, many of whom were rural spiritual teachers. To prepare for this practice, I invite clients to do the practice of *sacred holding,* in which they embrace their pain and anguish with tenderness. Feelings, laughter, and tears come from God, says the Qur'an (23:78; 53:43), and spiritual teachers infer from these verses that all feelings, whether happy or sad, are sacred and need to be acknowledged and honored.

Sacred Holding

As I lead bereaved individuals in the practice of *sacred holding*, I prompt them in the following ways:

1   Close your eyes, focus on your nostrils, and intend to inhale and exhale slowly. Gently, as you enter into a state of meditation, give yourself permission to experience your difficult feelings. Do this little by little with mercy for yourself.

2   Ask yourself, "Where do I hold this feeling in my body?" Feelings have a resting place, and we experience them in the physical body, most often in the heart, throat, or the pit of the stomach). By doing this you are patiently directing your consciousness in locating the site of what is called *physical holding*.

3   Once you have located the feelings as sensations in the physical body, acknowledge them with your consciousness. Talk to yourself with compassion by saying, for instance, "Dear one, I am sorry for what you are experiencing. Allow me to support you as you grapple with

this difficulty." Hold your sensations with the tender embrace of your heart. If the sensations move to another location, move your attention to that place. There is no need to fix or analyze the sensations. Simply be present with the holding as long as you want. The Qur'an has a metaphor for this light of gentle awareness that softens and transmutes, which is akin to "the dawn as it breathes away the darkness" (81:18).

4   Lovingly direct some questions to the center of sensations in your body: "Do you have a message for me?" Then, simply listen. Be attentive and respectful, even if you hear nothing.

5   Ask tenderly, "How may I befriend you? How may I love you and integrate you?" Again, listen carefully.

6   In the last step, be intentional about allowing your breath to flow through that physical locus of your feelings as you inhale and exhale. Allow the Divine Breath to caress that focal point.

Expression and Resolution

As I lead bereaved individuals in the practice of *expression and resolution*, I prompt them in the following ways:

1   Close your eyes and focus on your nostrils. Follow your breath as you inhale and exhale for a few minutes. Enter into a meditative, trance-like state. Then, focus on your heart and silently count from ten to one. At the count of one, usher into your sacred sanctuary. This is an imaginative place of infinite possibilities, either indoors or outdoors, that is absolutely safe and is filled with astonishing beauty and unconditional love.

2   In this sacred sanctuary, call out silently to the person you want to connect with. With an increased necessity of your heart's yearning, invite that person into your sanctuary. Allow yourself to visualize and feel that person arriving in your sanctuary. Use your imagination. Then, greet that person however you want. Remember that you are speaking to the person's soul, and souls love the truth. Whether you are feeling love, anger, or any other emotion, remember again that souls love the truth, and you have permission to articulate and convey fully any feelings that arise from within. This is healing and empowering not only for you but also for the soul of the other.

3   Reflect on your heart's need. What is it that you really want to convey or need in relation to this person? Put it in the form of a prayer. Then, express your sacred prayer to the person's soul in the presence of your soul and Divinity.

4   From your heart, acknowledge that this person has been in your life and is now in the embrace of Divinity. It's part of a larger story. We are not privy to the larger picture.

5   Allow for a sacred ritual to evolve. This might involve a ceremony of love, forgiveness, reconciliation, or letting go.
6   In the last step, from your heart, offer gratitude to the soul of the deceased, and allow it to return to the embrace of Spirit.

What about God?

When I first learned this technique of *expression and resolution*, I wondered whether I could use it if I were feeling angry at God for allowing such a cruel and unfair loss (see also Chapter 14). Wouldn't that be sacrilegious? To my surprise, my parents—my most treasured teachers—assured me through orally transmitted stories across many years that God loves the truth of our feelings and is our most intimate Beloved. If I cannot express my deepest feelings to my heart's Beloved, no matter what they are, to whom can I turn?

To illustrate the power of speaking directly to God even in anger, they repeatedly shared with me the story of a widow who had suffered the tragic and senseless loss of her two children. "Where is your compassion?" she screamed at God day and night, using words that were decidedly less than pious. And then one night she was graced by a dream in which she had died and the angels were escorting her to heaven. She was thrilled as the angels bore her higher and higher into paradise, and then suddenly she beheld the greatest joy of her life—her two children, radiant and exuberant, came rushing to greet her! In ecstasy she cried out, "O Allah, my children were lost to me, but they were not lost to you! O thank you, my Creator!"

Personal Experience

Much of what I have shared in these pages is based on my own experience of two grievous losses in 1991. My beloved mother, accompanied by my brother, had flown from Bangladesh to visit me in Seattle, but our joyful reunion turned to tragedy when she became violently ill the very evening she arrived. Desperate prayers, expert medical care, nothing availed, and seven days later she was gone! My father, shocked beyond belief to hear that his beloved wife would never return to Bangladesh, grieved for 20 terrible days and then died of a heart attack himself. My bond with my parents, which had been such a source of joy, comfort, and strength, seemed irretrievably broken and I could not bear the thought that they were gone from my life forever.

Somehow, I was able to convince myself to perform the heart practices that I have described in this chapter, and, although I never believed it would be possible, today I feel a greater intimacy with my father and mother than I did when they were alive. My practice of *sacred holding* and *expression and resolution* eased my pain, and I have seen and heard from my parents many times in my dreams, especially in the first two years following their death. The insights that I received during that period are invaluable, and in my heart and mind I know that there is indeed crucial, sacred activity going on in those invisible realms.

To this day, I send out light and love to my parents in my daily prayers, and this keeps my remembrance fresh. I honor them with an act of charity every Friday (the Muslim holy day), and, along with my brother and sister, have established and supported enduring charity work in our ancestral village in Bangladesh, dedicated to our grandparents and parents. All of these good deeds feed a palpable sense of connection with our beloved parents and a heart knowledge that they are blessing us every day.

In addition to the beautiful bond with the souls of my parents, these practices have dispelled all fear of my own death and have led to a lightness of heart, much like the Eastern mystics have expressed was possible with regard to death. We have no idea of the joy our souls will feel in returning home. "A lovesick nightingale among owls, you caught the scent of roses and flew to the Rose Garden," says the poet Rumi (as cited in Cowan, 1992, p. 101). And for those left behind, "Goodbyes are for those who love with their eyes, but for those who love with their hearts, there is no separation" (Rumi Quotes, n.d.).

"We are so afraid of passing into non-existence," Rumi says in another stroke of wisdom, "but if the truth be known, non-existence is trembling in fear that it might be given human shape!" (Helminski & Helminski, 1999, p. 89). And finally, several sages from a variety of traditions have remarked that when we die and go over to the other side and look back at our dramas and melodramas on earth, we shall laugh and laugh. Playfully, they ask, "Why wait? Why not laugh right now!" (Godman, 1989, p. 55). May our laughter and tears connect us to an inner, mysterious knowing of the heart, which is a sacred portal to the Unseen. Our heart knows that the souls of our departed loved ones are rejoicing as they journey into those heavenly realms.

Note

1 Dar al-Ifta Misriyah is considered among the pioneering foundations for fatwa (religious verdicts) in the Islamic world. It was established in 1895 by the high command of Khedive Abbas Hilmi, and affiliated in the Egyptian Ministry of Justice, on 21st November, 1895 by decree no. 10.

References

Ahmad, M.B. (1990). Contact with departed souls. *Review of Religions*, LXXXV (3), Retrieved March 7, 2021, from https://www.reviewofreligions.org/

Aksoy, G. (2017). On the astrological background and the cultural origins of an Islamic belief: The strange adventures of Munkar and Nakir from the Mesopotamian god nergal to the Zoroastrian divinities. Retrieved from: www.academia.edu

Al-Suhrawardy, A.M. (1905). *The sayings of Muhammad.* London: Archibald Constable Co. Ltd.

Badi, J.A. (2019). *Commentary on the forty hadith of Imam Al-Nawawi.* Jamaica, NY: Islamic Learning Foundation.

Barks, C. (2006). *A year with Rumi.* New York: Harper Collins.

Breton, D., & Largent, C. (1998). *Love, soul and freedom: Dancing with Rumi on the mystic path.* Center City, Minnesota: Hazelden.

Browne, E.G. (1893). *A year among Persians.* London: Adam & Charles Black.

Chittick, W.C. (1987). Eschatology. In S.H. Nasr (Ed.), *Islamic spirituality.* New York: Crossroad Publishing Co., pp. 378–409.

Cowan, J. (1992). *Where two oceans meet: A selection of odes from the divan of Shems of Tabriz.* Rockport, Massachusetts: Elements Books Ltd.

Dar Al-Ifta Al Misriyyah. (n.d.). *Does the deceased hear the salutations of the living?* Retrieved on February 17, 2021, from www.dar-alifta.org. Dar al-Ifta Misriyah is considered among the pioneering foundations for fatwa (religious verdicts) in the Islamic world. It was established in 1895 by the high command of Khedive Abbas Hilmi, and affiliated in the Egyptian Ministry of Justice, on 21st November, 1895 by decree no. 10.

Fadiman, J., & Frager, R. (1997). *Essential Sufism.* San Francisco: Harper.

Godman, D. (1989). *Be as you are: The teachings of Sri Ramana Maharshi.* London: Penguin Books.

Helminski, K. (1999). *The knowing heart: A Sufi path of transformation.* Boston: Shambala Publications.

Helminski, C., & Helminski, K. (1996). *Jewels of remembrance.* Putney, VT: Threshold Books.

Helminski, C., & Helminski, K. (1999). *Rumi daylight.* Boston: Shambhala.

Houston, J. (1987). *The search for the beloved: Journeys in mythology and sacred psychology.* Los Angeles: Jeremy P. Tarcher, Inc.

Kidwai, A.R. (2018). *Daily wisdom: Sayings of the Prophet Muhammad.* Leicestershire, UK: Kube Publishing, Ltd.

Krafess, J. (2010). *The influence of the Muslim religion in humanitarian aid. In International Review of the Red Cross.* Retrieved March 7, 2021, from https://www.icrc.org

Nurbakhsh, J. (1981). *Traditions of the Prophet.* New York: Nimatullah Publications.

Rumi Quotes. (n.d.). allauthor.com. Retrieved January 4, 2021, from https://allauthor.com/quote/5978/

Shah, I. (1990). *The way of the Sufi.* New York: Penguin Group.

Smith, J.I. (1980). Concourse between the living and the dead in Islamic eschatological literature. *History of Religions, 19(3).* Chicago University of Chicago Press.

7   Eternal Bond with the Deceased: A Hindu Perspective

Neena Verma

Introduction

The Hindu religion and philosophy are civilizations old, and have grown into countless branches and sects over time. As such there is a large number of prevalent versions of Hindu religious practices and rituals, varying across different schools of faith and philosophy, communities, and regions. I do not claim comprehensive accuracy of my descriptions. I acknowledge that my interpretations are based on my knowledge and understanding of the rather vast and diverse Hindu religion and practices, which by no means are exhaustive. This chapter explores: (1) the constructive effects of continuing bonds with the deceased; and (2) the role of Hindu traditions, practices, and rituals at the end of life, upon and after death, in facilitating the creation of eternal bonds with the deceased. The chapter draws the reader's attention to the essence and significance of the Hindu beliefs and rituals in eternalizing the bonds with the deceased, and the facilitative role thereof in helping the bereaved cope better with their loss, affirm their grief, and adapt in a healthy way.

Continuing Bond with the Deceased

It is not uncommon for bereaved people to desire and maintain a continued connection with the deceased. The body dies, the relationship does not. Love lives longer than loss. The deceased remains present in the heart and mind of the bereaved. Ejecting the deceased's presence out of the consciousness of the bereaved is a hard reality to contemplate. It is likely that such forced disconnection may end up proving counterproductive. In contrast, it is just as likely that maintaining a continued bond with the deceased could serve a good purpose in helping the bereaved affirm their grief and move toward meaningful reconstruction of their loss-altered life.

While sustaining such a bond with the deceased can be of meaning in integrating loss and grief, this has long been a matter of debate. A paradigm shift in bereavement studies was offered by Klass, Silverman,

DOI: 10.4324/9781003105077-9

and Nickman (1996), who argued that interactions with the deceased could be considered normal rather than pathological, and need not be broken to complete the grieving process. They explained that a continuing bond is an abiding association between the bereaved and their deceased loved one, emphasizing the adaptive function of such enduring bonds. For example, they held that some bereaved parents create an inner representation of their deceased child, and can preserve and integrate them into their lives in a new way (Klass et al., 1996).

Maintaining a continuing bond with the deceased likely not only offers solace to the bereaved but may also help them re-anchor themselves in their loss-altered life, and provide a greater sense of meaningfulness to their personal universe. Preserving continuing bonds with the deceased can have adaptive effects on the coping process and the well-being of the bereaved. In a ten-year follow-up study focused on bereaved parents, Rubin and Shechory-Stahl (2012–2013) found that improvement in biopsychosocial functioning was associated with the continuing connections the bereaved parents made to their deceased child. Reconstructing the bond enables preservation of the relationship beyond the mortal presence of the deceased. Neimeyer and Anderson (2002) highlight the interactive role of continuing bonds and meaning reconstruction in a study of two young mothers who both lost their infants to congenital heart disease. Both mothers reported a strong continuing attachment to their children. The Hindu belief of soul being eternal strengthens such a prospect of continued connection with the deceased.

Soul Is Eternal—A Hindu Belief

The Hindu philosophy emphasizes the eternal nature of the soul and maintains that like humans exchange old worn clothes for new ones, the soul also moves to a new body after death. While soul is eternal, death is certain. Death is the only absolute truth of life. Bhagwan (Lord) Krishna[1] avers in the *Bhagavad Gita* (2:27)[2]

> जातस्य हि ध्रुवो मृत्युर्ध्रुवं
> jātasya hi dhruvo mṛityur dhruvaṁ
> Death is certain for one who has been born.

The *Bhagavad Gita*, which has a revered space in the Hindu philosophy and consciousness, acknowledges death as the supreme truth of life, but lays emphasis on the undying nature of soul. Of the several shlokas (verse-texts) from the *Bhagavad Gita* (Prabhupada & Bhaktivedanta, 1972, 1986) that call attention to and explain the eternal nature of the soul, some of the most prominent ones include the following:

dehino'smin yatha dehe, kaumaram yauvanam jara
tatha dehantara-praptir, dhiras tatra na muhyati.
As the embodied soul continually passes, in this body,
from boyhood to youth to old age.
The soul similarly passes into another body at death
The self-realized is not bewildered by such a change. (2:13)
and
nainam chindanti sastrani, nainam dahati pavakah
na cainam kledayanty apo, na sosayati marutah.
The soul can never be cut into pieces by any weapon, nor burned
by fire,
nor moistened by water, nor withered by the wind. (2:23)

Loss, death, and grief are among the most central, timeless themes of the
Bhagavad Gita, which offers particularly profound wisdom in this context. The scripture starts with Bhagwan (Lord) Krishna's sermon about
the transience of the physical body, the abiding presence of the soul, and
the need to transcend grief and return to one's *dharma* (noble duty, as per
law of nature) and *karma* (noble deed). In emphasizing the eternal nature
of soul, the impermanence of the mortal body, and the possibility of
reunion in future lifetimes, the *Bhagavad Gita* offers solace to the bereaved (Bhatia, Madabushi, Kolli, Bhatia, & Madaan, 2013), and helps
them affirm their loss, maintain *dhairya* (forbearance, equanimity), heal,
and restore.

Although grief is an individual experience, it is often influenced by
socio-cultural influences. Sometimes death and bereavement can cause
one's assumptive world to be shaken to the core. Of the various things
that play a positive role in helping restore one's assumptive world,
spirituality holds particular importance. It is not uncommon to see
grief therapists with an openness to religious, spiritual, and socio-
cultural sensitivities and perspectives. In the same spirit, the practice of
psychotherapy in India often tends to incorporate *therapeutic pearls*
(Pandurangi, Shenoy, & Keshavan, 2014) from the *Bhagavad Gita*
in helping their clients accept their loss, understand the phenomenon
of mortal impermanence and the cyclical nature of birth and death,
and seek to connect with the deceased at the soul level because that
is eternal.

Eternal Bond with the Deceased: The Hindu View and Traditions

The Hindu religion affirms the eternal nature of the relationship, and
recognizes the possibility of an afterlife and reincarnation. Relationships
are thought to be lasting beyond lifetimes, as captured beautifully in the
common Hindi proverb of *janam-janam kaa saath*,[3] broadly interpreted

as *timeless togetherness over lifetimes*. The relationship stays alive even after the mortal journey has ended. The Hindu traditions and rituals commemorate the continuing bonds of love and legacy, thereby helping the bereaved meaningfully remember, sustain, and reconstruct their relationship with the deceased.

Thus, retaining an abiding relationship with the deceased is more than just a matter of emotional solace. It can also offer moral inspiration to bereaved individuals who may seek to imbibe and practice the values and beliefs of their deceased loved ones. The Hindu practices thus ensure an unbroken connection with the departed souls, who continue to hold a place of love and remembrance in the family they leave behind. In a particular tradition prevalent at some Hindu pilgrimage places, the priests maintain family tree records of their *yajamana* (ritual patron). The pilgrims are supposed to visit their family priests during their pilgrimage to such places, and get the details of recent births, marriages, deaths, and other such significant family events duly recorded in their family tree accounts. Many pilgrims express a surreal feeling when the priests surprise them with their family lineage details dating back several generations, much of which the pilgrims themselves may not be aware of.

It was a poignant experience for me and my family when we visited our family priest after immersing my son's ashes in the Ganges (Hindu holy river) at Hardwar (a major Hindu holy city in India). Though I do not relate to the regimented normative rituals, my participation in the above-mentioned practice, more with the intention to honor the family practice than for my own sake, offered a strangely positive experience. My eternal bond with my son got an external affirmation when the priest's fingers unwittingly reached the entry of my son's arrival in the world, before making the entry about his departure from the world. By an unconscious design, this Hindu tradition took me back to the time when my beloved child had entered my life and filled it with joy and richness. I promised myself in that very moment that my love would stay stronger than my grief, and that I would honor my child's eternal Presence in Spirit, more than lamenting his mortal absence. In this way, my bond with my child stays alive, deep, loving, and meaningful, notwithstanding his demise on September 24, 2014. Eternalizing my bond has been of immense help in affirming my grief and seeking deeper existential growth. I acknowledge the supportive role of the above-mentioned Hindu tradition and other rites of passage as discussed below, in facilitating my grief affirmation journey. Based on my own lived experience as a bereaved mother, and my experience of working with bereaved parents, I also find resonance with the work of a number of researchers whose findings are consistent with and help explain the role of continuing bonds following the loss of a child (e.g., Klass et al., 1996; Rubin & Shechory-Stahl, 2012–2013; and Neimeyer & Anderson, 2002).

The Therapeutic Value of the Rite of Passage

In the Hindu faith and tradition, various rituals or ceremonies serve as the rites of passage that enable and/or commemorate transitions over significant milestones or phases in life. In some contexts, they also serve a purificatory purpose. Building from the work of the French anthropologist, Arnold van Gennep, who coined the term "rite of passage" and studied their socio-cultural significance, Alexander and Norbeck (1998) explain three distinct elements or stages of the rites of passage: separation (pre-liminal, or before), transition (liminal,[4] implying, at, or passing-through), and re-incorporation (post-liminal, or after).

Rituals or rites of passage create an affirmatory space whereby one can pause, acknowledge, affirm, absorb, process, and integrate significant moments and events of life, which one may otherwise pass by, caught in the everyday humdrum of life. This argument holds greater meaning in the context of loss, death, and bereavement, where it is important to allow the shattering experience to sink in, be assimilated, processed, and healed, before returning to the busyness of life. The lack of such therapeutic pause and space may inhibit or suppress grief, and adversely impact grief affirmation, healing, and adaptive restoration.

In explaining therapeutic rituals, Doka (2012) highlights multi-fold restorative effects of rituals, that include allowing space to acknowledge the harsh reality of death, accept the loss, safely process or express feelings, find meaning by applying spiritual frameworks, validate the relationship, honor the continuing bond, and mark a transition in the grief journey. The rituals also offer integrative as well as regulatory support to the bereaved by facilitating a sense of structure in what otherwise feels like disorganized grief, offering order in relation to events, and enabling a shared ability to make sense out of a mutual loss (Neimeyer, Prigerson, & Davies, 2002). In essence, the rituals create a setting whereby the bereaved feel supported and facilitated to affirm grief and initiate restoration journey. The Hindu rituals go even beyond this, offering multi-level support to the bereaved by way of emotional solace, extending and/or reinforcing a sense of belonging and community, and offering practical help in the immediacy of loss.

Samskara: The Hindu Rite of Passage

The Hindu rites of passage are about invocation or initiation, stepping on to the lifespan thresholds, preparing for transitions, and moving to a higher realm. These rites of passages are called *samskara* (Hindi word for rites of passage, and *karmic* propensities). The Hindu samskaras represent each of the three elements or stages of the rites of passage—separation, transition and transformation, and re-incorporation. In honoring the enduring bond with the departed, they even extend beyond the mortal realm.

The Hindi word "samskara" captures the essence of the phenomenon of rite of passage. The word "samskara" has roots in the Sanskrit language, and although it is hard to find its literal English translation, given the sacred as well as complex nature of samskara, words such as sacrament, ritual, or rite of passage would come somewhat close. In Hindu philosophy, samskara is believed to have two broad connotations:

1   Rites and rituals at or before major transition life events or phases, which serve a purificatory, commemorative, or celebratory purpose, and support one in affirming one's identity as a practicing Hindu.
2   Karmic propensities, habitual tendencies, or mental impressions that one is supposed to have manifested and accumulated over several lifetimes, and which in turn influence one's unfolding fate. Yadav (2019) maintains that samskaras represent "the quality of consciousness that drives one's thoughts and emotions (embedded with intentions) for a particular *karma* (deed) while being guided by one's intelligence and discriminative wisdom (*viveka*)" (p. 656). In the context of this chapter, a greater relevance is found in the first connotation of samskara, which is the set of rites and rituals that one performs and undergoes at various stages in one's lifespan and even after death, in order to affirm one's Hindu identity, and become fit or ready for certain significant purposes or transitions in life.

In lifetime and even after death, a practicing Hindu is believed to have undergone or performed in at least two to three, if not more, of the 16–40 most typically prescribed and practiced rituals, varying in number and specific manner across different communities or sections within the Hindu religion (Mishra, 2019). Some of the most prominent Hindu samskaras include *vivaha* (marriage), *garbha-dharana* (conception or pregnancy), *annaprasana* (first solid food), *namakarana* (naming ceremony), *upanayana* (initiation into academics and contemplative studies), *antyeshti* (last or funeral rites), *pitru[5]-karma* (rituals to invoke, reconnect with, and worship the ancestors).

Beyond being defining rituals for purification or transition, the Hindu samskaras also represent preparation for the attainment of higher goals in life, viz. realization of the self or the absolute truth (Mishra, 2019). The Hindu rites relating to the death and deceased are performed at broadly four stages: on the *mrityu-shayya* (death-bed); at the antyeshti (last or funeral rites); during the 13-day mourning period to facilitate the departed soul's onward journey from *preta* (astral or bodyless) *swaroop* (form) to the realm of the ancestors; and the annual *pitru-paksha[6]* when the departed souls are invoked and worshipped. There is symbolic significance of samskaras performed at each of the above-mentioned stages. Each has its own meaning, and supports the bereaved in accepting the inevitably hard reality of the death, and affirming their grief.

The Hindu rituals performed on the mrityu-shayya (death-bed) mark a poignant start of the grief journey, allowing the family to hold their loved one's end of life in spiritual perspective, and prepare themselves for the inevitable. These rituals create a space whereby the family is able to have their last intimate and meaningful contact with the dying loved one, and offer a ceremonial affirmation to their relationship and bond. In some cases, these rituals even facilitate forgiveness and closure of unfinished relationship business, if any exists.

Antyeshti: The Antim Samskara (The Final Ritual)

Antyeshti (the last or funeral rites) is a Hindi word made by joining the Sanskrit words *antya* (last or final) and *ishti* (sacrifice or offering). Of the various Hindu sacraments and rites of passages, antyeshti is perhaps the most poignant samskara (Chaitanya, 2005), whereby the mortal remains of the deceased are offered to *Agni*, the sacred God-figure of the fire element. Symbolically speaking, the antyeshti rites are the dharma (noble duty) of the chief mourner, typically the oldest male child, or whoever is the legacy heir/successor of the deceased, be it spouse, child, friend, or anyone particularly important for the deceased.

Antyeshti is one of the oldest and most significant samskara that a practicing Hindu undergoes upon death. It is a solemn samskara, also called the *dah-samskara* (burning-ritual), whereby the God-figure, Agni, is invoked and urged to pacify the unfulfilled desires of the deceased, and purify and accept the mortal remains for disintegration. The Hindu philosophy maintains that the human body is made of *pancha-tattava*, a Sanskrit word, that means five (*pancha*) essential elements (*tattava*) of earth, water, fire, air, and ether/space. Hindus believe that upon death, the body must return to and dissolve into the *pancha-tattava*, and that, compared to other methods of disposing of the body, burning ensures better and faster disintegration into the pancha-tattava (Singh, 2015).

In the Hindu funeral practices, the deceased's body is placed on a pyre. The one performing the antyeshti walks around the pyre sprinkling water from an earthen vessel which is then broken, symbolizing the release of the soul. The pyre is lit, invoking Agni (Fire God) to disintegrate the mortal remains. The religious chants are recited to pray for the sacred return of the *jiva* (human being) to the *Param* (supreme being). The ritual of *kapal-kriya* (skull-disintegration process) is performed, whereby the burning *kapal* (skull) of the deceased is cracked open with a bamboo stick so as to release the remaining *prana* (life-energy) in the brain. Kapal-kriya is a poignant and powerful ritual that calls for psychological and moral courage. It is not for the fainthearted. It is common to see the funeral priests perform this ritual on behalf of the bereaved heir.

Worden (2009) underlines the role of rituals, especially the funeral, in facilitating a healthy grief process. In that sense, the Hindu funeral rites offer immense healing support to bereaved individuals. These rituals are not merely about disposal of the body. Rather, they are performed with great reverence and care to ensure the deceased's dignified release from the mortal world, and to facilitate their onward journey to the higher realm and/or next life. In honoring this purpose, the bereaved reaffirm their concern and responsibility toward their loved ones, even after their death, which often adds greater depth and meaning to their relationship with the deceased, which, in turn, can facilitate the ongoing bond between them.

Although in Hindu tradition, women are not supposed to perform the funeral and some other rites, there have been inspiring exceptions in recent times. For example, my family (my spouse, my younger son, and I) together performed the antyeshti and other rites for my deceased elder son. We received heart-warming support from the priests presiding over the rites. The whole experience brought the family closer, and proved immensely helpful in affirming our grief at individual and shared levels. The collective experience of performing the rituals together, also helped us create shared meanings of our loss and pain, and eternalize our bond with my deceased elder son.

Facilitating the Deceased's Onward Journey: The Hindu Enduring Bond

Traditionally the Hindu social mourning period begins with the funeral, and lasts 10, 13, or 17 days, varying across communities and regions. A day or two after the cremation, the bereaved family returns to the cremation ground to collect the *asthi* (ashes of the burnt body), which are carried in a purified urn for *visarjan* (immersion) in a holy river or waterbody. In a way, antyeshti, kapal-kriya, and visarjan mark the beginning of letting go, while still retaining the bond between the deceased and the survivors.

There is a belief in the Hindu philosophy that the soul of the dead is unable to abruptly break out of the mortal existence and attachments that formed its identity for an entire lifetime. The soul is thus believed to remain in the deceased's mortal world space in a preta (astral or bodyless) swaroop (form) for up to 12–13 days after death. The preta-swaroop is like a liminal state between *no longer* (*prithvi-loka*—the earth, or mortal realm) and *not yet* (*pitru-loka*—the ancestors' realm). It is considered to be the dharma (noble duty) of the deceased's family to perform rites during the mourning period to facilitate their transition and onward movement from the astral state to the pitru-loka. The holy scriptures like the *Bhagavad Gita* and the *Garuda Purana*[7] are read and recited, to provide emotional solace and spiritual anchors to the bereaved, and to pray for the salvation of the departed soul. This is an expression of the bereaved person's continued care for the deceased and their loving bond.

Presence Beyond Absence: Invoking and Re-bonding with the Deceased

Death takes away the body. But even in their absence, the deceased continue to remain present in the consciousness of the bereaved. An adaptive grief process allows the presence beyond absence to be affirmed and become remembrance. Remembering the altered reality can facilitate healthy continuous bonding with the deceased, as the bereaved evolve a new meaning in their relationship. Kristensen and Hedtke (2018) point to the therapeutic value that remembering can offer to the bereaved, by invoking the memories of the deceased person's life, which gives shape to the relationship by integrating the past and the future. It is a profound way to restore the sense of belonging, connection, and bonding between the deceased and the bereaved.

In Hindu tradition, respect and reverence for the pitrus (deceased) and their continued blessings are an integral part of the culture. The ancestors' rituals hold unique importance and meaning in honoring the presence beyond absence of the deceased. The annual pitru-paksha is considered to be a sacred time to invoke and honor the eternal presence of the pitrus, who are believed to descend down to the prithvi-loka during this phase, to spend time with their descendants (bereaved). The pitru-paksha is observed as a time to remember and venerate the pitru, pray for their salvation and well-being in their subsequent life forms, and seek their blessings.

Year after year, people wait for the pitru-paksha so as to reconnect and re-bond with their loved ones, despite the realization that the soul might have taken a new lifeform. Since the deceased is invoked as a collective of all those departed over the last three or more generations, it signifies a continued bonding even among the departed, not just between the deceased and the bereaved. Such ancestor rituals serve as scaffolds of the enduring bonds at individual, familial, and inter-generational levels. The bereaved feel rooted in their family tree, and experience the continued presence beyond absence of their deceased loved ones in their hearts and consciousness. This helps the bereaved in accepting, integrating, and adapting to their loss, while still maintaining a spiritual connection with their deceased loved ones.

The Hindu Way to Eternal Bonding with the Deceased

The Hindu samskaras are guided as much or even more by faith than they are by religious injunctions or traditions alone. They add meaning to transitions within one's lifetime and after death, and allow the connections and bonds with the deceased to remain alive, intimate, and meaningful.

The various Hindu rites performed at the end of life, upon and after death, are symbolic affirmations of the enduring bond of love. They represent the bereaved person's abiding sense of care and affection toward the deceased that extends beyond death, and inspires them to take responsibility for a virtuous dissolution of the deceased's mortal remains into the pancha-tattava, and facilitate their onward journey. This act of honoring their duties toward the deceased in death and even beyond, eternalizes the bond, and helps the bereaved affirm their grief, and give new meaning to their relationship with the deceased.

Notes

1 The Hindu God-incarnate.
2 The *Shrimad Bhagavad Gita* is the sacred Hindu scripture that chronicles the epic sermon on *dharma* (noble duty), delivered by Bhagwan (Lord) Krishna on the battlefield of Kurukshetra.
3 *"Janam"* is a Hindi word that means *birth* as well as *lifetime*. *"Saath"* is a Hindi word that means *togetherness*.
4 The word "liminal" has origin in Latin *limen*, which means *threshold*.
5 *Pitru* is a Hindi/Sanskrit word that means ancestor. It effectively represents all departed souls in the bereaved family.
6 *Pitru-paksha* is the 16-lunar-day-long ancestors' phase, which coincides with the waning moon fortnight in the Hindu month of *ashwin* (overlapping September/October).
7 *Garuda* (eagle-like bird) is the king of birds in Indian mythology that serves as the *vahana* (mount or carrier) of Lord Vishnu (the preserver God of the holy Hindu Trinity). The *Garuda Puran* is a Hindu holy scripture that is believed to have originated from the discourse between the Garuda and Lord Vishnu. It is broadly devoted to understanding of self, meaning of human life, soul, and the law of karma (noble deed).

References

Alexander, B.C., & Norbeck, E. (1998, September 19). Rite of passage. Britannica Online Encyclopaedia. Retrieved from https://www.britannica.com/topic/rite-of-passage

Bhatia, S.C., Madabushi, J., Kolli, V., Bhatia, S.K., & Madaan, V. (2013). The *Bhagavad Gita* and contemporary psychotherapies. *Indian Journal of Psychiatry*, 55(2), S315–S321. 10.4103/0019-5545.105557

Chaitanya, S. (2005). *Bereavement and final samskara (Antyesti)*. Tiruvannamalai, India: Purna Vidya Trust.

Doka, K.J. (2012). Therapeutic ritual. In R.A. Neimeyer (Ed.), *Techniques of grief therapy: Creative practices for counseling the bereaved*. New York: Routledge, pp. 341–343.

Klass, D., Silverman, P.R., & Nickman, S. (1996). *Continuing bonds: New understanding of grief*. Washington, DC: Taylor & Francis.

Kristensen, H.G., & Hedtke, L. (2018). Still alive: Counselling conversations with parents whose child has died during or soon after pregnancy. *The International Journal Of Narrative Therapy And Community Work*, 2018(1), 22–30.

Mishra, A. (2019). *Hinduism: Ritual, reason and beyond: A journey through the evolution of 5000-year-old traditions*. Mumbai, India: StoryMirror.

Neimeyer, R.A., & Anderson, A. (2002). Meaning reconstruction theory. In N. Thompson (Ed.), *Loss and grief*. New York: Palgrave, pp. 45–64.

Neimeyer, R.A., Prigerson, H., & Davies, B. (2002). Mourning and meaning. *American Behavioral Scientist, 46*, 235–251. 10.1177/0002764022366 76

Pandurangi, A.K., Shenoy, S., & Keshavan, M.S. (2014). Psychotherapy in the *Bhagavad Gita*, the Hindu scriptural text. *American Journal of Psychiatry, 171*(8), 827–828. 10.1176/appi.ajp.2013.13081092

Prabhupada, Swami, & Bhaktivedanta, A.C. (1972; 1986). *Bhagavad-Gita: As it is*. Mumbai, India: Bhaktivedanta Book Trust.

Rubin, S.S., & Shechory-Stahl, M. (2012–2013). The continuing bonds of bereaved parents: A ten-year follow-up study with the two-track model of bereavement. *Omega: Journal of Death and Dying, 66*(4), 365–384. 10.2190/OM.66.4.f

Singh, K.V. (2015). *Hindu rites and rituals: Origins and meanings*. India: Penguin Books.

Worden, J.W. (2009). *Grief counseling and grief therapy*. New York: Springer.

Yadav, S.K. (2019). Human samskaras and the psychic process in coherence to ideosphere and impulses for unethical actions. *International Journal of Indian Psychology, 7*(3), 656–666. 10.25215/0703.071

Section II
Clinical Implications

8   Restorative Internalization

Edward (Ted) Rynearson

When my patient, Gloria, announced that her husband Ralph had cancer of the pancreas, I worried. How would she manage her future without him? I knew enough of her history and vulnerabilities to be concerned.

We began treatment 15 years earlier, after her first panic attack in the middle of the night, trapped in a Europe-bound airplane, certain that she was dying. As an international executive, she was accustomed to stress and as a seasoned traveler she wasn't threatened by flying. However, further assessment revealed a possible source of more immediate distress---her elderly parents' impending deaths coincided with her fear of imminent death in the airplane.

However, distress of her own death was more ascendant than the fear of her parents' dying. If she died, she worried her husband would be lonely and emotionally unmoored without her. Her altruistic commitment to her husband in adulthood was in direct contrast to her parents' lack of commitment to Gloria and her younger sister in childhood. Gloria's primary emotion during her childhood was intense loneliness and now, instead of anticipatory distress about her parents' deaths, she resented their demands for financial support and caregiving that she never received from them.

Our monthly supportive visits continued for the next two years. When both of her parents died within the first year of Gloria's therapy, she felt relief more than sadness or remorse knowing she had "…done all I could, and they didn't die alone." She didn't visit their graves and denied any persistent need for continuing bonds. There was no conversation with their presence within absence or dreams or visitations from them. After her short-lived course of bereavement, she stopped seeing me for support for the next eight years.

Shortly after the discovery of Ralph's cancer, I saw Gloria and Ralph together for a visit to be of support during his treatment. Ralph recognized his slim odds of surviving but remained optimistic. While they were together in session, Gloria shared his optimism, but in our individual sessions she dreaded his dying and death. His treatment included surgery followed by aggressive chemotherapy, and for the next four years he remained cancer free. Ralph and Gloria assumed active roles in Ralph's treatment, becoming patient advocates and board members of the pancreatic treatment project at

DOI: 10.4324/9781003105077-11

his treatment center, and volunteering to give public lectures supporting pancreatic cancer advancements. The same week they celebrated his five-year survival, radiologic signs of metastasis to his lungs and abdomen were found. He refused to consider further treatment. In the last six months of his life, he accepted his imminent death and actively prepared Gloria for his absence and her potential loneliness. They had long conversations about Gloria's future, discussing practical details of their wills and finances and having comforting interchanges of their shared belief that their separation was temporary—death promised a spiritual reunion, to which Ralph emphasized, "I will never leave you."

Ralph died at home. Gloria spent an entire day with his body before calling the funeral director. Her comforting conversations with his presence within absence began that day. She never believed his voice was imaginary, "Ralph never left me." Their interchange remained particularly intense at night when Gloria was alone; and, occasionally, she felt his physical embrace while lying awake and during her dreams of reunion.

In our supportive visits the year after Ralph's death, Gloria experienced isolated episodes of sadness and tearfulness but no remorse, intense loneliness, or recurrence of panic. Her conversations and visitations with Ralph remained comforting and hopeful. She continued to live alone in the home they had built 40 years before and supportively engaged with her business associates and friends. Attending a two-day national meeting featuring lectures and workshops on spiritual reconnection with deceased loved ones she discovered, "Everyone there seemed to be having the same sort of experiences I have been having."

The week before he died, Ralph gave her ten sealed envelopes to be opened over the next five years at times of her birthday and their wedding anniversary.

Principles of Restorative Adaptation

The focus of this chapter is to clarify the restorative internalization of the deceased, not its pathological fixation. Through spontaneous processing and retelling of their loss, the vast majority of bereaved adults and children do not require treatment following the death of a loved one (Thimm, Kristoffersen, & Ringberg, 2020). While object relation theorists have written extensively on the genesis of pathological internalization as basis for psychopathologic responses with grief in adults (Schafer, 1968), and children (Furman, 1983; Oltjenbruns, 2001), their conceptual models are designed for longer-term therapy for patients with underlying disturbances of self-identity or character disorders (see Chapter 11). Only a minority of children and adults remain distressed and disabled by grief where the persistent internalization of the presence/absence has a dominating external vitality of its own and becomes less available for internal change (Johannsen et al., 2019; Rosner, Kruse, & Hagl, 2010).

In contrast, Ralph's presence within absence during Gloria's bereavement served a spontaneous and restorative purpose, adaptive to her underlying fear of loneliness. In Gloria's case, this restorative process did not require a structured therapy beyond opportunity for retelling and replaying the private metacommunication with Ralph, with me as listener. To understand Gloria's restorative processing, there are several levels of adaptive principles to consider: neurobiological, neuropsychological, and neurodevelopmental.

Neurobiological

The neurobiological function of the central nervous system (CNS) is to maintain continuous registration and readjustment of the body. A basic CNS reorganization occurs after the loss or amputation of a body part that, like grief, includes phenomena of presence within absence. For instance, if your arm was amputated you likely would maintain a *phantom limb*, an active, somatosensory representation of your arm, not only evoking its illusory presence, but its movements and sometimes pain.

In simplest terms, following amputation, sub-cortical and cortical CNS synaptic patterns representing the dismembered arm undergo a predictable reactivation, continuing to register its presence as a phantom limb. A more detailed neural model suggests an underlying neuromatrix, a structured network of neurons in interconnected brain areas (i.e., thalamus, somatosensory cortex, reticular formation, limbic system, and posterior parietal cortex), establishing a functional foundation for the representation of the physical body. Despite the absence of somatosensory input from the amputated arm, its altered CNS reverberation continues registering the arm's phantom presence. Fortunately, because of substantial plasticity of cortical interconnections, the brain's neural patterning of the arm reorganizes over time and the epiphenomena of phantom limb sensation diminishes, although never fully disappears (Ratcliffe, 2019).

Neuropsychological

The neuropsychological *amputation* of a stabilizing loved one often changes the representation of the survivor's self-identity associated with the kind and degree of shared attachment with the deceased. Based upon the degree and quality of psychological attachment, variable neuropsychological changes in self-identity may range from brief changes in self-identity with weak attachment with the deceased, to enduring and intense changes in self-identity with strong attachment with the deceased. Like the neural circuitry of physical amputation, changes in self-identity with the death of an emotionally valued attachment figure are based upon similar principles of CNS neural patterning and stabilization. After death, the dying and living representation of an attachment figure (i.e., a part of self *amputated* rather than the amputation of a body part) is often predictably followed by *phantom* psychological phenomena. However, different from the somatosensory representation of the body, the human mental representation of the self and relationships is primarily conveyed through narrative memory. Cortical and sub-cortical neural patterns of self-identity continue to signal the presence within absence through private behaviors of searching, pining, and continued communication with the deceased (O'Connor, 2019; Parkes, 1975; Pengmin & Northoff, 2011). Similar to the process of reorganization after the physical amputation of an arm, the neural patterning of the *dis-membered* attachment figure would be *re-membered*, and the narrative memory reorganized over time, to diminish but never fully disappear.

Though phantom and self-identity phenomena of grief are associated with functional MRI changes (O'Connor, 2019), these CNS changes are currently unresponsive to medication (Shear et al., 2016). Instead, therapeutic interventions that proceed through psychotherapies have a functional role in *reorganizing* CNS reverberations (Collerton, 2013). There are intriguing functional MRI studies showing that the CNS changes associated with grief (e.g., fixation on the presence within absence of the deceased) are responsive to retelling therapies combined with mindfulness techniques (Jain et al., 2019).

Neurodevelopmental

The enactment of a highly imaginative and retentive attachment has a neurodevelopmental precursor in the interactive dynamics of separation in preverbal children that may be relevant in adults as well. Donald Winnicott, a British pediatrician and psychoanalyst, introduced the term *transitional object* (1953) to describe blankets, soft toys, and bits of cloth to which some young children (i.e., 9–18 months) develop phase-specific attachments, particularly at times of separation from their attachment figures. Winnicott discovered that transitional attachments can be intensely positive and imperative. The object must be physically held and fondled to ensure safety, can never change (i.e., cannot be washed or repaired), and must be readily available throughout the day and particularly at night while the child is alone.

Transitional objects in young children are common and ubiquitous (Malhalski, 1985), but Winnicott (1953) was the first to cite its formal description and dynamic. The object is transitional because it represents a psychological simultaneity of both *not me* (the object) and *me* (my safe self) representations. Winnicott theorized that transitional attachments are associated with an essential phase of ego development leading to the processes of healthy separation/individuation of children from their primary caregivers. Winnicott further suggested that transitional phenomena originate in a psychological *third space* between infant and mother, in which the infant develops a nascent capacity for self-autonomy and separateness and that this imaginary space is basis for subsequent play (i.e., imaginative processing), by which the infant develops a more stable self-identity at times of separation from the mother. What exists between subject and object is in some sense a metaphorical zone or a permeable boundary with constant two-way traffic between the processing of internal and external experience. Thus, repetitive replay of the *internal* experience of loss and separation porously experienced in the comforting repetition of an *external* experience with transitional objects is an early sign of self-soothing (Winnicott, 1971).

The third space is normative and engages the individual in the perpetual task of keeping inner and outer reality separate yet interrelated. Opportunity for imaginative play alone or with others promotes novel and enriching interchange. The maturing capacity for play within the third space remains crucial in the normal development of personal and social identity and is widely encouraged in restorative replay with traumatized and grieving children (Kaplow, Saxe, Putnam, Pynoos, & Liberman, 2006; Pynoos et al., 1987; Salloum, 2015). Bereavement presents an analogous separation/individuation challenge in older children and adults, where attachment revitalization replaying in the third space may serve a transitional function within a resuscitated me/not me attachment. Linkage with the presence within absence may include inert, transitional objects belonging to the deceased to be worn or fondled (Volkan, 1981), and at a later developmental phase may include maintenance of a private, imaginary relationship through conversation or visitation (Kamp et al., 2020; Wakenshaw, 2020).

Recognizing the commonality of communication with the deceased as a normative and spontaneous adjustment to the death of a loved one, grief therapists often include imaginary exercises to reconstruct a verbal and non-verbal reframing of the connection (e.g., see Chapter 9). Multiple techniques of expressive exposure have been applied to readjust the internal presence of the deceased through a variety of exercises (e.g., writing, music, dance, art, drama, directed empty chair conversations). A recent compendium volume of therapeutic grief techniques (Neimeyer, 2015) details these and additional exercises. The common element to each is the opportunity for therapist and patient to enter the third space with the presence within absence and to *play* with and replay the real and symbolic representation of the deceased, not as a means of extinguishing or relinquishing but of rebuilding a more generative internalized bond to be carried forward.

Restorative Retelling of the Presence within Absence

Understanding the transitional dynamic within its visionary time and space between the bereaved and the deceased can be conceptually illuminating.

Prior to his death, Gloria and Ralph created a third space of communication to master the neurological and psychological reverberations of threatened separation. At first, Ralph's optimism of survival was mutually self-soothing, but as his dying became irrefutable, Ralph promised that while Gloria lived, she could always reach out to him through his presence within absence, and through their eventual reunion when she died. Entering this third space, I participated as listener and occasional questioner, to affirm the importance of our replaying to widen and deepen its frame. To be more specific, the goal of our collaborative retelling was not to extinguish the presence within absence as a semi-fiction, but to encourage its retelling between us in a shared time, space, and action. Once shared, Gloria's retelling was suspended between us, and once external became less literal. By joining in the retelling, I became an ally rather than repudiator or director in the movement of retelling and reframing. What had been intensely private and unedited, was now open for commentary and revision. Challenging or disregarding this spontaneous narrative as unreal or the product of cognitive distortion likely would have been counterproductive for Gloria in her bereavement journey. Instead, through our imaginary replay, Gloria realized a more capacious change in her perspective—by appreciating that each of our viewpoints within the story was somewhat different, the story might be changed. That new perspective, her semi-detached presence as narrator, enabled Gloria to prevail above and beyond the story. Instead of recovering who she had been before (i.e., merged in the presence within absence), now as narrator, she had developed ownership of a revised story no longer fixed in time and space, a story that could now be summoned and carried forward.

The Third Space with the Presence within Absence

Shaman, clergy, and therapist all intervene within the third space of separation and individuation through an inter-subjective interchange of words, behaviors, and images with the presence within absence. Since the third space is the ground or base where change is sought and reinforced, it first must be opened and joined. As always, it is wise to create such a collaboration with the griever by asking open-ended questioning during the first visit, such as, "What do you believe happens after death?" Asking directly about "what happens" allows an early glimpse into the presenting concept of death, which may include such beliefs as a dogmatic certitude of a resurrected afterlife, a plausible spiritual continuation, an affirmation of its mystery, or a certitude that any belief would be specious. The presence of death beliefs may introduce a generative and hopeful context (Moules, Simonson, Fleiszer, Prins, & Glasgow, 2007) within the third space, for instance, that the deceased still exists in some form in space and time.

Beyond the belief system of death, explaining the normality of the phantom presence of the deceased may be a reassuring way to introduce its focus. Early emphasis on the similarity between the amputation of a body part and the loss of an attachment relationship with one's CNS responses of phantom projection of a continuance may be a basic way for a counselor or therapist to structure an opening to the third space. For example, it could be explained like this:

> There is nothing abnormal about sensing that your loved is still here. Losing someone you love is like an amputation or losing a part of your identity. If your foot was amputated, you would never lose the feeling that it was still there. It's similar when you lose someone you love. Your brain is telling you that they still exist even though they are not physically present. After their death, they remain in your memory as a part of you and sometimes their presence is so real that they seemingly revisit you while you're awake or while you dream and sometimes you continue talking with them. What has been your experience? How do you remain connected with your deceased loved one?

Normalizing the phenomena of the phantom presence within absence can be an important aspect of bereavement to convey to the griever. In fact, validating the internalized presence within absence can relieve the misdirected fear that the phantom experiences of the deceased are pathologic. Once introduced as a common experience, the supportive conversation may magnify the third space to not only introduce the presence of the deceased but also to help the mourner appreciate how the deceased might serve in stabilizing their own self-identity.

But first, the deceased needs a name and a face to enliven their presence, which comes from asking the griever something like, "I want to know the name and see the face of the person you lost. Can we look at their picture together?" This serves as an opportunity to invite a shared processing of the attachment relationship with the deceased. Sharing their image (often summoned from an iPhone) and knowing their name introduces fundamental rudiments of early childhood attachment and transition—a comforting face and the power of naming. Now seen and named, the deceased may visually and verbally materialize within the conversation to become an active player in retelling. Thus, the therapist could say, "I know that [name of the deceased] can't be physically here with us, but if they were what would they do or say to help you?" Encouraging the voice and presence of the deceased in early support may introduce a familiar caregiver as an ally in a triadic conversation leading to readjustment. In subsequent sessions, elaboration of who the deceased was while alive may strengthen a coherent and meaningful presence through photos and writings, celebrating their vitality before considering the distress of their absence.

Gloria's Restorative Separation and Individuation

The first year after Ralph's death, Gloria and I met every three to four months. Each session celebrated her progress, encouraged by daily conversations with Ralph. I listened and reinforced the positive purpose of Ralph's voice and his visitations in her dreams. Functioning as a collaborative listener, I formed an associative alliance, listening and questioning for novel and generative change in the representation of Ralph's presence within absence as a way to include his voice (Attig, 1996; Beyers, Rallison, & West, 2017). In this way, my engagement in Gloria's retelling was now triadic between the three of us. By retelling this imaginative, collaborative trialogue, Gloria created an active role for herself as narrative moderator. The story of Ralph's death and his presence within absence did not change in our shared retelling; instead, Gloria's identity as moderator adjusted her role from participant to a more integrated and prevailing presence. By combining the voices and viewpoints from Ralph and me in the retelling, she began to establish an emancipated perspective over the presence within absence now carried forward as part of her renewed self-identity. Becoming a moderator reinforced her capacity for detachment and release from her earlier viewpoint that Ralph's presence within absence could not change.

Before our last visit, Gloria had opened several of Ralph's sealed envelopes. When we met, she said, "I can hardly wait to open the next one." Then she paused and said, "He left envelopes for only five years. I guess he thought we might not need them after that." I silently wondered if her voice as narrator was suggesting, "I might not need them after that, either."

References

Attig, T. (1996). *How we grieve: Relearning the world.* New York: Oxford University Press.

Beyers, J.M., Rallison, L., & West, C. (2017). Dialogical space in grief work: Integrating the alterity of loss. *Death Studies, 41*(7), 427–435.

Collerton, E. (2013). Psychotherapy and brain plasticity. *Frontiers in Psychology, 4,* 548.

Furman, E. (1983). Studies in childhood bereavement. *The Canadian Journal of Psychiatry, 28*(4), 241–247.

Jain, F.A., Connolly, C.G., Moore, L.C., Leuchter, A.F., Abrams, M., Ben-Yelles, R.W. Chang, S.E., Ramirez Gomez, L.A., Huey, N., & Lavretsky Haicoboni, M. (2019). Grief, mindfulness and neural predictors of improvement in family dementia caregivers. *Frontiers in Human Neuroscience, 13,* 1–12.

Johannsen, M., Damholdt, M.F., Zachariae, R., Lundorff, M., Farver-Vestergaard, I., & O'Connor, M. (2019). Psychological interventions for grief in adults: A systematic review and meta-analysis of randomized controlled trials. *Journal of Affective Disorders, 253,* 69–86.

Kamp, K., Steffen, E., Alderson-Day, B., Allen, P., Austad,A., Hayes, J., Larøi, F., Ratcliffe, M., & Sabucedo, P. (2020). Sensory and quasi-sensory experiences of the deceased in bereavement: An interdisciplinary and integrative review. *Schizophrenia Bulletin, 46*(6), 1367–1381.

Kaplow, J., Saxe, G., Putnam, G., Pynoos, R., & Liberman, A. (2006). The long-term consequences of early childhood trauma: A case presentation and discussion. *Psychiatry, 69*(4), 362–374.

Malhalski, P. (1985). Children's attachment to soft objects at bedtime, child-rearing, and child development. *Journal of the American Academy of Child Psychiatry, 24*(4), 4442–4446.

Moules, N.J., Simonson, K., Fleiszer, A.R., Prins, M., & Glasgow, R.B. (2007). The soul of sorrow work: Grief and therapeutic interventions with families. *Journal of Family Nursing, 13*(1), 117–141.

Neimeyer, R.A. (Ed.). (2015). *Techniques of grief therapy: Assessment and intervention*. New York: Routledge.

O'Connor, M. (2019). Grief: A brief history of research on how body, mind, and brain adapt. *Psychosomatic Medicine, 81*(8), 731–738.

Oltjenbruns, K.A. (2001). *Developmental context of childhood: Grief and re-grief phenomena*. In M.S. Stroebe, R.O. Hansson, W. Stroebe, & H. Schut (Eds.), *Handbook of bereavement research: Consequences, coping, and care*. Washington, DC: American Psychological Association, pp. 169–197. 10.1037/10436-007

Parkes, C.M. (1975). Psycho-social transitions: Comparison between reactions to loss of a limb and loss of a spouse. *The British Journal of Psychiatry, 127*(3), 204–210.

Pengmin, Q., & Northoff, G. (2011). How is our self related to midline regions and the default mode network? *NeuroImage, 57*(3), 1221–1233.

Pynoos, R., Frederick, C., Nader, K., Arroyo, W., Steinberg, G., Eth, S., Nunes, F., & Fairbanks, L. (1987). Life threat and posttraumatic stress in school-age children. *Archives of General Psychiatry, 44*(12), 1057–1063.

Ratcliffe, M. (2019). Grief and phantom limbs: A phenomenological comparison. *New Yearbook for Phenomenology and Phenomenological Philosophy, XVII*, 77–96.

Rosner, R., Kruse, J., & Hagl, M. (2010). A meta-analysis of interventions for bereaved children and adolescents. *Death Studies, 34*(2), 99–136.

Salloum, A. (2015). *Grief and trauma in children: An evidence-based treatment manual*. New York: Routledge.

Schafer, R. (1968). *Aspects of internalization*. Washington, DC: International Universities Press, Inc.

Shear, M.K., Reynolds, C.F., Simon, N.M., Zisook, S., Wang, Y., Mauro, C., ..., & Skritskaya, N. (2016). Optimizing treatment of complicated grief: A randomized clinical trial. *JAMA Psychiatry, 73*(7), 685–694.

Thimm, J.C., Kristoffersen, A.E., & Ringberg, U. (2020). The prevalence of severe grief reactions after bereavement and their associations with mental health, physical health, and health service utilization: A population-based study. *European Journal of Psychotraumatology, 11*(1). 10.1080/20008198.2020.1844440

Volkan, V.D. (1981). *Linking objects and linking phenomena: A study of the forms, symptoms, metapsychology, and therapy of complicated mourning*. Washington, DC: International Universities Press, Inc.

Wakenshaw, C. (2020). The use of Winnicott's concept of transitional objects in bereavement practice. *Bereavement Care, 39*(3), 119–123.

Winnicott, D. (1953). Transitional objects and transitional phenomena: A study of the first not-me possession. *International Journal of Psycho-Analysis, 34*, 89–97.

Winnicott, D. (1971). *Playing and reality*. Middlesex, England: Penguin Books.

9 From Retelling to Reintegration: Narrative Fixation and the Reconstruction of Meaning

Robert A. Neimeyer and
Edward (Ted) Rynearson

Introduction

Human beings are not only seekers of *knowing* (homo sapiens) but also speakers of *narratives* (homo narrans), as it is through stories and their retelling that we establish and convey our unique capacity for knowing and meaning. *Storying* experience, we integrate disparate and challenging events, position ourselves as the tellers, protagonists or victims of the account, attribute sense and significance to what has transpired, and find an audience for what might otherwise be a silent story that merely haunts our private consciousness. Thus, what begins in a monological relating of a story bridges into its dialogical extension with others, inviting compassion, understanding, and integration that may have been unvoiced, unvalued, and unvalidated. Accounts of the traumatic death of a loved one are among the most anguishing of such narratives, calling for a trauma-informed restorative retelling (Rynearson, 2001) to help bereaved clients process the *event story* of the dying and its implications for their ongoing lives (Neimeyer, 2019).

This chapter is premised on a narrative quest for meaning in tragic loss, at levels that are both intimately personal and intricately interpersonal. We also seek to expand this frame to encompass not only the *narration* of stories of loss in dialogue with living others but also the *performance* of stories of relationship with symbolically invoked others—in this case the deceased. Doing so in therapy typically promotes an encounter with the ongoing bond with the deceased, as well as greater mastery of the haunting or traumatizing particulars of the narrative of their dying and death. In this way, grief therapy also includes attachment-informed access to the *backstory* of the relationship to the deceased (Neimeyer, 2019), frequently recovering it as a resource for accommodating the trauma of the loss itself (Rynearson, 2012).

Our goal in this chapter is threefold. First, we acknowledge the spontaneous adaptation to narratives of dying and death that serves as a major mechanism for our characteristic human resilience. Second, we attempt to identify potential risk factors for maladaptive grieving in the face of traumatic loss,

DOI: 10.4324/9781003105077-12

suggesting some practical clinical probes for revealing vulnerabilities to protracted impairment in survivors' psychosocial adjustment. And third, we suggest some guidelines for facilitating both restorative processing of the event story of the death and performative accessing of the *presence within absence* of the deceased, illustrated through a case vignette. We engage these issues in the form of a dialogue between authors, questioning one another about our thoughts and experiences relevant to the three broad objectives.

Narrative Resilience: The Anatomy of Adaptation

Ted: Bob, it could be wise to first review the dynamics of spontaneous adaptation since therapy is often focused on reinforcing our clients' existing skills. Can you give us a general understanding of adaptive meaning making, whether a person is trying to accommodate a traumatic narrative of loss or the anguishing absence of the deceased loved one?

Bob: Certainly, Ted. Almost 70 years ago, the founding father of clinical constructivism, George Kelly (1955), developed his whole psychology around the idea that all human beings, not merely scientists, spent their lives building and testing theories, not so much about such abstruse topics as sub-atomic particles or the farther reaches of astrophysics, but about the everyday realities of human life, and especially our relational lives with others. Like scientists, we seek patterns and regularities in the flow of experience and weave the plots of our lives through with themes that help us understand, predict, and, at least in some measure, control the events that we confront. The result, he proposed, was a system of personal constructs, a framework of meaning that constitutes our individually constructed, but socially situated, assumptive world.

The difficulty, of course, is that life so frequently invalidates our constructs, and sometimes shatters our world assumptions altogether (Janoff-Bulman, 1992), as when it is our baby who is stillborn, our child who overdoses, our partner who dies by suicide, or our parent who dies in isolation on a ventilator from COVID-19. In such cases, core constructs of life—the assumption that our future is in some measure predictable, that the universe is just, and that we ourselves are capable agents who can protect our loved ones—are cruelly revealed to be fragile illusions. None of it makes sense. We can't wrap our heads or our hearts around what has happened, and we struggle to reconstruct a system of meaning capable of integrating the tragic turn of events and capable of restoring a semblance of connection to who and what we've lost. Simply put, we've been caught with our constructs down (Neimeyer, 1987, p. 14).

A meaning reconstruction approach to loss is built on this conceptual foundation (Neimeyer, 2019, 2020). Human beings are inveterate meaning makers. But too often, especially in the face of tragic loss, we are forced to make sense of a world that doesn't. Mostly, as we noted at the outset, we do so in storied terms, constructing accounts of past, present, and future events that render them intelligible. But when faced with tragic bereavement following traumatic death loss (e.g., homicide, suicide, fatal accident), we face two losses simultaneously, and with them a welter of others: the loss of a loved one in horrific and incomprehensible circumstances, and the loss of a meaning system that failed to anticipate the trauma that has befallen us.

Ted: Okay, but when we observe ourselves and others in the wake of troubling losses, we typically see a good deal of adaptive retelling of the narratives of what happened between family members, close friends, co-workers, and the spiritual community. And all of this spontaneous grappling with the loss story usually initiates a normative return of stability and meaning within weeks or months of the dying and death. However, both the ruminative retelling of meaningless dying (as when the death is sudden or violent) and overly dependent or ambivalent attachment to the deceased can distort the restorative synthesis in a significant minority, roughly 10%, of mourners (Lundorff, Holmgren, Zachariae, Farver-Vestergaard, & O'Connor, 2017).

Bob: I agree with you, Ted, and so do the data. For example, when others in our social world are able to validate us in our efforts to reaffirm or reconstruct a world of meaning that has been challenged by such loss, we tend to move toward post-traumatic growth, whereas when we confront social invalidation of our meaning making, we are far more likely to struggle with intense symptoms of prolonged grief (Bellet, Holland, & Neimeyer, 2018). In essence, we typically make sense of what we've gone through as we spontaneously retell our adversity to others, who serve as witnesses and resources for the reconstruction of our world of meaning.

Moreover, as you also imply, ruminative preoccupation with the event story that does not lead to meaning making prospectively predicts poor bereavement outcomes (Milman et al., 2019), just as insecure forms of attachment to the deceased interact with the quality of the relationship to them in life to predict more complicated grief symptomatology (Smigelsky, Bottomley, Relyea, & Neimeyer, 2020). This trifecta of tragedy—a close but conflicted relational history, a ruminative impasse in sense making, and social invalidation—is a recipe for trouble, often leading mourners to turn to professionals who can help them reconstruct their worlds and bonds and find new footing in a changed life.

Signs of Risk for Maladaptive Grieving

Ted: Before considering therapy, let's clarify the narrative signs that forecast difficulty in assimilating the story of the dying and death. Narrative fixation—the intense, prolonged, and repetitive interchange with the presence/absence of the deceased—is a sign of maladaptation as well as signage of the need for therapy. Understanding the purpose of the fixation, as well as the frozen and spectral time, space, and action of the story, is essential. While the intensity and redundancy of the story of attachment to the deceased may compensate for the voided role of care giving and receiving following their dying and death, the narrative remembrance of their living and dying can become so absorbing and prolonged that it impedes adaptation to a changed world. The timing, setting, and manner of dying shapes and shades the narrative remembrance of the dying in several ways. For instance:

- When a loved one dies from a *natural* cause (e.g., lengthy illness), there typically is time, space, and action to enact a dying narrative with closeness, caring, respect, and finally relinquishment. There is a place for the survivor in the unfolding death narrative, made painful but also meaningful because it is anticipated.
- If instead a loved one dies *suddenly and unexpectedly*, their bereaved survivors are further traumatized because of the lost opportunity to care for and mutually and meaningfully relinquish one another. This lost opportunity also is common for loved ones with the enforced isolation associated with dying from COVID-19.
- If the dying is not only sudden and unexpected but also *violent*, the narrative of the dying may be a solitary enactment of horror and helplessness, isolated from the care, respect, and protection that close supporters feel mandated to offer. As a result, the narrative is retold as an alienated event, a surreal story that supporters cannot own because they played no role in its unfolding, and the account is rendered meaningless and socially stigmatized because it never should have happened.

Bob: Good points. The suddenness, unexpectedness, and violence of traumatic death have long been counted as evidence-based risk factors for painful and protracted grieving (Burke & Neimeyer, 2013), and recent research has suggested why. Both contemporaneous (Burke & Neimeyer, 2014; Currier, Holland, & Neimeyer, 2006; Rozalski, Holland, & Neimeyer, 2016) and longitudinal (Milman et al., 2018, 2019) studies have documented that violent deaths lead to greatly more anguishing and prolonged grief, and that this outcome is substantially or entirely mediated by its adverse impact on meaning making regarding the dying or death. It's as if our inability to wrap our hearts or minds around the reality of what has befallen us is the very definition of trauma. Our current research on bereavement to COVID-19 further supports this conclusion, as ten distinctive circumstantial risk factors associated with the surreal narrative of dying (e.g., rapid progression of the illness, images of the loved one dying alone or struggling for life on a machine) or the disengagement or disempowerment of the mourner (e.g., inability to be there for the loved one at the end of life, impossibility to prevent the illness and death) make independent and cumulative contributions to the prediction of dysfunctional grief and impairment of functioning in family, social, and work roles (Lee & Neimeyer, 2020; Neimeyer & Lee, 2021). In other words, both the traumatic story of violent dying and the abrogated attachment mandate to care for the loved one at a point of great vulnerability may nullify our efforts to enact a meaningful narrative of transition, ushering in an ongoing struggle to assimilate the loss adaptively. This is precisely where restorative retelling of the dying story and restorative internalization of the relationship come in.

Ted: Yes. But despite their risk, each form of narrative fixation also may allow a fragile adjustment to impaired autonomy, that is, "I cannot be without you" or "I cannot be with the events of your dying." But suspended in a fixated narrative of denial of loss, the mourner also pays a price, unable to commit to valued activities, relationships, and a meaningful future.

A major challenge in the therapeutic reconstruction of fixation narratives of grief is the over-determined quality of approach toward the alluring and meaningful story of relational attachment contrasted with avoidance of the aversive and meaningless story of traumatic dying. Reconstructing these fixations with the presence in absence may be further challenged when comforting themes of attachment are admixed with aversive themes of transgression, remorse, dishonor, and reenactment with the dying event. This combination may place the therapist and griever in a para-doxical impasse—how to unravel a meaningless narrative of dying that eclipses a meaningful narrative of attachment to the presence/absence. Earlier, I suggested that the primacy of fixation narrative(s) could serve as signage for the ordering and staging of therapy. You have had extensive clinical experience in deconstructing and restoring grief-related fixations with the presence/absence of the deceased. So, let me pose three relevant questions before considering a case illustration:

- How do you establish a trusting and collaborative therapeutic relationship for retelling in terms of its focus and staging?
- Clarifying and reinforcing resilient resources for adaptation is requisite, but are there other basic principles of history taking that you include at the start of therapy?
- What are the specific procedures with which you set the stage for restorative retelling or reintegration?

Evaluating the Client's Need and Readiness

Bob: Fair questions, and I'm happy to engage them. First a further word about fixations. I share your perspective that symptoms have significance, and fixations have functions. Fixations are not simply a nuisance or pathology to be eliminated, but a sub-intentioned means of preserving something essential to the person's core sense of identity or way of being in the world, in other words, their core meaning systems. This calls for the kind of stance that Bruce Ecker (2012) advocates in his Coherence Therapy, as we seek the significance of the suffering, the implicit or non-conscious meaning of mourning in fixation that makes it more important to maintain than to eliminate, despite the very real pain it entails. For example, clients with prolonged and disabling grief often seem to resist reducing or relinquishing their anguish, as if doing so represented a betrayal of their loved one. This also fits with your notion that preoccupation with or fixation on the dying or the relationship allows a kind of fragile adjustment, in a sense freeze framing a world that has changed radically and ruptured a key attachment bond. In such cases, the intense grief sometimes seems to become the bond, as if the pain is what keeps them connected, and it gets written into the terms of attachment. This is a partial answer to your first question.

If we ask TerryRando's (2012) question to people in prolonged and pre-occupying grief, "Would it be okay for you to be okay?" and they hesitate, and then stammer out, "Well ... no, I don't think it would," then we know we are in the zone of a fixation inviting more therapeutic attention. As therapists, we are eager to reduce our client's suffering but until we understand deeply and intimately what our clients are holding on to and why, we have no business urging them to let go. Premature advocacy to release their fixation on transitional presence within absence could result in their fear of plunging into a meaningless void. The question, of course, is how one can work within Winnicott's third space (Keenan & Miehls, 2008) that you described in the previous chapter, that transitional world between the life that was and whatever life will now become.

You further raise the crucial precondition to both restorative retelling of the loss and restorative internalization of the relationship, which is establishing a trusting and collaborative therapeutic relationship. Elsewhere, I've written about how this entails an authentic offer of therapist presence to the client's suffering—a non-anxious, attuned, and, in a sense, vulnerable stance of showing up compassionately, patiently, respectfully, to whatever emerges, which in effect invites the client to do the same (Neimeyer, 2012a). This is akin to beginner's mind in Buddhism, a relinquishment of, or at least holding only lightly to, our case conceptualization, in order to meet clients in this moment, in all of their unpredictable uniqueness. In this place of stillness, we offer what Winnicott would call a holding environment (Winnicott, 1960) a secure base, a container for difficult and emotionally collaborative work. As we attune to the intersubjective process that unfolds between us, we can then discern more clearly the two essential markers that direct our therapy: what the client most deeply needs in this very moment, and what the client is ready for in relation to this need (Neimeyer, 2019). It is at the crosshairs of this need and readiness that we can most accurately target a therapeutic opening or opportunity, one that calls for restorative retelling when the client seems ruminatively fixated on the dying narrative, or for restorative reintegration when the client is anxiously clinging to a concrete relational narrative that was tragically terminated by the death. Thus, presence is the precondition for attunement to process, and a process reading of need and readiness is the precondition to selecting a particular therapeutic procedure. For me, these constitute the three P's of psychotherapy (Neimeyer, 2012a). So, this is another concrete response to your question: Grow still and attentive, and the client's signal of enmeshment with the traumatic story of the death or the concrete attachment to the loved one will come through clearly. This is the signage that points to the work we are about to describe in greater detail.

Staging the Intervention

Bob: In your systematic questions about structure and staging, I hear you calling for a judicious stepwise staging of intervention with emphasis on history taking, which can indeed offer useful cues of client resources and vulnerabilities and is fully in line with best practice medical guidelines. But your emphasis on thoughtful evaluation and implementation is something I usually identify with only in hindsight. In the moment, immersed in the flow of give and take with the client, I'm not focally aware of signs or stages, intentions or interventions. I suppose I'm functioning more like a jazz musician riffing off the offering of another player, than I am a surgeon reaching for a clamp or scalpel at a particular point in the operation. I'm not advocating an "anything goes" eclecticism, far from it. Instead, I believe our clients are telling us exactly what they need and are ready for in every conversational turn of therapy, and at non-verbal and co-verbal as well as verbal levels. However, I can offer some concrete steps and guidelines:

> Focus on fixation. *Listen deeply between the words of the client's story to determine whether and where the mourner is fixated. Remember that research demonstrates that most grievers are resilient* (Bonanno, 2009), *and although they may benefit from bereavement support, they do not require grief therapy* (Neimeyer & Currier, 2009). *But when clients meet ICD-11 or DSM 5-TR criteria for prolonged grief disorder, by definition they are preoccupied by either the tragic story of the dying or an anguishing effort to hold tight to an attachment with the deceased that has been assaulted by death. Traumatic arousal and rumination about how the loved one died points toward a fixation on the narrative of dying and calls for restorative retelling. Alternatively, corrosive separation anxiety and loneliness indicate the relevance of restorative integration. Of course, a mourner may suffer from either or both in various admixtures. But simple open probes like, "What is the hardest part of this terrible experience for you?" will usually reveal the crucial initial focus. This is what I mean by reading the client's implicit need that directs the work.*

> Recruit resources. *Restorative work of either kind calls for a strong therapeutic foundation, as it is inherently emotional work, undertaken at a time of great vulnerability. Offering an engaged but unhurried holding environment characterized by high therapist presence provides the secure base in the therapeutic alliance that the client requires to contain and process strong affect. Recognize that, although this can sometimes be established in a very short time when clients are trusting and therapists are highly attuned, it commonly takes a couple of sessions for this relational grounding to be established. So, the best advice is, when in doubt, wait it out. A client's deepening disclosures of highly vulnerable material will tell you when you are there. At that point, building a firmer frame for the work by assessing the client's self-care capacities (e.g., ability to emotionally down-regulate without repressive self-inhibition in the wake of strong emotion, personal practices of meditation, exercise, or other means of coping with high stress, recourse to religious beliefs of a consoling kind, social and familial support) is useful. In my therapies, I commonly lead clients in some closed-eyed, deep diaphragmatic breath work, inviting them with*

a slow and measured voice across a span of just a few minutes to attend to and release some of the tension they discern in their bodies. As I breathe in synchrony with them, slowing our breath cycles, we also slow the clients' racing thoughts and feelings. We are then poised to consider staging the restorative work itself.

Assess acceptance. *Offer a succinct description of the restorative work you are proposing and evaluate the client's readiness to engage it. For example, if the fixation focuses on the event story of the dying, I might say something like:* "It sounds like the experience of finding your son's body after the overdose was a living nightmare to you, leaving you replaying random parts of the story or being flooded with images of the scene of his dying as you try to make sense of what happened and why. I'm also guessing that a lot of that plays out as a silent story inside you [client nods her head slowly and sadly], *so that you are left alone in the story, trying to find a way through it or out of it.* [Brief pause to allow the client to further consider this.] *I wonder how you'd feel about our walking through that story together, from the moment you opened his bedroom door, slowing down to notice what captured your attention, what emotions arose in you at each point, and what questions or thoughts about what was happening rose up in response. We might find that we just do this for 10–15 minutes, just taking in one short chapter of the longer story, or we could spend as much time as you need, as long as we save at least 15 minutes to step back from that story, arrive back in the room together, and see what steps to take from there. How does that sound to you?" I usually allow clients to begin the story in the verb tense of their choice, which 90% of the time is the more natural and perhaps emotionally regulated past tense. But occasionally, I will suggest a present-tense telling to promote greater immediacy and engagement when the client seems emotionally distant in the telling, unless this appears to reflect a means of managing their vulnerability.*

Similarly, if the client is fixated on the backstory of the relationship with the deceased, I might say: "It sounds like there was so much more that needed to be said to your father, so much more life you wanted to share with him. And so, dealing with his very present absence is anguishing for you. But one of our goals in therapy is to bend the rules of usual social life and make space for things we usually don't —like reopening a conversation with a loved one that was prematurely closed by death. If I were to support you in that, being able to say 'hello again,' in a sense, rather than a final 'goodbye,' how would that *be for you, just to be able to say some of what is in your heart directly to him, as if he could hear you and respond to you? How would you feel about giving that a try together for a few minutes, just to see what comes of it—to talk to him in a sense, rather than just about him?"*

With this brief acceptance check, we're poised in either case to move forward with the staging of the restorative retelling or integration itself. Note that I don't expect the client to feel comfortable with either form of restorative work. Anxiety is to be expected, precisely because this pushes into the sort of novel territory where change becomes possible. But when accompanied by trust and courage, moderate anxiety is actually a positive signal of readiness for the work, a sign that we are on the growing edge of therapeutic change.

Bracing, Pacing, and Facing

Ted: Can you say more about how you manage that anxiety as the retelling or reintegration gets underway, so that it doesn't become retraumatizing? Can techniques for stress moderation or exposure be categorized and how are they staged in actual practice?

Bob: I'm glad you emphasize that, as it is crucial that we help clients stay within their window of tolerance for distressing emotion (Ogden, 2010) throughout the work, precisely to avoid re-immersing them in the trauma of the dying. The goal in restorative work of any kind is to accompany mourners to the hard places to help them process and integrate what they find there. Elsewhere, I've used the mnemonic of bracing, pacing, and facing to convey this stance and its intentions (Neimeyer, 2019). So, let me summarize the essence of each concept to offer some concrete guidance in how to move forward.

> Bracing. *Bracing refers to the support we give clients, not merely the macro-level support of recruiting their religious or philosophical beliefs, reaffirming their ties to family and friends, or rekindling their self-care practices prior to staging the restorative work, but also the micro-level support we provide when their distress begins to crest and spill beyond their window of tolerance during the retelling or revisiting itself. Some categories of bracing interventions could include visualization, such as viewing the scene or the loved one not as if at arm's distance, but rather from across the room, or as if in a football stadium, as the scene being engaged is unfolding on the field as*

seen from the highest bleacher. Another category could be labeled grounding, inviting a client beginning to experience overwhelming emotion in a closed-eyed encounter with the scene of dying or the loved one to re-open his or her eyes and make visual contact with us, or to pause and notice the security with which his or her body is held in the chair, to ground the client more safely in the present moment. Yet another that I use with some frequency is breath work, pausing the restorative re-enactment to soothe the turbulent stream of the emotion and slow the racing thoughts that are threatening to drag the client like an undertow into a sea of panic or grief. The possibilities are really endless and depend largely on the skill set of the clinician. But the crucial point is to use each of these practices not to interrupt or avoid the retelling or re-enactment, but rather to stay with it in a safer way. The other two mnemonic guidelines reinforce this goal.

Pacing. *The second mnemonic, pacing, refers to the speed of the work, and the advice here is straightforward: Go slow. You almost can't go too slowly, whereas you can easily go too fast. Only the former permits the deliberative conscious and collaborative review and integration of the story or the relationship in a way that is restorative, that allows for meaning reconstruction. By contrast, the familiar story told in the client's typical storytelling pace is merely ruminative, and the accelerated telling, like a runaway truck with failed brakes on a mountain road, is a recipe for re-traumatization. With their eyes closed to minimize distraction and more easily access episodic memories, invite the client to visually set the scene by asking prompting questions like: What did the hospital room look like when you arrived? Who was there? Where was your attention drawn? When you took the hand of your dying mother as she lay in that hospital bed during that last visit, how did it feel? Can you show us how you held your mother's hand with your own? Witnessing the tears that come with this, we might ask, What emotion rises in you now, like a tide? If those tears had words, what would they say? Marinating in the moment, we open the door not merely to the external narrative, the plot of the objective story unfolding before the client, but also to the subjective, internal narrative, the emotion-focused story that is unfolding within the client, while a succession of significant events is occurring around her. As we do so, from time to time the client might wrinkle her brow, frown thoughtfully, or phrase a specific question that suggests engagement with the third strand, the reflexive or meaning-oriented narrative. For example, seeing the flicker of puzzlement on the client's face, we might ask, "What comes to you now?", and learn that, at that moment in the story, she was just beginning to take in the reality that her mother actually was dying, or that she felt a strange admixture of emotion, an amalgam of grief and relief. It is with this slow, methodical review of the narrative of the dying, or, correspondingly, the enactment of a conversation with the deceased, that we delicately braid together the external, internal, and reflexive strands of narration, giving the client a stronger through-line to traverse the experience* (Neimeyer, 2019).

Facing. *The final mnemonic, facing, refers to both the process and goal of the restorative work: to stand in the presence of something difficult with courage, witnessed by a compassionate guide or fellow traveler (or in group settings, several such). The intention in doing so is to promote mastery of a difficult narrative, or to resolve unfinished business in the case of a relational enactment with the deceased where too much was left undone or unsaid prior to the death. Ultimately, with appropriate bracing and pacing, facing such challenges with new resources in the presence of a stalwart ally in the therapist and often in the deceased, fosters empowerment of the client, in place of the helplessness and horror that predominated before the restorative work began.*

Restorative Reintegration: A Case Example

Ted: Can you give us a fuller view of how this interchange might operate in a session by illustrating techniques of restorative reintegration? Perhaps where a client has been trapped for many months or years in a fixation or a troubling rupture in an attachment bond?

Bob: I can. Here's a real-life therapeutic vignette that follows procedures for chair work that I detail elsewhere (Neimeyer, 2012b):

Rob had entered therapy to sort out his younger brother Jimmy's overdose death which had occurred several years before. Rob recalled jettisoning both his faith and family (including Jimmy) as he pursued his university and ultimately law school studies with a fierceness and ego that seemed the clearest alternative to the sanctimonious atmosphere of his past. Now, however, Rob realized that his cut-off from family had left his little brother Jimmy without a buffer from an unhealthy and alcoholic home environment. As Jimmy slipped into an adolescence characterized by severe substance abuse,

Rob recalled that "I judged him ... and he felt it", expressing in these words a deep form of remorse for actions toward his brother that now seemedunresolvable. But his fixation on the death and his abrogated big brother role continued to haunt him. A full decade after Jimmy's ambiguous overdose, Rob still felt deep remorse but was stymied how to address it. As he described it, "It's like an itch I can't scratch."

Having established a strong working alliance in the preceding three sessions, I asked Rob if these were experiences that he felt ready to address with Jimmy now, were his brother able to join us in the session, ready to hear what he had to say. Rob nodded his head. Gesturing to the empty chair positioned opposite him, I asked him to close his eyes for a moment and envision Jimmy there, and then to open his eyes and speak to the broken heart of their relationship. His eyes growing moist, Rob said, "I'm sorry I didn't help you. As 10 years have gone by, my perspective has changed so much. I'm sorry forjudging you. You were always good to me, never judged me. I want to pay that forward with my own children." "Try telling him," I suggested, "I am loving my kids for you." Pausing and nodding seriously, Rob repeated this, and continued, "Yes. Your memory is still part of my family. You are forever in my life." "Try saying," I offered, "You are still my brother." Tears welling, Rob repeated this, then fell silent with private emotion.

Gesturing to Jimmy's chair, I then directed Rob to sit in Jimmy's seat and respond to his older brother's comments. Responding as Jimmy, Rob answered, "Rob, I've missed you too and I am so sorry about my addiction. I just lost the battle. Grieve me. I'm happy you found beauty and purpose in your life. Love your children. Thanks for keeping me in their minds and hearts. I accept your apology."

Moving Rob to a third chair at right angles to the two he had used in the dialogue, I asked him from this witness position what he had observed about the conversation that had just taken place. Taking this meta-perspective, Rob responded that he was struck by the "sincerity in the relationship, the feeling. The relationship is tremendously important. I think I carry it with me wherever I go." As we sat with this recognition, Rob was suddenly flooded with emotion, and sobbing deeply, stammered out, "Of all my family, my brother loved me thebest. Now I see so much of my brother in me. Jimmy never had my mean streak, my severity." Recognizing the seeds of love that his brother had planted in him, Rob concluded, "So now I tell my children every time I see them that I love them just the way they are." Nine months later, as our therapy drew to a close, Rob reflected on that pivotal fourth session, which seemed to resolve a long-standing sense of guilt, install more securely a brother's love, and begin to prompt a more compassionate witnessing of those wounded souls, including his parents, who remained physically present for a deeper dialogue.

Conclusion

In their attempts to find orientation and meaning in what may feel like a senseless loss, bereaved individuals sometimes become fixated on a ruminative engagement with the event story of the loss, or on an anguishing rupture in the backstory of a bond of attachment to the deceased. In such cases, we have found that a compassionate and methodical retelling of the event of the dying can help clients face and find greater meaning in the dying narrative, just as the performance of carefully facilitated symbolic conversations with the deceased can promote reintegration of the relationship in a way that is healing without requiring denial of the death. We hope that our attempt to outline clinical principles and practices to guide this work will invite the engagement of other clinicians in this restorative approach to grief therapy, ultimately supporting clients to find greater coherence and connection in the wake of tragic loss.

References

Bellet, B.W., Holland, J.M., & Neimeyer, R.A. (2018). The Social Meaning in Life Events Scale (SMILES): A preliminary psychometric evaluation in a bereaved sample. *Death Studies, 43*, 103–112. 10.1080/07481187.2018.1456008

Bonanno, G.A. (2009). *The other side of sadness*. New York: Basic.

Burke, L.A., & Neimeyer, R.A. (2013). Prospective risk factors for complicated grief: A review of the empirical literature. In M.S. Stroebe, H. Schut, & J. van der Bout (Eds.), *Complicated grief: Scientific foundations for healthcare professionals*. New York: Routledge.

Burke, L.A., & Neimeyer, R.A. (2014). Complicated spiritual grief I: Relation to complicated grief symptomatology following violent death bereavement. *Death Studies, 38*, 259–267. 10.1080/07481187.2013.829372

Currier, J.M., Holland, J.M., & Neimeyer, R.A. (2006). Sense making, grief, and the experience of violent loss: Toward a mediational model. *Death Studies, 30*, 403–428.

Ecker, B. (2012). Overt statements for deep work in grief therapy. In R. Neimeyer (Ed.), *Techniques of grief therapy: Creative practices for counseling the bereaved*. New York: Routledge, pp. 152–154.

Janoff-Bulman, R. (1992). *Shattered assumptions: Towards a new psychology of trauma*. New York: Free Press.

Keenan, E.K., & Miehls, D. (2008). Third space activities and change processes: An exploration of ideas from social and psychodynamic theories. *Clinical Social Work Journal, 36*(2), 165–175.

Kelly, G.A. (1955). *The psychology of personal constructs.* New York: Norton.

Lee, S.A., & Neimeyer, R.A. (2020). Pandemic Grief Scale: A screening tool for dysfunctional grief due to a COVID-19 loss. *Death Studies,* 1–11. 10.1080/07481187.2020.1853885

Lundorff, M., Holmgren, H., Zachariae, R., Farver-Vestergaard, I., & O'Connor, M. (2017). Prevalence of prolonged grief disorder in adult bereavement: A systematic review and meta-analysis. *Journal of Affective Disorders, 212,* 138–149.

Milman, E., Neimeyer, R.A., Fitzpatrick, M., MacKinnon, C.J., Muis, K.R., & Cohen, S.R. (2018). Prolonged grief symptomatology following violent loss: The mediating role of meaning. *European Journal of Psychotraumatology, 8*(Suppl 6), 1503522. 10.1080/20008198.2018.1503522

Milman, E., Neimeyer, R.A., Fitzpatrick, M., MacKinnon, C.J., Muis, K.R., & Cohen, S. R. (2019). Rumination moderates the role of meaning in the development of prolonged grief symptomatology. *Journal of Clinical Psychology, 75*(6), 1047–1065. 10.1002/jcp.22751

Neimeyer, R.A. (1987). An orientation to personal construct theory. In R.A. Neimeyer & G.J. Neimeyer (Eds.), *Personal construct therapy casebook.* New York: Springer, pp. 3–19.

Neimeyer, R.A. (2012a). Presence, process and procedure. In R. Neimeyer (Ed.), *Techniques of grief therapy: Creative practices for counseling the bereaved.* New York: Routledge, pp. 3–11.

Neimeyer, R.A. (2012b). Chair work. In R. Neimeyer (Ed.), *Techniques of grief therapy: Creative practices for counseling the bereaved.* New York: Routledge, pp. 266–273.

Neimeyer, R.A. (2019). Meaning reconstruction in bereavement: Development of a research program. *Death Studies, 43,* 79–91. 10.1080/07481187.2018.1456620

Neimeyer, R.A. (2020). What's new in meaning reconstruction? Advancing grief theory and practice. *Grief Matters: The Australian Journal of Grief and Bereavement, 23*(1), 4–9.

Neimeyer, R.A., & Currier, J.M. (2009). Grief therapy: Evidence of efficacy and emerging directions. *Current Directions in Psychological Science, 18,* 352–356.

Neimeyer, R.A., & Lee, S.A. (2021). Circumstances of the death and associated risk factors for severity and impairment of COVID-19 grief. *Death Studies,* 1–9. 10.1080/07481187.2021.1896459

Ogden, P. (2010). Modulation, mindfulness and movement in the treatment of trauma-related emotion. In M. Kerman (Ed.), *Clinical pearls of wisdom.* New York: Norton, pp. 1–13.

Rando, T.A. (2012). Is it okay for you to be okay? In R. Neimeyer (Ed.), *Techniques of grief therapy: Creative practices for counseling the bereaved.* New York: Routledge, pp. 149–151.

Rozalski, V., Holland, J.M., & Neimeyer, R.A. (2016). Circumstances of death and complicated grief: Indirect associations through meaning made of loss. *Journal of Loss and Trauma, 22,* 11–23. 10.1080/15325024.2016.1161426

Rynearson, E.K. (2001). *Retelling violent death.* New York: Routledge.

Rynearson, E.K. (2012). Invoking an alliance with the deceased after violent death. In R. Neimeyer (Ed.), *Techniques of grief therapy: Creative practices for counseling the bereaved*. New York: Routledge, pp. 91–94.

Smigelsky, M.A., Bottomley, J.S., Relyea, G., & Neimeyer, R.A. (2020). Investigating risk for grief severity: Attachment to the deceased and relationship quality. *Death Studies, 44*, 402–411. 10.1080/07481187.2018.1548539

Winnicott, D.W. (1960). The theory of the parent-infant relationship. *International Journal of Psycho-Analysis, 41*, 585–595.

10 Grieving in the Wind Telephone Booth

Craig Van Dyke

Introduction

In the Tohoku region of northeastern Japan resides a disconnected black rotary telephone that relies on the wind to transmit spoken messages from grieving individuals to the dead. As a psychiatrist who assists individuals and communities recovering from natural disasters, I was invited to its formal dedication in May 2014, slightly more than three years after the region was devastated by a massive tsunami, the likes of which had not been experienced since 869 CE. The experience sent me on a journey to understand how speaking to the dead through the Wind Telephone, as it is now referred to (or in Japanese as *kaze no denwa*) can bring relief to thousands of grieving individuals.

The 2011 Japanese Disaster

At 2:46 pm on Friday, March 11, 2011, Japan experienced a cascade of events that threatened its very existence as a functioning state. A magnitude 9.0 earthquake, the fourth most powerful ever recorded, moved Japan's main island, Honshu, eight feet eastward and caused much of the coastline in the Tohoku region to subside 2–3 feet. The earthquake produced a massive tsunami that in less than an hour flooded the villages and cities along the coast. At the Fukushima Daiichi nuclear power plant, it overtopped the 46-foot high seawall and flooded multiple reactors, triggering the second-worst nuclear power plant accident after Chernobyl. While the nuclear accident commanded the world's attention, the tsunami was the real culprit for the Tohoku people. Village after village along the coast of Fukushima, Miyagi, Iwate, and Aomori Prefectures were completely destroyed. The massive flooding reached heights of 40–120 feet and arrived onshore so quickly that people had little time to reach safety. The tsunami claimed most of the 15,894 confirmed deaths, while an additional 2,500 remain missing. Searches for the missing continue to this day and include survivors diving in bays across the region hoping to find the remains of their lost loved ones.

DOI: 10.4324/9781003105077-13

On that fateful day in the remote fishing village of Otsuchi, people instantly knew the earthquake was more powerful than any they had experienced previously. Instinctively, they understood that the epicenter was near and that a tsunami would soon follow. People were shouting, running, jumping in cars, and racing for high ground. Children were confused, crying, and panic-stricken. Others stood transfixed. In short order, an innocent white ribbon of waves appeared, stretching across the bay, moving inexorably toward the village. As it approached, the bay began to fill and quickly overtopped the 30-foot-high seawall and submerged the low-lying village center to a depth of 40–60 feet. The tsunami pushed inland, crushing houses and floating other structures off their foundations. Cars and trucks were destroyed, and fishing boats cast adrift. The flooding relented only after it reached a steep slope at the far side where the village cemetery rested. For several days as the water receded, a black liquid conveyor belt transported the flotsam out to sea and left in its wake the jetsam as a large debris field that covered the area where the village center once stood. The gutted two-story concrete town hall where the mayor and his staff perished remained standing as a forlorn symbol of the devastation. Of its 15,000 inhabitants, 799 people died and another 608 remain missing.

Survivors in Otsuchi faced unimaginable loss of family members, friends, pets, housing, livelihood, cars, fishing boats, and their way of life. Their sense of place in the world and the village where the history of their families stretched back multiple generations had disappeared in the blink of an eye. Emblematic of the rent in the village's social fabric was the cemetery where the grave markers and remains of their venerated ancestors were scattered over the hillside. It was a disorienting and painful end to the life they had known. After this horrible experience, how could the survivors mourn their personal losses, recover their way of life, and embrace the future?

Grieving in the Wind Telephone Booth

Otsuchi had no mental health services at the time of the disaster and like much of rural Japan its residents harbored stigmatizing attitudes toward anyone manifesting psychological symptoms or aberrant behaviors that might be expressions of a mental illness. To address the town's emotional needs, Dr. Mitsuru Suzuki, a psychiatrist at the Ministry of Foreign Affairs in Tokyo formed Kokorogake, a non-profit mental health team. This was a heartfelt undertaking, but not an easy task given the day-long travel from Tokyo, where most of the team was based and the villagers' long-standing distrust of strangers. But over several years and numerous trips, the team gained their trust and engaged Otsuchi residents in a communal healing process, combining group art projects with discussions of what they had experienced and how their lives had changed.

However, the emotional burden of the villagers proved overwhelming and beyond the capacity of the Kokorogake team to address everyone's needs. A year after the tsunami, in what can be best described as *deus ex machina* (an unexpected solution to a seemingly unsolvable problem), the Wind Telephone miraculously appeared at Belle Gardia Kujirayama, the estate of Itaru Sasaki in the foothills outside Otsuchi. Mr. Sasaki had created a beautiful English garden that blended seamlessly with the native trees and surrounding flora. Standing elegantly in the middle of the garden was a white British-style telephone booth with multiple window-panes and a light aquamarine roof. In 2007, Mr. Sasaki rescued it from a Pachinko parlor that was being demolished in Kamaishi, a nearby town. Initially, he intended it as a decorative element, but following the death of his cousin from stomach cancer in 2010, he installed a rotary telephone so that he could talk to his cousin with the wind carrying his love and sorrowful messages to him. Approximately a year after the tsunami, he realized the Wind Telephone could be helpful to others in communicating their sorrow to those they had lost.

The dedication day was crystal clear, and from the estate it was easy to see Otsuchi Bay in the far distance where so many people had lost their lives. Mr. Sasaki was a gracious host and with his gray hair, ready smile, and calm demeanor he made everyone feel welcome. He was clearly pleased that his inspiration, the Wind Telephone, was receiving formal recognition. The ceremony occurred under a vine-encrusted trellis with a small bell hanging in the center. Mr. Sasaki, Dr. Suzuki, and village elders spoke about loss, and several children read passages from a book about pets using a telephone to communicate with lost pets. One of the Kokorogake team played an Irish harp and sang traditional Irish ballads. At first hearing, Danny Boy in English felt out of place, but as I listened to the lyrics it captured the moment perfectly as it described the mourner kneeling at the gravesite speaking of their love and how this allowed Danny to rest in peace until the mourner could reunite in the afterlife (Weatherly, 1913).

In the solemn mood that followed, approximately 30 of the 60–70 people in attendance headed to the Wind Telephone to speak with those they had lost. Children went first. The line moved slowly, the glass booth allowed little privacy, yet the pent-up urge to communicate with those in the afterlife took control.

After the ceremony, I thought the Wind Telephone was a sensitive-yet-practical approach for survivors to reestablish a one-way communication link with their lost loved ones. I very much appreciated being included in the ceremony, but I had no reason to imagine that it would have much impact on a wider grief-stricken population, especially given the re-moteness of Otsuchi. For a couple of years, I thought little about it until 2016 when my younger son, Lucas, a San Francisco Bay Area psychiatrist, mentioned to me that he heard an episode of *This American Life* on

National Public Radio (NPR) about grieving individuals making a pilgrimage to the Wind Telephone in a small town in northeastern Japan (Glass & Meek, 2016). Knowing that I was working on the recovery effort following the Fukushima disaster, he wondered if I knew about it. Needless to say, I was flabbergasted by the power of the Wind Telephone to attract grieving individuals (now more than 25,000 mourners) from all parts of Japan and from distant corners of the world. And, of course, I was more than a little humbled by the limitations of my predictive powers.

In the years since the ceremony, many people have recorded their emotional sentiments in a series of notebooks that Mr. Sasaki keeps in the Wind Telephone:

> I am crying secret tears...; Terrible heart ache and sadness...; Debris in my heart that lingers...; Helps bring closure...; Dad I hold you in my heart...; I want to hug you again and hear your voice...; Dad, you are my best friend and I miss your intelligence...; I think of you every day...; You are my angel watching over me...; I can now find peace after anger...; I feel sadness and grief...; I can feel your presence...; Mom, please watch over me so that I can keep going until the day I am able to see you again. I want to see you, even if in a dream, I want to see you. (Yanaga & Sasaki, 2018)

Most of the many thousands of visitors to the Wind Telephone come alone and have a solitary communication with their cherished loved one. Certain people confine their communication to personal updates, reassurances they are managing well, and inquiries about the quality of the afterlife. Some are unable to speak, as if words cannot do justice to the moment. A silent and frequently tearful shared reverie is all that matters. But most speak of their overwhelming heartache and sorrow accompanied by bouts of sighing and sobbing. They speak of a desire to reunite so they can hold their loved ones again, ask questions about why fate selected their loved one to die, express regrets about certain aspects of their relationship, and contemplate whether life is worth living without them. And for those whose loved ones remain missing, they express deepfelt concerns about the location of their loved one, apologies about being unable to find them, and pledges to never stop searching until they are able to bring them home (Glass & Meek, 2016; Yanaga & Sasaki, 2018).

Relationship to Psychotherapy

As an approach to relieving the pain of unresolved grief, the Wind Telephone is remarkable in how quickly it can unleash a torrent of emotion and verbal outpouring of the survivor's longing and sadness. It is as if a switch is thrown in the psyche and the suppressed feelings surge into open expression. By contrast, it often requires multiple psychotherapy sessions for a grieving individual to feel comfortable releasing these same thoughts and feelings in the presence of a therapist. It made me realize how powerful the Wind Telephone experience is for grieving individuals and how little I understood about its compelling nature. Why would grieving individuals make a journey, including many from distant places, to enter a phone booth in a remote region of Japan to speak to a dead loved one over a disconnected telephone and expect to gain relief from suffering in a single session (although local people often come multiple times)? On top of this, they were going through this experience without the benefit of a psychotherapist to assist them. Couldn't the grieving individual just think or speak these same thoughts and express the same emotions regardless of their location and do so without utilizing a device such as the Wind Telephone?

Accompanying my bewilderment was a moderate unease about the implications of the Wind Telephone experience for the foundations of a variety of psychotherapies requiring multiple sessions. As a psychiatrist with a 45-year professional investment in the critical role that a psychotherapist plays in psychological healing, how could I understand the widespread appeal of a phone booth session *sans* psychotherapist for those who are grieving? Is the benefit that grief-stricken individuals derive from the Wind Telephone a statement about the lack of specificity of individual psychotherapy? Are traditional psychotherapies nothing more than a generic balm applied weekly to the psychic wound? Or do psychotherapists rely on a transference cure where the grieving individual benefits from being accepted without criticism or from an idealized belief that the therapist is omnipotent and possess the answers to all their concerns? This set me on a path to understand the relationship of the Wind Telephone to psychotherapy and the nature of human cognition and communication through speech.

The Wind Telephone shares a confidential setting, audible speech, and emotional catharsis with more standard psychotherapies, but it lacks a psychotherapist. No therapist is present to provide practical advice, accurate empathy, reframing of problematic situations, or help in resolving inner conflicts or in untangling issues the individual has ignored or resisted facing. Nor is a therapist available to provide psychological insight about emotions, motivations, or behaviors, or to point out and correct cognitive distortions.

However, the Wind Telephone does share certain features with psychodrama and Gestalt therapy. Psychodrama is a type of individual therapy that occurs in a group setting with a trained psycho-dramatist. The most common technique utilizes role-playing and dramatized enactments drawn from an individual's life to gain insight and understanding. The soliloquy technique is less well known and more closely resembles what occurs in the Wind Telephone. It requires one member of the group to speak about a life situation or express their inner thoughts and feelings about a personal issue and then listen to the perspectives, insights, and descriptions of similar experiences and feelings from group members. Psychodrama therapy has three phases, namely, a warm-up phase, where the psycho-dramatist conducts a number of group exercises to put the participants in the proper frame of mind for the action and discussion phases that follow.

One of the benefits of the Wind Telephone is that it does not require a directed warm-up phase. Mr. Sasaki has set the frame. Those who self-select to make the journey do so for the sole purpose of speaking to their lost loved one over the Wind Telephone. The pilgrimage allows time for rehearsal and for the psychological pressure to mount so that, after dialing the number, pent-up thoughts and emotions are released in a climactic soliloquy. For many, the soliloquy moves beyond acting out a situation and is an authentic connection with their lost loved one. Mr. Sasaki has orchestrated a dramatic enactment, but unlike psychodrama it is not encumbered by the presence of others or by any intrusive or objectifying feedback. It is a private moment, with the conviction that the message was heard and understood by their lost loved one.

Gestalt therapy emphasizes experience in the moment especially the phenomenology and the dialogue between the individual and the therapist. It relies on the individual discovering or becoming aware of aspects of self rather than feedback or interpretations, and from that perspective it is a cognitive therapy. One common approach is for the therapist to assume the role of someone in the individual's life and for the two of them to have a dialogue about a problematic issue. Or the therapist might have the individual discuss an emotionally charged issue with an empty chair, as if the person in question is sitting in it (see also Chapter 9). These approaches allow the individual to express thoughts and feelings that have been locked inside. They experience this in the moment as authentic interactions and, as a result, often grow psychologically. The Wind Telephone closely resembles Gestalt therapy but without the dialogue with a therapist. It is a form of expressive or imaginative therapy—a self-psychotherapy (i.e., without a therapist) but not a solitary therapy because the dyadic communication with the lost loved one is the focus.

Human Cognition and Speech

I realized that the final considerations in understanding what transpires in the Wind Telephone relate to human cognitive processing and the critical role of spoken language in communication. Human cognition has three components, namely unconscious processing and two types of conscious processing (i.e., global availability and self-monitoring or introspection; Dehaene, Lau, & Kouider, 2017). Most of our intelligence resides in unconscious processing (i.e., out of our awareness and not available for self-reporting or self-monitoring). Sensory and emotional inputs are combined with conscious inputs to make sense of the world and to guide our conscious thinking and action. Unconscious processing is often parceled out to different brain regions and performed in parallel. It is the domain of imagination, creativity, pattern recognition, problem-solving, and validating and judging sensory and emotional inputs for their relevance to self. Einstein believed the true sign of intelligence was not knowledge but imagination. He made the point that his major discoveries did not emanate from rational thinking. Most of the time, we are completely unaware of unconscious processing because it is constantly feeding information to our conscious awareness without a trace. But occasionally it reveals its existence in "Aha" moments, when a solution to an intractable problem pops into our mind. Often it occurs out of context when we are consciously thinking about an unrelated issue, and it is so sudden and unexpected that we wonder where it came from and whether we can take ownership. An example of this comes from the Nobel laureate, Bob Dylan, who recently told historian Douglas Brinkley:

> Those kinds of songs for me just come out of the blue, out of thin air. I never plan to write any of them. But in saying that, there are certain public figures that are just in your subconscious for one reason or another. None of those songs with designated names are intentionally written. They just fall down from space. I'm just as bewildered as anybody else as to why I writethem. (Brinkley, 2020)

Conscious processing has two components. Most familiar and prominent is the information that dominates our thoughts and is available for self-reporting (i.e., globally available). This process analyzes content, makes predictions about the future, and decides on a course of action. The second component of conscious processing is meta-cognition or introspection that is involved in self-awareness and self-monitoring. Do I have confidence that I know something? Did what I say make sense? Are my motivations and emotions in agreement with the content of my verbal output?

Human cognitive processing is both bottom-up and top-down, since information flows bi-directionally between the unconscious and conscious components. A major function of cognitive processing is error detection, namely, the difference between what we thought was going to happen and what actually happened. The detection is triggered by both factual discrepancies and by emotions that flood our awareness.

But why is the opportunity to speak out loud to the dead over the Wind Telephone so irresistible? Speaking to oneself is considered peculiar, yet many of us do it on occasion. This may be nothing more than an aside or minor editorial comments, brief expressions of frustration, surprise, or joy, instructions to self in working out practical problems, practicing for a future conversation, or weighing the evidence on an emotional or conflicted situation. Hamlet's famous soliloquy, "To be or not to be," is not only a device to let the audience know his inner ambivalence about whether it is better to live or to die, but it is also a way for both the audience and Hamlet to hear the oral argument. Rather than being trapped in the inner reaches of his tortured mind, Hamlet depersonalizes and objectifies his dilemma by speaking about his shared problem with *we* humans so he can listen to the weight of the evidence as an impartial jury member.

Humans have the unique ability to communicate thoughts and feelings to others through speech. A spoken dialogue between individuals is usually thought of as an iterative process, a back and forth with individuals either talking or listening. But when speaking, we are also listening and monitoring our verbal output. Are we making ourselves clear? Is it rationale? Is it a valid representation of what we believe and feel? Or do we suddenly realize our words are ineffective and not communicating the point, that the real issue is something else entirely. Are we rambling and have no idea what we are talking about? Occasionally, we may note a discrepancy between our expressed emotion and the content of our speech. Detecting these mismatches allows us to adjust our thinking and behaviors and to gain valuable insights about self.

At the same time, when the other person is speaking, we are not only listening to the content, but we are also mentalizing about what is going on in the other person's mind. What is the intent and emotional state of the other person? Are they making sense? Is their point valid? And, most critically, what are the implications or affordances of their verbal output for me? How does their communication alter my predictions about the future and shape my response? Deciphering even deeper meanings of what is being transmitted may be enhanced by our inner associations, reveries, and emotional reactions. Sometimes we understand what is being said and its full implications, and sometimes we misunderstand or are badly deceived. We are entitled to both our good and bad judgments.

What transpires in the Wind Telephone experience is quite different from spoken language. Thought is silent and private while spoken language is audible and primarily social. Language not only transmits information, knowledge, and predictions about the future, but it also builds interpersonal connections, community, and a cumulative history and culture. Spoken or signed language is the dominant mode of our social interactions. Without language, we are isolated and alone (Scott, 2019). By contrast, the conscious component of thinking involves mental images, partially formed ideas, small phrases, and occasionally complete sentences. But speaking about our thoughts requires additional cognitive processing. Blank spaces in our thoughts need to be filled and the narrative dots connected to produce cogent and coherent speech. Speaking requires selection of words, syntax, sentence structure, background information, explanation, and rationale so that the other person understands (Hagoort, 2019). Moving ideas and emotions from the silent inner world into the audible external world unlocks unconscious compartments of the mind. Each verbal representation, emotional display, and physiologic expression produces a feedback loop that allows the grieving individual to monitor, examine, and gain information about self. The process is a revelation that provides grist for introspection, unconscious mental processing, and creative imagination. It allows the grieving individual to synthesize and integrate the new information, to detect and correct errors, to develop new formulations of self, and to bring partial order to a disordered part of the psyche, and to heal.

Lastly, how should we think about communication? The standard definition of communication is to express thoughts and feelings to another person in a form they understand. When it is not understood, it is defined as miscommunication. Does speaking out loud over the Wind Telephone, knowing full well that it is not physically connected to the lost loved one, represent communication? Is it necessary for the message to be received and understood by the intended party to be therapeutic? Or is the mere belief that this has occurred sufficient? One potential advantage in speaking to the dead is that there is little likelihood of a rebuttal that interferes with the conviction that the message was received, understood, and accepted.

Conclusion

The attraction and therapeutic power of the Wind Telephone reside in the commitment to make the pilgrimage, and the socially sanctioned permission to express thoughts and feelings that have been bottled up inside, especially for grievers who are unable to find a proper mode of expression until the sanctity of the Wind Telephone is reached. It is entering a miniature cathedral where the shackles of society are removed, allowing the grieving individual to enter a state of reverie where time is suspended, speaking to the dead becomes real, and the tension of grief can be released. Speaking out loud reinforces the emotional attachment to the lost loved one, promotes introspection, and instills confidence that the message was sent and received. It is self-directed grief work where audible communication of innermost thoughts and feelings occurs with both the self and the lost loved one, who for that moment is brought back to life by the power of the human imagination.

References

Brinkley, D. (2020, June 12). Bob Dylan has a lot on his mind. *New York Times*, *12*, pp. AR, 8–9.

Dehaene, S., Lau, H., & Kouider, S. (2017). What is consciousness, and could machines have it? *Science, 358,* 486–492.

Glass, I., & Meek, M. (Producer). (2016, September 23). One last thing before I go: Really long distance. *This American Life: National Public Radio.* Retrieved from https://www.thisamericanlife.org/597/one-last-thing-before-i-go/act-one-0

Hagoort, P. (2019). The neurobiology of language beyond single-word processing. *Science, 366,* 55–58.

Scott, S.K. (2019). From speech and talkers to the social world: The neural processing of human spoken language. *Science, 366,* 58–62.

Weatherly, F.E. (1913). *Danny boy.* New York: Boosey & Co.

Yanaga, Y., & Sasaki, I. (Eds.). (2018). *Kaze no Denw–Daishinsai Kara Rokunen, Kaze no Denwa wo Tooshite Mieru Koto.* Tokyo: Kazama Shobo.

11 Limitations of Traumatic Grief Therapy: The Palliative Embrace of a Homicidal Dying

Edward (Ted) Rynearson and John E. Ruark

Frequency of Successful Outcome with Grief Interventions

The dying and death of someone loved is culturally accepted as a timeless and ubiquitous *rite of passage*, a socially prescribed change in self-identity associated with loss and dislocation, different from the enhancement of self-identity celebrated with passages of life's progress, such as birth, baptism, adolescence, graduation, marriage, or retirement (Van Gennep, 2019). Usually, there is a restorative vector of change in self-identity that is associated with the rite of passage of dying and death and often comes without a healing intervention. With time and the support of family, friends, spiritual and work communities, a majority (85–90%) of children and adults show spontaneous improvement and reengage with their community, work, and valued relationships within a year or two following a loss (Bonanno & Mancini, 2006).

But what about the 10–15% who remain distressed and disabled by loss (Shear, Ghesquiere, & Glikman, 2014)? Do they seek assistance with their losses, and, if so, from whom? To our knowledge, there is no well-documented follow-up of this cohort of grievers to know what proportion seeks help. Presumably, for spiritually inclined grievers, clergy offer relevant pastoral support at the time of death and memorialization, as might a funeral director; however, licensed mental health professionals, such as counselors and psychologists, who may be more professionally endorsed as *helpers*, are often consulted, as are shaman and spiritualists.

What is the rate of treatment response? It would be relevant for helpers to know what proportion of those seeking help showed no improvement with grief intervention.

While, to our knowledge, there are no empirical studies of unimprovement with grief interventions led by shaman, clergy, or non-licensed therapists, a small number of controlled, prospective, empirically based studies of focused and time-limited grief interventions document that a significant minority (25–30%) remain unimproved (Cameron, 2006; Rosner, Lumbeck, & Geissner, 2011; Shear, Frank, Houck, & Reynolds, 2005). Clarifying the signs of unimprovement before or during the early

DOI: 10.4324/9781003105077-14

phase of intervention might allow shaman, clergy, or therapist to adjust their role and revise their helping objectives. For instance, there are well-documented, recognizable demographic risks associated with unimprovement that should be considered before an intervention begins. Additionally, some grievers appear to internalize or take on the life and death of the deceased. Studies show that the internalized presence within absence of the deceased first emerging in the narrative interaction is also predictive of poor treatment outcome (Boelen, Keijsers, & van den Hout, 2012; Horowitz, Wilner, Marmar, & Krupick, 1980). So, how do we identify and assist someone who remains unhelpable (Rynearson, 1975), especially those whose struggle involves the presence within absence of their deceased loved one?

For some mourners, it is as though their grief response has become a fixation. Whether you are a shaman, clergy, or a therapist, you might confer with your colleagues about challenging cases in the hallway or over lunch, but chances are their recommendations do not include the more subtle and unarticulated fixation with presence within absence of the deceased. Rather, their suggestions likely fall along these lines:

- "Maybe it's time for a psychiatric evaluation and possible medication?"
- "Have you tried adding eye movement desensitization and reprocessing (EMDR) or Dialectical Behavior Therapy (DBT) techniques?"
- "What about a support group?"

Regardless of these well-intentioned suggestions, and even with their trial, little progress likely will result in the treatment of grievers who struggle with the internalized presence within absence of the deceased. In fact, both the therapist and patient often begin to feel stuck in the time, space, and action of a fixation within the internalized presence within absence of the deceased.

A relevant principle in understanding the basis of grief fixation is the incapacity to alter or release the presence within absence presaged by lifelong attachment conflicts (Kosminsky & Jordan, 2016). Therapeutic progress likely will be stymied by relational traumas (Boelen, Smid, Mintima-Verloop, Keijser, & Lenferink, 2019; Hagman, 2016), which often are represented by a co-morbid attachment conflict of unbearable separation distress (e.g., "I cannot live without you") and/or trauma distress (e.g., "I cannot forgive myself for your dying"). In either event, the presence within absence of the deceased cannot change or be released. Grief interventions alone generally cannot help someone who is unable or unwilling to engage in treatment techniques to address their fixation of an unalterable narrative of the dying and death of the deceased. Long-term attachment, trauma, and identity conflicts require more intense and longer-term interventions.

One of my (ER) cases of limited improvement highlighted below provides a dynamic introduction to this challenging interchange between therapist, patient, and the resistance to change associated with a griever's struggle with the internalized presence within absence of the deceased.

"I Don't Think Anything Is Going to Help Me"

Pam, a 37-year-old social worker moved to Seattle from the East Coast two months prior to our first session. She lived alone with her two cats in a rented apartment and recognizing, "I'm in no shape to be a social worker," was working full time as a receptionist in a medical clinic. Her sister, Bev, had been murdered a year and a half before. She found our center's specialized service for traumatic grief after violent dying through an Internet search and initiated individual therapy sessions with me. Pam could not contain her crying while introducing herself and could offer only fragmentary pleas between her sobs:

> I can still work, but when I'm home by myself and start thinking about my sister's killing I get numb and my mind shuts down. I can't remember what happens after that for hours.

> If she died from a bad heart or kidney failure, I could understand that.

> I don't think anything is going to help me.

She was so emotionally dysregulated and traumatized that I suspected that she was having flashbacks of her sister's dying and dissociating while alone. I reassured her that we need not talk directly about the murder until she was feeling calmer and safer. And that, instead, I needed more details about her relationship with Bev before the killing. I learned that her move to Seattle from the East Coast was more a quest than a choice. Years before the murder, she and Bev planned to live together in the Pacific Northwest, away from a time and place of repeated traumas shared during their childhood and later in abusive relationships and marriages. Seattle would be a new beginning for both of them.

Pam felt some relief as our supportive weekly sessions continued that first month. In addition to stress management exercises, I asked her to focus on her relationship with her sister with images and stories that were meaningful and comforting before her dying. We enlisted Bev's recorded voice on her phone and added recordings of my guiding voice of relaxation to divert her mind from flashbacks while alone at night.

While reviewing pictures from her family album (in an effort to search for comforting images to dispel and counterbalance the surrealistic flashbacks of her sister's murder), I gathered a few details about the family. There were images of Pam and Bev smiling together, but conspicuously few images of their parents, who were alcoholics and abusive of one another and the children. Pam was seven and Bev was three when their mother died. The details and cause of her dying were not shared or explained by their father, and within a year he remarried, again to an alcoholic. Their sisterhood was a sustaining and shared identity. They were always there for one another, and, as the older sister, Pam felt obligated to protect Bev.

During the second and third months of scheduled weekly sessions, Pam was more stabilized and her dissociative experiences became less frequent. At this point, I had not encouraged an open inquiry about the events of Bev's dying narrative. I was not confident that Pam's fragile autonomy could tolerate its retelling and full exposure to the traumatic memories. Instead, I encouraged a return to meaningful activities (e.g., external and performative changes she was seeing in herself) for further stabilization.

Over time, Pam began missing sessions, calling minutes before the appointment to announce a crisis at work or with one of her cats, requiring her immediate attention and caregiving. Returning after a missed visit, she assured me that she had been able to manage the crisis on her own but that is becoming more active in caring for others she now felt a greater sense of loneliness. She wanted our visits to continue "because I have no one else," but was unwilling to establish a list of treatment objectives because she would "never recover." When I asked what she meant by "recover," she answered, "Bring back my sister. Thirty years ago, you might have saved us, but not now."

In that moment, I more fully recognized the emptiness of Pam's self-identity without Bev, and that our narrow focus on her grief was probably going to be insufficient. Pam's self-identity was beyond despairing—in a state of near collapse—and the chance for improvement seemingly had passed 30 years before when Pam and Bev were little girls, the year their mother died. Presumably Bev's death resonated with the unresolved grief that Pam shared during their childhood. I reflected her despair, but I worried about being drawn into the highly metaphorical tangle of childhood trauma and her mother's death beneath her presenting grief. To widen the metaphor, I now had two *fused* children, Pam/Bev, as my patients.

Two years before Bev's murder, their father died from a malignancy. Within months of his death, the need for one another's support was so strong that Pam relocated to live with Bev.

Initially it was blissful, "We had never been so happy." They had long talks about their father and childhood abuse, "I had never talked with anyone but Bev about that." However, in the next 18 months, Bev began to abuse drugs, was agoraphobic, and became suicidal. Pam became desperate when faced with Bev's lack of improvement, despite Bev's multiple consultations with medical professionals, long list of medications, and treatment trials for multiple diagnoses, including alcohol dependence, attention deficit disorder, bipolar disorder, post-traumatic stress disorder, multiple personality disorder, and panic disorder. Before losing her insurance coverage, Bev also failed time-limited treatment trials with eye movement desensitization and reprocessing (EMDR), trauma-focused cognitive behavioral therapy (TFCBT), and trauma survivor groups. A month before her murder, Bev became overtly psychotic with active delusions and hallucinations. Pam called the police to begin psychiatric commitment, but Bev fled their home before the police arrived. The last thing Bev said to Pam was, "Just let me die. I don't need a psychiatric hospital. I need a psychiatric hospice." A week later she was murdered.

As therapist for Pam/Bev, I feared that we were in a metaphoric blind alley. Pam and I shared the abundant evidence that she was reenacting and identifying with Bev's psychological decompensation and failed trials of therapy before her violent dying and death, despite my efforts to interrupt this fusing. Our relationship was stabilizing, but over the next few months there was no substantive change in her status. Anytime I suggested ancillary supports, such as medication or group therapies, they were quickly waved aside. Those had not worked for Bev, thus, they would not work for Pam/Bev either. I was willing to continue supporting her but recognized that our relationship would probably be measured in many months or years based on her current level of fixation. Reassurance that I would continue seeing her supportively was threatened by my suggestion that we arrange for consultation with another clinician for a second opinion. Could a consultant offer us a fresh perspective and possible guidance? It was worth a try. However, not surprisingly Pam/Bev refused. Perhaps Bev's presence within absence in a state of psychiatric hospice was Bev's active wish for dying and death and behind her refusal to accept any intervention to save herself. Despite this level of unconscious resistance, Pam was insightful enough to accept the possibility that she was reenacting Bev's tragic collapse. In addition to offering that insight in my own solitary voice, I wondered if Bev's voice might be more decisive. I knew that Bev and Pam often advised one another, so I asked, "What would Bev say if she knew you were following in her footprints—trapped in her dying?" Pam began crying and said, "She would say go home and get your old job back!"

At our next office visit, Pam began making plans for her own future. Home meant returning to the East Coast and her career as a social worker. With that decision, she began separating from me and Seattle. She continued having conscious, imaginary conversations with Bev and continued making preparatory changes. I purposely did not interrupt her planning. Leaving Seattle represented the surrender of her wish for merger with Pam/Bev in Seattle but returning to the East Coast represented a confrontation with Bev's tragic dying. I worried that she was going from one blind alley to another, but I was encouraged to see that the planning encouraged Pam's self-identity to become more confident and autonomous.

The last two months of our office visits included a series of emails and phone calls between Seattle and her East Coast professional work contacts and friends to prepare the transition. She could not return to her former position but was confident she would find a job and arranged to stay with an acquaintance until she found her own apartment. She resisted committing herself to another therapist but wanted continued contact with me by phone should she need support. It took two weeks for her cross-country drive with her two cats. She called several times when her car had major mechanical problems, but arrived safely, found an apartment, and was actively looking for a job. Pam has not called since that last conversation. I tried to contact her several times, but her cell phone number was deactivated. That was over three years ago.

A Case Review

My co-author, John Ruark, is a seasoned psychiatrist with clinical expertise as a national authority in thanatology and has extensive experience treating patients with disabling complex trauma. I invited John to review my year-and-a-half attempt to help Pam. Below is the conversation between us:

Ted: John, let me begin this review with the dilemma I felt from the beginning of the intervention. Even at our first meeting, Pam questioned the possibility of improvement in terms of her grief. She said that Bev's dying and death from heart failure would have been bearable, but her homicidal dying killed a crucial attachment within her. We subsequently spent more time stabilizing her dislocated self-identity from the shattering incorporation of Bev's presence within absence than on re-engagement with Pam's life without her.

John: The metaphor "dislocated self-identity" is particularly germane and insightful here. Dislocation injuries of the body are often very violent and undermine the sufferer's sense of personal/bodily integrity. What is required to enable healing from an orthopedic dislocation is an energetic intervention that in some ways repeats the original trauma in order to restore the parts of the dislocated joint (or self) to a natural alignment in which effective healing can take place with proper support. The psychotherapeutic paradigm for a robust intervention such as this has been outlined by several researchers (Herman, 2015; Terr, 1990; Van der Kolk, 2014).

These clinicians emphasized the need for an even more robust multidisciplinary intervention with individuals presenting with an underlying identity disorder, referred to as complex post-traumatic stress disorder (CPTSD), associated with multiple childhood developmental traumas. Pam's identified merger with her sister apparently served as a psychological joint, a stabilizing union of safety and caring, a fantasied haven of protection from their abusive parents. With Bev's violent death, her traumatized presence within absence dislocated Pam's vulnerable sense of safety. If Pam was to be helped, her underlying CPTSD needed early recognition and treatment tailored to the rigors of that condition.

Ted: Let's try amplifying the metaphor of an orthopedic dislocation. Most of us have strained or sprained one of our joints where the pain from stretched and inflamed ligaments is short lived. But the dislocation of a shoulder or a hip, or the tearing of an underlying ligament often is disfiguring and disabling. Were there signs and symptoms during the early evaluative phase of our traumatic grief intervention that might have alerted me to an underlying dislocation of self-identity?

John: There might be demographic risk factors with Pam to enumerate, such as a history of developmental abuse/neglect or previous psychiatric diagnoses/treatments (Kristensen, Weisaith, & Heir, 2012); however, the first therapeutic task should be the reinforcement of psychological resilience or re-alignment of self-identity (Field & Filanosky, 2009). During the early sessions, when you recognized Pam's dissociative denial of Bev's murder as a sign of fragile identity, you observed the need for a shift in the therapeutic paradigm. Pam's dissociation lasting more than a year after Bev's murder was a sign of Pam's underlying CPTSD. Her dissociative episodes and panic were unbearable without the psychological essentials of resilience (Rynearson, 2018), which include:

1   Emotional regulation or pacification
2   Spatial regulation or partition
3   Time regulation or perspective

Presumably, Pam and Bev's childhood history of abuse and emotional neglect superimposed on the death of their mother cemented a shared identity for both of them, providing a basic level of trust, comfort, and safety in the moment, and hope in a shared future. With reenactment flashbacks of Bev's murder, Pam's self-identity disintegrated with dissociation. Emotional dysregulation, boundary dysregulation, and temporal fixation were important to address during the introductory phase of intervention for Pam's psychological trauma (Pearlman, Wortman, Feuer, Farber, & Rando, 2014). Your introduction of non-verbal stress management exercises, and review of images and recordings of their living and meaningful relationship was stabilizing by enhancing emotional and boundary regulation. Then, you both became challenged by the regulation of time as she began missing appointments. Tell me more about that.

Ted: To further encourage stabilization and in an effort to reinforce her self-confidence, I suggested that she initiate and reestablish relationships and activities that had been individually meaningful apart from Bev. She began volunteering at a pet shelter and wrote journal entries describing times in her life that she deemed positive and fulfilling. Then, she began missing appointments. She usually had an explanation—some emergent event taking priority over our therapy. How might I have guided Pam beyond this phase of early stabilization to then reinforce a meaningful self-identity and an autonomous future without Bev?

John: This intense experience of fusion required even more than the most empathic support could possibly provide. Your support was enough to hold Pam in treatment for a while.

However, if Pam's identity was as highly bound up with Bev's as seems to be the case, establishment of a more autonomous self-identity (Boelen, 2017; Ryan & Deci, 2005) would have required a more intense treatment to foster a powerful attachment to you as her therapist. This gradually could have supported Pam's self-identity as being more autonomous, not dominated by her connection to her sister. Anything less would be psychologically regarded by Pam as palliative. You also would have needed to help her overcome her aversion to risking more intense attachment with you, which likely explains her missing appointments. You recognized her underlying identity disorder and guarded prognosis but were overly encouraged by her capacity for professional success and altruistic caring for others—a prevailing strength she could no longer maintain without Bev. Perhaps you felt handicapped by your unwillingness to devote yourself to the long-term demands of supporting Pam and were not confident that she would improve with the short-term focus of your clinic for traumatic grief.

Ted: Yes, as her therapist I felt stuck in time as well. It remained difficult for us to make therapeutic movement in our futile acknowledgment that she could no longer hope for a future within Bev's palliative grief fixation. Each time I recommended ancillary therapies, such as EMDR, TFCBT, or grief support groups, Pam would explain that she and Bev had tried those treatments before the murder. How might I have guided the two of us along this therapeutic tightrope—suspended between the merger of Pam's living and Bev's dying?

John: You identify the projective identificatory helplessness and despair that you both were feeling. The only intervention I suspect that might have turned the tide early on would have been a recognition of the robustness of treatment necessary to give Pam a believable (to both of you) pathway toward improvement. Perhaps a protocol for identifying such severely traumatized patients and diverting them toward a more comprehensive trauma and grief center featuring more ancillary therapies would have increased her chances for improvement.

Ted: Pam needed more specialized and long-term care than our clinic could offer her. I suggested a second opinion, which she refused. And we considered a referral to another therapist, but finding such a resource is challenging and, if available, there is usually a long waitlist. Pam and I were in a confounding impasse. Introducing Bev's voice as an advisory ally between Pam and me was decisive, or at least catalyzed movement. Pam's decision to leave Seattle represented a pseudo release from Bev's palliative presence, and, for me, it reflected an unspoken disappointment in my limitations in helping her improve. Preparing for termination, she was unable to talk directly about leaving me, but beneath her questioning, "Can my car make the cross-country trip without breaking down?" and "How will my cats adjust to the move?" was an expression of her separation anxiety. While she had attained enough autonomy to make a geographic move, my recommendation for identifying a continued source of therapy reflected my concern about an early relapse. Unfortunately, Pam did not maintain a connection after our final phone call, leaving me to wonder if she would call me for help. I wondered, "Can she survive on her own? Was I a helpful presence in the re-establishment of her self-identity?" Overall, I was left with a professional dislocation between my concern for her future and my inability to ensure her psychological safety and sense of hope. John, could the transitional triad (Ted/Pam/Bev's palliative presence) have been more productively restored and released for all three of us? Given that one of the greatest impediments to identifying people who will not improve with any type of psychotherapy is the therapist's failure to recognize it, perhaps I inadvertently failed to "do no harm" as her helper.

John: I think that the only way in which such a triad could have been restored is by making good on the offer of potentially adequate treatment. Patients with this degree of identity impairment need to be seen two or three hours a week. Indeed, when we offer an insufficient therapeutic alliance with patients whose improvement requires deep repair and healing, we are inadvertently harming them. You actually had the compassionate presence and psychological sturdiness that Pam needed but you couldn't provide enough of it. That necessitated her finding a way out of your care in order to avoid further disappointment in the therapy she was receiving, as many CPTSD patients experience with their psychiatric care (Heeke, Kampisiou, Niemeyer, & Knaevelsrud, 2019).

Pam's traumatic grief after her sister's murder was superimposed on a serious and disabling identity disorder. Outcome studies of outpatient therapy with these patients document a high rate (i.e., 20–40%) of dropout or non-response with long-term individual intervention (Mohr, 1995). The treatment of disabling identity disorders under more optimal conditions (e.g., 18-month, day hospitalization combined with intensive daily therapies) remains marginally successful (Laurenssen, Smits, Bales, & Feenstra, 2018). I would encourage you to forgive yourself for letting Pam down in spite of your sincere and best efforts.

Ted: Summarizing my understanding, John, Pam's diminished resilience and inability to differentiate herself from reenacting her sister's murder presented as an early sign of her unstable identity. She could not tolerate the horror and helplessness of her sister's murder resonating the underlying horror and helplessness of her childhood, a childhood shared with Bev. Their idealized and fused identity compensated for Pam's underlying CPTSD. Without Bev, and now fixated on Bev's palliative presence within absence, Pam could no longer maintain mastery over her underlying CPTSD. My hope is that our readers will recognize the possibility of underlying co-morbid disorders that might challenge a mourner's ongoing adjustment to traumatic dying and death. During the early phase of a traumatic grief intervention might be the time to suggest a second opinion for confirmation of your diagnostic suspicion. If your suspicion is confirmed, you will need to decide if you are able to offer an intervention for the underlying disorder as well. If you are not prepared to assume care because of constraints of time and professional competence, this may be the time to declare your limitations and not commit yourself beyond the boundaries of an intervention focused on traumatic grief, if at all. Engaging in a longer-term commitment could reinforce dependence and regression, possibly echoing developmental traumas, disappointment in a lack of progress, and dread of abandonment during or after the intervention. Committing your practice or your agency to an intervention with little promise of payment is another challenging limitation—and this might be the most challenging limitation of all. Unfortunately, our health care system does not recognize mental health parity for individuals requiring intensive long-term interventions.

Thank you, John. This written interchange has been helpful in clarifying an intervention complicated by limited improvement and a tangled termination. However, in this writing and sharing of my role as Pam's helper, I remain burdened with the unresolved triad of Ted/Pam/Bev. Unfinished interventions like this are the most difficult for me to work through.

References

Boelen, P. (2017). Self-identity after bereavement. *Journal of Nervous and Mental Disease, 205*(5), 405–408.

Boelen, P., Keijsers, L., & van den Hout, M.A. (2012). The role of self-concept clarity in prolonged grief disorder. *Journal of Nervous and Mental Disease, 200*(1), 56–62.

Boelen, P., Smid, G., Mintima-Verloop, H., Keijser, J., & Lenferink, L. (2019). Patterns, predictors and prognostic validity of persistent complex bereavement disorder symptoms in recently bereaved adults. *Journal of Nervous and Mental Disease, 207*(11), 913–920.

Bonanno, G.A., & Mancini, A.D. (2006). Bereavement-related depression and PTSD: Evaluating interventions. In L. Barbanel & R.J. Sternberg (Eds.), *Psychological interventions in times of crisis.* New York: Springer, pp. 37–55.

Cameron, C. (2006). Brief psychotherapies: A brief review. *American Journal of Psychotherapy, 60*(2), 147–152.

Field, N., & Filanosky, C. (2009). Continuing bonds, risk factors for complicated grief, and adjustment to bereavement. *Death Studies, 34*(1), 1–29.

Hagman, G. (Ed.). (2016). *New models of bereavement theory and treatment: New mourning.* New York: Routledge.

Heeke, C., Kampisiou, C., Niemeyer, H., & Knaevelsrud, C. (2019). A systematic review and meta-analysis of correlates of prolonged grief disorder in adults exposed to violent loss. *European Journal of Psychotraumatology, 10*(1), 1583524. 10.1080/20008198.2019.1583524

Herman, J. (2015). *Trauma and recovery: The aftermath of violence—from domestic abuse to political terror.* New York: Basic Books.

Horowitz, M., Wilner, N., Marmar, C., & Krupick, J. (1980). Pathological grief and the activation of latent self-images. *American Journal of Psychiatry, 137*(10), 1152–1157.

Kosminsky, P., & Jordan, J.R. (2016). *Attachment-informed grief therapy: A clinician's guide to foundations and applications.* New York: Routledge.

Kristensen, P., Weisaith, L., & Heir, T. (2012). Bereavement and mental health after sudden and violent losses: A review. *Psychiatry, 75*(1), 76–97.

Laurenssen, E., Smits, M., Bales, D., & Feenstra, D. (2018). Day hospital mentalization-based treatment versus intensive outpatient mentalization treatment for patients with severe borderline personality disorder: Protocol of a multicenter randomized clinical trial. *Psychological Medicine, 48*(15), 2522–2529.

Mohr, D. (1995). Negative outcome in psychotherapy: A critical review. *Clinical Psychology: Science and Practice, 2*(1), 1–27.

Pearlman, L.A., Wortman, C.B., Feuer, C.A., Farber, F.H., & Rando, T.A. (2014). *Treating traumatic bereavement.* New York: Guilford Press.

Rosner, R., Lumbeck, G., & Geissner, E. (2011). Effectiveness of an inpatient group therapy for comorbid complicated grief disorder. *Psychotherapy Research, 21,* 210–218.

Ryan, R., & Deci, E. (2005). The significance of autonomy support in psychological development and psychopathology. *Developmental psychology, Vol. 1: Theory and method* (2nd ed.). 795–849.

Rynearson, E. (1975). The helpful physician and the un-helpable patient. *Post Graduate Medicine, 58*(2), 145–150.

Rynearson, E. (2018). Disabling reenactment imagery after violent dying. *Death Studies 42*(1), 4–8.

Shear, K., Frank, E., Houck, P., & Reynolds, C. (2005). Treatment of complicated grief: A controlled trial. *Journal of the American Medical Association, 293*(21), 2601–2608.

Shear, K., Ghesquiere, A., & Glikman, K. (2014). Bereavement and complicated grief. *Current Psychiatry Reports, 15*(11), 1–11.

Terr, L. (1990). *Too scared to cry.* New York: Basic Books.

Van der Kolk, B. (2014). *The body keeps the score: Brain, mind, and body in the healing of trauma.* New York: Penguin.

Van Gennep, A. (2019). *Rites of passage.* Chicago: University of Chicago Press.

Section III

Research Considerations

12 Sensory and Quasi-Sensory Experiences of the Deceased in Bereavement: An Overview of the Literature

Edith Maria Steffen and Karina S. Kamp

I had gone to bed, and I just, I felt like there was someone in the room, and I felt this sensation on my scalp, you know, where [grandmother] used to, she always used to love like kind of playing with our hair, my sister and I, I just felt this sensation, and I remember sitting up in bed and saying, "[Grandmother], I know you're there." And um, and I said, "I'm not scared." And "I know you're just trying to tell me everything's all right." And, actually, it was actually quite comforting in a way. And um just feeling that sort of sense she was there. It was almost like she was saying goodbye, because I wasn't there when she actually died. It was almost like she just come to say, "You'll be fine. Everything will be fine. And I just want to say bye-bye." And it was actually it was a really nice feeling. (Elaine; bereaved interview participant; previously unpublished data)

Introduction: A Common Yet Controversial Phenomenon

The above quotation by Elaine, who took part in a research interview about sensory experiences of deceased loved ones (Steffen & Coyle, 2011), stands for many similar reports from bereaved people who have experienced the presence of a deceased loved one through sensory perception or a feeling of near-physical presence. The above instance includes many elements that may be part of such an experience, for example, a sensory perception such as being touched by her deceased grandmother, a difficult-to-define feeling of her presence, and an understanding of the possible meanings of her presence, such as her grandmother coming to say goodbye and reassuring Elaine. Furthermore, the comforting impact of the experience is emphasized. Later in the interview, Elaine also explored how this experience fitted with her global belief system and how, while remaining somewhat sceptical, she felt that this suggested there is an afterlife and that her grandmother, like a benevolent spiritual being, is watching over her.

Experiences like the one recounted by Elaine are not at all rare. Forty-seven to eighty-two percent of bereaved individuals report having had a sensory or quasi-sensory experience of the deceased (SED) involving any one or several of the five senses and/or a more difficult-to-define feeling or awareness of the deceased's presence (Datson & Marwit, 1997; Grimby, 1998;

DOI: 10.4324/9781003105077-16

Hayes & Leudar, 2016; Kamp et al., 2020; Rees, 1971). SED first became the focus of systematic scientific interest in the late 19th century when they were explored as part of a census on hallucinations (Sidgwick, Johnson, Myers, Podmore, & Sidgwick, 1894). Much of the research since then has taken place in Western contexts, but SED have also been reported across many cultures (Sabucedo, Evans, & Hayes, 2020), and recent decades have seen a general increase in SED research, including in non-Western cultures (e.g., Chan et al., 2005; Shimizu, Kikuchi, Kobayashi, & Kato, 2017). However, for much of the 20th century, SED were mostly researched or written about from Western and particularly psychiatric perspectives, for example, viewing SED as symptoms of pathological grief and getting in the way of the clinical goal of *letting go* and *moving on* in grief (Freud, 1917; Parkes, 1972) or, from an attachment theory perspective, as getting in the way of integrating the loss in adaptive ways (Field, 2006). Drawing on cross-cultural research that suggested the potential adaptiveness of SED in non-Western cultures such as Japan (Yamamoto, Okonogi, Iwasaki, & Yoshimura, 1969), a radical shift in perspective occurred toward the end of the 20th century with the seminal publication of *Continuing Bonds: New Understandings of Grief* (Klass, Silverman, & Nickman, 1996), a book that marked a paradigm shift in bereavement scholarship. Grounded in qualitative research, SED were shown to be often comforting and helpful events welcomed by perceivers (e.g., Conant, 1996). SED could thus be understood as expressions of an ongoing dynamic relationship with the deceased rather than as pathological grief or unresolved loss. In the years following the publication by Klass et al., further qualitative research into the phenomenology and meanings of SED was conducted (Keen, Murray, & Payne, 2013b; Steffen & Coyle, 2011), and quantitative research focused on trying to establish when SED or continuing bonds broadly might be more or less adaptive (e.g., Field & Filanosky, 2010; Neimeyer, Baldwin, & Gillies, 2006).

What Are Sensory and Quasi-Sensory Experiences of the Deceased Like?

Sensory experiences of the deceased have been reported as occurring through all of the five senses, sometimes through only one of the senses and at other times through multiple senses (Kamp, Steffen, Alderson-Day, et al., 2020). For example, the voice of the deceased may be heard or there may be a visual perception of the deceased in combination with, for example, a sound or feeling of touch (e.g., Hayes & Leudar, 2016; Keen et al., 2013b; Steffen & Coyle, 2011). Experiences can be distinct and clear or vague and diffuse, involving a whole or partial perceptual experience of the deceased. For instance, the deceased may be seen in full body, or only a glimpse of their face may be seen (Woollacott, Roe, Cooper, Lorimer, & Elsaesser, 2021). The experience can also involve indirect perception such as hearing the footsteps of the deceased or the smell of tobacco or perfume as characteristic of them when they were alive (e.g., Sormanti & August, 1997; Steffen & Coyle, 2017). While taste experiences are very rare, they do occur and can, for example, involve the taste of a favorite dish associated with the deceased (e.g., Hayes, 2011).

The most commonly reported experience of the deceased tends to be, however, not a sensory experience as such but, what has been called, a *quasi-sensory* experience of presence (Steffen & Coyle, 2011), which is difficult to pin down in terms of one of the five senses but which is clearly felt as an awareness or feeling of the deceased somehow being *there* (Bennett & Bennett, 2000; Datson & Marwit, 1997; Grimby, 1998). The feeling of presence frequently involves a sense of location of the deceased (Woollacott et al., 2021), for example, just above one's shoulder or to one side of the bereaved. But it can also be a general awareness of the deceased being somehow *around* or the griever feeling *watched over* by the deceased from a more distant location, such as heaven (Bennett, & Bennett, 2000; Conant, 1996; Steffen & Coyle, 2011). The latter kind of experience also points to a continuum between SED and feelings of connection between the deceased and the bereaved person that are of a less sensory or tangible nature (e.g., Ratcliffe, 2020). Very often sensory experiences and presence occur in combination. Elaine's experience of feeling her grandmother caressing her as well as sensing her presence in the room illustrates this (see also Table 12.1).

One distinctive feature of the experience is the sense of veridicality that tends to accompany the phenomenon; that is, people experience their perception as *real*, although they do not tend to think that others would necessarily share their experience (Grimby, 1998). This sense of veridicality appears to be part of the phenomenon and seems to occur independently of what perceivers themselves believe with regard to the possibility of post-death contact. A common feature in some cases is that people *recognize* the deceased or immediately understand the experience to be of the deceased even when only catching a fleeting glimpse (Woollacott et al., 2021). Although hearing the voice of the deceased can be compared to hearing voices outside of bereavement, the voice is usually clearly identified as that of the deceased, whereas in voice-hearing more generally the connections between the voices and persons or events in the hearer's life may be less clear (Hayes & Leudar, 2016). This sense of *knowing* in bereavement that the experience is of the deceased may be particularly interesting as a feature in cases of a more diffuse or vague feeling of presence. There are many examples in the published literature that highlight this combination of certainty of identity with uncertainty or vagueness of the perceptual quality of the experience (e.g., Steffen & Coyle, 2011).

In terms of whether SED are experienced as welcome or unwelcome, the vast majority of SED are described as positive (Kamp et al., 2020). People often experience them as comforting or beneficial (e.g., Chan et al., 2005; Conant, 1996; Steffen & Coyle, 2011). However, a small

Table 12.1 Prevalence, perceptual content, and examples of sensory and quasi-sensory experiences of the deceased

Sensory modality-prevalence range	Perceptual content	Examples reported by perceivers
Sense of presence	The deceased as felt presence that can be located in space	"I just completely relaxed inside this car [.] He was with me. It was as if he was sitting next to me really" (Steffen & Coyle, 2011).
	The deceased as non-specific yet "felt" presence/awareness	"Sometimes I just know he's around, you know. And other times I don't. But when I do think that he is it's such a strong feeling that I'm sure of it" (Tyson-Rawson, 1996).
Auditory SED	Hearing the voice of the deceased	"And I heard my grandma say, 'it's at the back, it's at the back'. And [.] as I looked toward the back, I could see there was like a, thing that needed, needed to be turned" (Hayes & Leudar, 2016).
	Hearing sounds of the deceased	"I've heard odd noises once and once I was frightened. I said, 'Stop that dad,' and it did stop" (Keen et al., 2013).
Visual SED	Seeing the deceased in full figure	"And all of a sudden, from nowhere, he appeared! I mean, I just – a vision of him was right in front of me. I mean, it lasted a split second. But, it was there" (Conant, 1996).
	Partial visual perception of the deceased	"Well this was an eye and a nostril, it filled the whole of my, my vision bit there, my vision that you can see, and like a nostril, and it was all, sort of, floaty and I thought that looked like my mum when she was young" (Keen et al., 2013).
Tactile SED	Feeling touched on specific part of the body	"When I sat alone at the dining table, I felt how she put her arm around my shoulders as she used to do when she served me food" (Grimby, 1998).
	Feeling held/being enveloped by the deceased	"And then he gave me this big hug ... and it was just this intense feeling of peace ... everything was going to be okay because my grandpa was going to make it okay" (Nowatzki & Kalischuk, 2009).
	Touching the deceased	"I was reading, when suddenly a figure floated over me about a foot above my head. She was wearing a white, long-sleeved night-dress, and her hair looked as brilliant read as it really

(Continued)

Table 12.1 (Continued)

Sensory modality-prevalence range	Perceptual content	Examples reported by perceivers
		was. I reached out and stroked her face, which felt just like any other face. The figure at once faded away" (West, 1948).
Olfactory SED	Smells emanating closely from the deceased	"I started to smell cigar smoke, and then out of the corner of my eye I saw someone sitting in the chair. And it scared me, and then I realized it was my grandfather and I felt surprised. Now whenever I travel I smell that cigar smoke and that's how I know he's around" (Parker, 2005).
	Smells more broadly associated with the deceased	"At about 9 p.m., two weeks after Stacy's death, I was in bed and I started smelling Noxzema; this went on for about two hours. [.] This happened for the entire week. Finally, thinking I was losing my mind, I asked my husband at 9 p.m. one evening if he smelled Noxzema. He said yes, that he thought I had started putting it on like Stacy used to every night before she went to bed" (Sormanti & August, 1997).
Gustatory SED	Perceived taste of food linked to deceased (in combination with smell)	"And, it was a very strong, powerful smell. Which, I knew wasn't in the room but I could definitely smell it none the less. Erm, and, erm, sort of a few seconds after that, I could really taste like the food" (Hayes, 2011).

minority report negative or distressing experiences, and some experiences may be described as neutral or ambivalent (Rees, 1971; Sabucedo, Evans, Gaitanidis, & Hayes, 2020). The impact that SED have on bereaved perceivers is closely connected with the meanings that SED may have for them (Keen et al., 2013a), which will be discussed below.

Who Experiences Sensory and Quasi-Sensory Experiences of the Deceased?

The limited research exploring who may be more likely to experience SED has begun to show a tentative picture. Studies show that SED may be more likely to occur for women, older people, and those for whom the pre-death relationship was considered good (Grimby, 1998; Kamp, O'Connor, Spindler, & Moskowitz, 2019; Kamp, Steffen, Moskowitz, & Spindler, 2020; Rees, 1971). In addition, a higher level of personality traits such as extraversion, openness to experience, and neuroticism have also been found among experiencers of SED (Datson & Marwit, 1997; Kamp et al., 2019; Rees, 1971). However, these studies have focused on bereavement following spousal loss, and none of the results have been replicated; as a consequence, the implications are still unclear.

SED have been reported following losses of many kinds of relationships, including death of a spouse, child, parent, friend, teacher, or even an acquaintance (Hayes & Leudar, 2016; Klugman, 2006; Steffen & Coyle, 2011). In addition, SED have been reported by children, as well as adults across age groups, and regardless of gender (Datson & Marwit, 1997; Rees, 1971). A recent study by Kamp et al. (2020) also found SED to be more likely if the bereaved person reported an interpersonal trauma, such as a violent assault or sexual abuse, which concurs with similar associations found among voices hearers outside of bereavement (e.g., Read, van Os, Morrison, & Ross, 2005). A more frequently asked question is whether SED are more likely to occur if people are religious or from a specific culture. SED are clearly a cross-cultural phenomenon (Sabucedo, Evans, & Hayes, 2020), and generally, studies have also not shown an association to specific socio-economic or ethnic groups, nor for specific geographic locations or living circumstances (e.g., Datson & Marwit, 1997; Klugman, 2006; Rees, 1971). In addition, SED have been reported among people with different religious and spiritual beliefs (Ata, 2012; Datson & Marwit, 1997), with a recent study finding SED to be more likely if the bereaved person holds a stronger religious or spiritual conviction (Kamp, Steffen, Moskowitz, et al., 2020).

How Do Experiencers Make Sense of SED at a Personal and Situational Level?

How SED are experienced and what they mean to perceivers has been the main focus of a number of qualitative studies into the phenomenon (e.g., Conant, 1996; Hayes & Leudar, 2016; Parker, 2005). A study by Steffen and Coyle (2011), which employed a thematic analysis of interview transcripts of 12 participants who had reported having sensed the presence of the deceased, identified a number of themes that showed how perceivers derived meaning from the experiences at a personal, situational, and relational level. Participants identified characteristic features within the experiences that suggested to them the continuation of the deceased as they had been in life, for example, the deceased coming to check on the bereaved to make sure they are okay as suggestive of the deceased's caring nature, or having the experience in a specific location as associated with the relationship between the deceased and the bereaved to indicate the continuing bond between them. In the case of Elaine, she felt stroked as she had in the past by her grandmother, who was coming to *say goodbye* because they had not been able to see each other before the death. Thus, SED could thus function as a means to completing *unfinished business* with the deceased.

Another theme around personal meaning-making showed how the bereaved could derive guidance and purpose from the experience for their lives going forward, providing a sense of affirmation of self. Other positive themes to do with the comforting and beneficial presence of the deceased were identified by Keen et al. (2013b), who interviewed eight female bereaved participants and conducted an interpretative phenomenological analysis of the data. However, they also offered examples of more distressing or hostile experiences, which, seemed to be continuous with the unpleasant characteristics the deceased appeared to have when alive.

An aspect of meaning that has been particularly emphasized in a study by Hayes and Leudar (2016), which employed ethnomethodological conversation analysis, concerns pragmatic aspects of SED. The study showed how meaning is often derived from the immediate situation in which SED occur and the consequences these experiences have within that context. For example, it was shown how perceivers who hear the deceased's voice may use the linguistic features of the voices to make sense of them or draw on the current context as a source of meaning. Thus, a voice can refer to objects or features in the context and may even provide practical help to the bereaved person, such as fixing a blocked sink or finding a lost object. Similarly, Steffen and Coyle (2011) described an example where a widow experienced the presence of her deceased husband in the car next to her and found that he was helping her become more confident with driving. In a study of family meaning making, Steffen and Coyle (2017) provided an example of a mother receiving advice from her deceased husband with regard to childrearing (see also Woollacott et al., 2021).

These examples of the deceased as a helpful agent in the here and now provide evidence against one of the concerns that have sometimes been raised with regard to the continued presence of the deceased, namely, that this might suggest a fixation of the bereaved with the deceased as *frozen* in the past or simply as signifying *unresolved loss* (Field, 2006). Contrary to such understandings, many of these examples show that the relationships with the deceased can be fluid and dynamic, relating to current situations and that they often are amenable to change. However, this is not necessarily always the case. Just as relationships between the living can be more or less constructive, so can relationships between the living and the dead. Additionally, the presence of the deceased may not always be welcome, in which case SED may be experienced as troublesome (Hayes & Steffen, 2018).

How Do Experiencers Make Sense of SED at an Existential and Global Level?

As described above, recent research suggests that perceivers often have a relatively quick sense of the meanings of SED at a situational level. Within the immediate context of the occurrence, specific meanings, such as the deceased coming to say goodbye or reassuring the bereaved, are sometimes part and parcel of the experience itself and do not require an intensive interpretative effort on the part of the perceiver. When it comes to making sense of SED at a more global level, this is, however, rather different. While experiencers may make sense of SED situationally as an actual encounter with the deceased, this may conflict with global beliefs about the possibility of post-death contact, leading to a cognitive dissonance between a person's situational and global beliefs (Park, 2008). This points to the complexity of assimilation and/or accommodation processes that may be involved when attempting to integrate SED into one's assumptive world (Parker, 2005). Furthermore, challenges may be posed by discrepancies between an individual's beliefs and their socio-cultural context, which may not offer conceptual frameworks in which SED can be meaningfully integrated (Steffen & Coyle, 2010, 2011, 2012), for example, due to possible stigma associated with so-called *anomalous* experiences in many cultural contexts (Steffen, Wilde, & Cooper, 2018). There is a well-documented reluctance to disclose having had SED in Western contexts for fear of being dismissed or ridiculed (e.g., Rees, 1971; Steffen & Coyle, 2011). SED may be condoned and even welcomed in some cultural contexts (Chan et al., 2005; Yamamoto et al., 1969) where they may be made sense of in terms of spiritual, religious, and/or cultural understandings around after-death contact. However, spiritual meaning making has not been straightforward in Western contexts, particularly in Protestant traditions, where spiritual bonds other than the bond with God/Christ tends not to be permitted (Klass & Goss, 1999; Steffen & Coyle, 2010, 2012). Those who are able to negotiate these ontological challenges may, however, derive not only personal and relational benefits from the experiences but also report existential meaning making and post-traumatic growth (Steffen & Coyle, 2011; Tedeschi & Calhoun, 2006). For some, this provides confirmation or even proof of life after death, a reduction in death anxiety, an increase in spiritual growth, and hope for a reunion with the deceased (Kwilecki, 2011; Steffen & Coyle, 2011).

Recent qualitative studies have also pointed out that existential meaning making does not need to be based on spiritual beliefs.

Austad (2014) showed that sense making of SED can involve a mixture of religious and non-religious interpretative resources. Hayes observed a similar tendency in her sample and referred to *epistemic pluralism* (2011, p. 211), similar to the idea of *ontological flexibility* as recently developed in connection with SED and the afterlife (Steffen, in Press), meaning that people seem to draw on a range of different narratives and frameworks, which may or may not be in conflict when making sense of SED.

Are SED Associated with Distress?

This question has been raised repeatedly in the literature, and several authors have suggested that SED should be viewed as part of a maladaptive response to bereavement (Field & Filanosky, 2010; Kersting, 2004). This perspective is often accompanied by a conceptualization of SED as hallucinations, and may as such be viewed in light of a historic link between hallucinations and pathology (Kamp, Steffen, Alderson-Day, et al., 2020; Moskowitz, Mosquera, & Longden, 2017). However, research on hallucinations in non-clinical populations has made it apparent that hallucinations are not necessarily equal to a need of care or treatment (e.g., Johns et al., 2014). By the same token, most people reporting SED consider the experiences as welcome, and do not seek help. This may also be the reason several of the case descriptions of SED presented in some of the research on SED are from a psychiatric context in which these experiences had been noticed (Baethge, 2002; Kersting, 2004; Shimizu et al., 2017). These descriptions are often characterized as being distressing, for instance in content, such as a study from Japan (Shimizu et al., 2017), which described a widow who heard her deceased husband's voice telling her to stop eating and to harm herself. Moreover, a recent survey into psychotherapy with distressing SED found that approximately two-thirds of the 70 practitioners who completed the survey had seen at least one case of ambivalent or distressing SED in their practice, with 20 having seen more than five cases over the course of time (Sabucedo, Evans, Gaitanidis, et al., 2020).

A related question is whether reporting SED are associated with higher levels of bereavement-related distress, such as grief symptoms, anxiety, loneliness, or depression. Overall, studies show that SED are associated with higher levels of bereavement-related distress (Field & Filanosky, 2010; Kamp et al., 2019; Simon et al., 2011). However, the studies vary in their methodology and in how SED are assessed, and as such, the implication of this association remains unclear. For instance, only experiences of seeing or hearing the deceased were assessed in two studies among 1,321 and 782 bereaved people, respectively (Boelen & Hoijtink, 2009; Simon et al., 2011). So while frequent occurrence of this subset of experiences was almost exclusively found among participants categorized with complicated grief, the generalizability of this result to SED overall is unclear. Moreover, in a recent study among 175 widowed people, experiencers of at least one SED displayed significantly higher symptom levels of depression, prolonged grief, and post-traumatic stress disorder (PTSD), compared to non-experiencers four years following the loss of a spouse (Kamp et al., 2019). However, whether these differences were of clinical significance was not assessed. Taken together, these studies point to a noticeable association between SED and bereavement-related distress, but more research is needed to understand the causality, as well as the clinical significance, of this association (Kamp et al., 2020). Furthermore, it is worth keeping in mind, that most experiencers find the experience a positive one, as well as the noticeable discrepancy between the estimated prevalence of SED mentioned above (i.e., 47–82%) and, for instance, prolonged grief disorder (i.e., 10%). This makes it questionable to view SED *per se* as an indicator of a pathological grief reaction. In contrast, we advocate that SED should be considered in light of the consequences of SED to the individual (Kamp, Steffen, Alderson-Day, et al., 2020).

Implications for Practice

The majority of SED are benign experiences that do not give any cause for concern in themselves. Instead, they may often be beneficial to the bereaved experiencer, provide comfort, hope, and help and potentially hold important personal, relational, and existential and/or spiritual meanings. However, these meanings may not always be straightforward. They may lead to conflicts with personal or cultural and religious meaning systems. There may be societal stigma around having such experiences, and, thus, those supporting bereaved experiencers may play an important role in normalizing SED, facilitating their exploration, and even providing affirmation. However, it should be noted that these experiences may not always be welcomed by the griever and/or they could, in very rare cases, be connected to pre-existing mental health problems or be suggestive of some kind of clinical deterioration (Sabucedo, Evans, Gaitanidis, et al., 2020). As these more negative outcomes are extremely rare, they should not be assumed, and it is recommended that an open-minded and non-judgmental attitude be taken. Based on the current knowledge base on SED, as well as some case studies and reports from therapists and clients regarding what may be helpful or unhelpful when encountering SED in practice (Hayes & Steffen, 2018; Sanger, 2009; Sluzki, 2008; Steffen et al., 2018; Taylor, 2005), recommendations for practice have been compiled in Table 12.2.

Table 12.2 Clinical recommendations for assessing and working with SED

1. Assessment, diagnosis, and risk

1.1 Assessment of SED	When SED have been disclosed, clinicians should: • be welcoming of clients disclosing SED • allow detailed narrative retelling of the event(s) • assess for the impact of the experience on the client • explore the meaning of SED to the client
1.2 (Pre-existing) mental health problems	In cases of (pre-existing) mental health problems, or clinical deterioration, clinicians should: • assess (prior) mental health problems and possible links to current context • be cautious as in some cases distressing SED may be linked to pre-existing mental health issues or clinical deterioration • be aware of the risk of misdiagnosis, given that the vast majority of SED tend to be benign

2. Therapeutic strategies

2.1 Psychoeducation	If bereaved disclose concerns for their sanity due to SED, clinicians are advised to: • normalize SED by sharing information, e.g., the high prevalence of SED • provide reassurance that SED are not normally linked to mental health problems
2.2 Relationship re-processing	Working with the relationship, e.g., in grief therapy: • SED can be used as a catalyst for working on the relationship with the deceased • SED can lead to developing a helpful continuing bond, although not necessarily in all cases
2.3 Working with welcome SED	When SED are welcome: • SED can be used for drawing on the continuing bond with the deceased as a resource for coping with grief • meanings and messages can be taken forward into the client's ongoing life
2.4 Working with unwelcome or ambivalent SED	When SED are unwelcome or ambivalent SED, practitioners should: • carefully assess the circumstances of SED • assess the current context of the client • assess the context of the pre-death relationship • explore potential to work on unfinished business with the deceased person • offer opportunities for exploring different ways of responding to SED

(Continued)

Table 12.2 (Continued)

2.5 Addressing existential crisis/cognitive dissonance	Practitioners should be willing to explore issues such as: • struggle to make sense of SED • lack of available conceptual frameworks within which the experience can be understood • clashes between experience of SED and beliefs including spiritual and religious beliefs
3. General guidelines for clinicians	
3.1 Non-judgmental exploration	Clinicians should approach clients' experiences: • with openness • in a non-judgmental manner • with respect for the client's perception and interpretation
3.2 Cultural sensitivity	Clinicians should: • pay careful attention to how clients make sense of the experience • pay attention to the language clients use to frame their experiences • respect the worldview of the client • be sensitive toward clients' social and cultural context • be open to diverse perspectives
3.3 Affirmative stance (if relevant)	If appropriate and relevant, clinicians should: • adopt an affirmative stance toward SED • help clients find the transformative potential in SED • reinforce post-traumatic growth if naturally occurring in client's response to SED

References

Ata, A. (2012). Bereavement anxieties and health amongst the Australian-Italian Catholic community. *Mental Health, Religion & Culture, 15*(6), 555–570. 10.1080/13674676.2011.599370

Austad, A. (2014). *"Passing away—passing by": A qualitative study of experiences and meaning making of post death presence.* (PhD). MF Norwegian School of Theology, Oslo.

Baethge, C. (2002). Grief hallucinations: True or pseudo? Serious or not? *Psychopathology, 35*(5), 296–302. 10.1159/000067067

Bennett, G., & Bennett, K.M. (2000). The presence of the dead: An empirical study. *Mortality, 5*(2), 139–157. 10.1080/713686002

Boelen, P.A., & Hoijtink, H. (2009). An item response theory analysis of a measure of complicated grief. *Death Studies, 33*(2), 101–129. 10.1080/07481180802602758

Chan, C.L., Chow, A.Y., Ho, S.M., Tsui, Y.K., Tin, A.F., Koo, B.W., & Koo, E.W. (2005). The experience of Chinese bereaved persons: A preliminary study of meaning making and continuing bonds. *Death Studies, 29*(10), 923–947. 10.1080/07481180500299287

Conant, R.D. (1996). Memories of the death and life of a spouse: The role of images and sense of presence in grief. In D. Klass, P.R. Silverman, & S.L. Nickman (Eds.), *Continuing bonds: New understandings of grief.* London: Taylor & Francis, pp. 179–196.

Datson, S.L., & Marwit, S.J. (1997). Personality constructs and perceived presence of deceased loved ones. *Death Studies, 21,* 131–146.

Field, N.P. (2006). Unresolved grief and continuing bonds: An attachment perspective. *Death Studies, 30*(8), 739–756. 10.1080/07481180600850518

Field, N.P., & Filanosky, C. (2010). Continuing bonds, risk factors for complicated grief, and adjustment to bereavement. *Death Studies, 34*(1), 1–29. 10.1080/07481180903372269

Freud, S. (1917). Mourning and melancholia. In J. Strachey (Ed.), *The standard edition of the complete psychological works of Sigmund Freud* (Vol. XIV, pp. 252–268). London: Hogarth Press.

Grimby, A. (1998). Hallucinations following the loss of a spouse: Common and normal events among the elderly. *Journal of Clinical Geropsychology, 4*(1), 65–74.

Hayes, J. (2011). *Experiencing the presence of the deceased: Symptoms, spirits, or ordinary life?* (PhD). University of Manchester, Manchester.

Hayes, J., & Leudar, I. (2016). Experiences of continued presence: On the practical consequences of "hallucinations" in bereavement. *Psychology and Psychotherapy, 89*(2), 194–210. 10.1111/papt.12067

Hayes, J., & Steffen, E.M. (2018). Working with welcome and unwelcome presence in grief. In D. Klass & E.M. Steffen (Eds.), *Continuing bonds in bereavement: New directions for research and practice.* New York: Routledge/Taylor & Francis Group, pp. 163–175.

Johns, L.C., Kompus, K., Connell, M., Humpston, C., Lincoln, T.M., Longden, E., …, Larøi, F. (2014). Auditory verbal hallucinations in persons with and without a need for care. *Schizophrenia Bulletin, 40*(Suppl 4), 255–264. 10.1093/schbul/sbu005

Kamp, K.S., O'Connor, M., Spindler, H., & Moskowitz, A. (2019). Bereavement hallucinations after the loss of a spouse: Associations with psychopathological measures, personality and coping style. *Death Studies, 43*(4), 260–269. 10.1080/07481187.2018.1458759

Kamp, K.S., Steffen, E.M., Alderson-Day, B., Allen, P., Austad, A., Hayes, J., …, Sabucedo, P. (2020). Sensory and quasi-sensory experiences of the deceased in bereavement: An interdisciplinary and integrative review. *Schizophrenia Bulletin, 46*(6), 1367–1381. 10.1093/schbul/sbaa113

Kamp, K.S., Steffen, E.M., Moskowitz, A., & Spindler, H. (2020). Sensory experiences of one's deceased spouse in older adults: An analysis of predisposing factors. *Aging & Mental Health,* 1–9. 10.1080/13607863.2020.1839865.

Keen, C., Murray, C., & Payne, S. (2013a). Sensing the presence of the deceased: A narrative review. *Mental Health, Religion & Culture, 16*(4), 384–402. 10.1080/13674676.2012.678987

Keen, C., Murray, C.D., & Payne, S. (2013b). A qualitative exploration of sensing the presence of the deceased following bereavement. *Mortality*, *18*(4), 339–357. 10.1080/13576275.2013.819320

Kersting, A. (2004). The psychodynamics of grief hallucinations: A psychopathological phenomenon of normal and pathological grief. *Psychopathology*, *37*(1), 50–51. 10.1159/000077020

Klass, D., & Goss, R.E. (1999). Spiritual bonds to the dead in cross-cultural and historical perspective: Comparative religion and modern grief. *Death Studies*, *23*(6), 547–567. 10.1080/074811899200885

Klass, D., Silverman, P.R., & Nickman, S.L. (Eds.). (1996). *Continuing bonds: New understandings of grief*. Bristol, UK: Taylor & Francis.

Klugman, C. (2006). Dead men talking: Evidence of post-death contacts and continuing bonds. *Omega: Journal of Death & Dying*, *53*, 249–262.

Kwilecki, S. (2011). Ghosts, meaning, and faith: After-death communications in bereavement narratives. *Death Studies*, *35*, 219–243.

Moskowitz, A., Mosquera, D., & Longden, E. (2017). Auditory verbal hallucinations and the differential diagnosis of schizophrenia and dissociative disorders: Historical, empirical and clinical perspectives. *European Journal of Trauma & Dissociation*, *1*(1), 37–46. 10.1016/j.ejtd.2017.01.003

Neimeyer, R.A., Baldwin, S.A., & Gillies, J. (2006). Continuing bonds and reconstructing meaning: Mitigating complications in bereavement. *Death Studies*, *30*(8), 715–738. 10.1080/07481180600848322

Nowatzki, N.R., & Kalischuk, R.G. (2009). Post-death encounters: Grieving, mourning, and healing. *Omega: Journal of Death and Dying*, *59*(2), 91–111. 10.2190/OM.59.2.a

Park, C.L. (2008). Testing the meaning-making model of coping with loss. *Journal of Social and Clinical Psychology*, *27*(9), 970–994. 10.1521/jscp.2008.27.9.970

Parker, J.S. (2005). Extraordinary experiences of the bereaved and adaptive outcomes of grief. *Omega: Journal of Death and Dying*, *51*(4), 257–283. 10.2190/FM7M-314B-U3RT-E2CB

Parkes, C.M. (1972). *Bereavement: Studies of grief in adult life*. London: Tavistock.

Ratcliffe, M. (2020). Sensed presence without sensory qualities: A phenomenological study of bereavement hallucinations. *Phenomenology and the Cognitive Sciences*, *20*(4), 601–616. 10.1007/s11097-020-09666-2.

Read, J., van Os, J., Morrison, A. P., & Ross, C.A. (2005). Childhood trauma, psychosis and schizophrenia: A literature review with theoretical and clinical implications. *Acta Psychiatrica Scandinavica*, *112*(5), 330–350. 10.1111/j.1600-0447.2005.00634.x

Rees, D. (1971). The hallucinations of widowhood. *British Medical Journal*, *4*(5778), 37–41.

Sabucedo, P., Evans, C., Gaitanidis, A., & Hayes, J. (2020). When experiences of presence go awry: A survey on psychotherapy practice with the ambivalent-to-distressing "hallucination" of the deceased. *Psychology and Psychotherapy: Theory, Research and Practice*. 10.1111/papt.12285.

Sabucedo, P., Evans, C., & Hayes, J. (2020). Perceiving those who are gone: Cultural research on post-bereavement perception or hallucination of the deceased. *Transcultural Psychiatry*. 10.1177/1363461520962887

Sanger, M. (2009). When clients sense the presence of loved ones who have died. *Omega: Journal of Death and Dying, 59*(1), 69–89.

Shimizu, K., Kikuchi, S., Kobayashi, T., & Kato, S. (2017). Persistent complex bereavement disorder: Clinical utility and classification of the category proposed for Diagnostic and Statistical Manual of Mental Disorders, 5th edition. *Psychogeriatrics, 17*(1), 17–24. 10.1111/psyg.12183

Sidgwick, H., Johnson, A., Myers, F.W.H., Podmore, F., & Sidgwick, E.M. (1894). Report on the census of hallucinations. *Proceedings of the Society for Psychical Research, 34*, 25–394.

Simon, N.M., Wall, M.M., Keshaviah, A., Dryman, M.T., LeBlanc, N.J., & Shear, M.K. (2011). Informing the symptom profile of complicated grief. *Depression and Anxiety, 28*(2), 118–126. 10.1002/da.20775

Sluzki, C.E. (2008). Saudades at the edge of the self and the merits of "portable families." *Transcultural Psychiatry, 45*(3), 379–390.

Sormanti, M., & August, J. (1997). Parental bereavement: Spiritual connections with deceased children. *American Journal of Orthopsychiatry, 67*(3), 460–469. 10.1037/h0080247

Steffen, E.M. (in press). Interacting with the afterlife: Continuing bonds with deceased loved ones. In T.R. Byerly (Ed.), *Death, immortality, and eternal life.* Abingdon, UK: Informa UK.

Steffen, E., & Coyle, A. (2010). Can "sense of presence" experiences in bereavement be conceptualised as spiritual phenomena? *Mental Health, Religion & Culture, 13*(3), 273–291. 10.1080/13674670903357844

Steffen, E., & Coyle, A. (2011). Sense of presence experiences and meaning making in bereavement: A qualitative analysis. *Death Studies, 35*(7), 579–609. 10.1080/07481187.2011.584758

Steffen, E., & Coyle, A. (2012). "Sense of presence" experiences in bereavement and their relationship to mental health: A critical examination of a continuing controversy. In C. Murray (Ed.), *Mental health and anomalous experience.* Hauppauge, NY: Nova Science Publishers, pp. 33–56.

Steffen, E., & Coyle, A. (2017). "I thought they should know ... that daddy is not completely gone": A case study of sense-of-presence experiences in bereavement and family meaning making. *Omega: Journal of Death and Dying, 74*(4), 363–385. 10.1177/0030222816686609

Steffen, E.M., Wilde, D.J., & Cooper, C.E. (2018). Affirming the positive in anomalous experiences: A challenge to dominant accounts of reality, life, and death. In N.J.L. Brown, T. Lomas, & F.J. Eiroa-Orosa (Eds.), *The Routledge international handbook of critical positive psychology.* New York: Routledge/ Taylor & Francis Group, pp. 227–244.

Taylor, S.F. (2005). Between the idea and the reality: A study of the counselling experiences of bereaved people who sense the presence of the deceased. *Counselling and Psychotherapy Research, 5*(1), 53–61. 10.1080/14733140512331343921

Tedeschi, R.G., & Calhoun, L.G. (2006). Time of change? The spiritual challenges of bereavement and loss. *Omega: Journal of Death & Dying, 53*(1/2), 105–116. 10.2190/7MBU-UFV9-6TJ6-DP83

Tyson-Rawson, K. (1996). Relationship and heritage: Manifestations of ongoing attachment following father death. In D. Klass, P.R. Silverman, & S. Nikman (Eds.), *Continuing bonds: New understandings of grief.* Bristol, UK: Taylor & Francis, pp. 125–145.

West, D.J. (1948). A mass-observation questionnaire on hallucinations. *Journal of the Society for Psychical Research, 34*(644–645), 187–196.

Woollacott, M., Roe, C.A., Cooper, C.E., Lorimer, D., & Elsaesser, E. (2021). Perceptual phenomena associated with spontaneous experiences of after-death communication: Analysis of visual, tactile, auditory and olfactory sensations. *EXPLORE.* 10.1016/j.explore.2021.02.006.

Yamamoto, J., Okonogi, K., Iwasaki, T., & Yoshimura, S. (1969). Mourning in Japan. *American Journal of Psychiatry, 125,* 1660–1665. 1660.pdf

13 Internet Resources for the Bereaved: Facebook's Influence on the Grieving Process

Camille B. Wortman[1]

Introduction

Over the past decade, the process of grieving had been fundamentally changed by the Internet, by technology, and especially by social media. This chapter focuses on how the mourning process has been affected by Facebook, arguably the most influential media platform in the world. There is no doubt that Facebook has revolutionized the way we mourn. As Wiederhold (2017) noted, social network sites like Facebook "allow us to grieve in new ways, both public and private, within communities that aren't limited to family members and close friends" (p. 585).

The first section of this chapter provides background information about Facebook and describes options for the deceased person's Facebook profile after they die. The next section examines how Facebook has influenced the grieving process. The advantages and disadvantages of expressing grief on Facebook are compared to the use of traditional mourning practices. This is followed by a review of empirical research on Facebook and grief. Finally, the authors propose future research questions that could significantly enhance our understanding of the role that Facebook plays in the grieving process.

Background

Since its inception, Facebook has been a significant site for communication, as it offers the opportunity for people to cultivate, maintain, and strengthen relationships with one another. Essentially, it provides a vehicle for users to create, share, reflect on, and revise their life narratives (Lincoln & Robards, 2017) through use of text, photos, videos, news articles, etc. Facebook was founded in 2004 by Mark Zuckerberg and three of his classmates at Harvard University. By the end of 2004, the precursor to Facebook (thefacebook.com) had over one million registered users. Its name was changed to Facebook in 2005. The site continued to grow exponentially, and in the summer of 2012, Facebook became the first social media platform to have over one billion monthly

DOI: 10.4324/9781003105077-17

active users (Facebook, n.d.). By the end of 2020, Facebook had 2.8 billion users who visited the site at least monthly (Richter, 2021). According to a recent survey conducted by the Pew Research Center (Perrin & Anderson, 2019), about seven in ten US adults (69%) use Facebook. Among adult users, around three-quarters (74%) visit the site at least once a day (Perrin & Anderson, 2019). The average US user spends 37 minutes on Facebook per day (Statista, 2021). Nearly half of adults who are 65 and older (46%) use Facebook, and this demographic group is the most fast-growing (Perrin & Anderson, 2019). Facebook's net worth as of March 12, 2021 was nearly $780 billion (Macrotrends, 2021).

Given the ubiquitous presence of Facebook in many peoples' lives, it is not surprising that it would play a notable role in how we mourn our dead. Over the years, the Facebook staff has made an effort to accommodate those who wish to make posts in remembrance of a loved one. Facebook's policies about what happens to a profile after a person dies have been modified several times and are still evolving. At present, people can choose how their Facebook profile is handled upon their death. They can have their account permanently deleted or designate a "legacy contact," giving permission for a specific person to manage their account after their death. If no such option is selected, family members or close friends have three alternatives regarding how to deal with their loved one's profile: they can have it removed, leave it as is, or convert it into a memorialized account (Facebook Help Center, n.d.).

When a profile is removed, all of the deceased person's posts, photographs, and videos are permanently deleted. However, loved ones will still have access to messages they received before their loved one died. If the profile is left as it was before the death occurred, family and friends are able to post their condolences on that site. However, they will continue to receive notifications such as birthday reminders, memories of the past year, and friendship anniversaries, just as if the person were still alive, which may be disconcerting to some people. For those with a close relationship to the deceased, these can be profoundly upsetting. One bereaved father indicated that he never knew when he would be subjected to photos of his deceased daughter, and these unexpected images made him feel like he was being haunted by her (Lambert, Nansen, & Arnold, 2018).

In response to the growing sentiment among the bereaved about these notifications, Facebook added the option for a profile to be converted into a memorialized account. Once the profile has been memorialized, the Facebook staff adds the word "Remembering" next to the person's name on their profile. Depending on the deceased person's privacy settings, family members and friends can continue to post on the person's timeline; however, they do not receive notifications about friendship anniversaries or birthday reminders (Facebook Help Center, n.d.). In 2019, Facebook Chief Operating Officer, Sheryl Sandberg, noted that "over 30 million people view memorialized profiles every month," which suggests that

Facebook users find the memorialization option to be a valuable avenue for expressing their grief. At the same time, she announced the creation of a Tributes section, "a separate tab on memorialized profiles where friends and family can share posts" (Sandberg, 2019).

Grieving a Loved One: Facebook vs. Traditional Mourning Practices

Facebook can be utilized for many aspects of the mourning process. It may be used to inform people about the death and funeral arrangements, pay tribute to the deceased, express feelings of sorrow, and connect with others to create a sense of community and support. Individuals can convey their sentiments through a wide variety of types of posts, including comments, poems, photographs, videos, and artwork. By its very nature, Facebook offers easy ways to share these messages. Facebook also offers a convenient forum for surviving family members to raise awareness for a specific illness or cause. In addition, events arranged to honor the deceased, such as a celebration of life or the one-year anniversary of the death, can be publicized easily.

Prior to the rise of social media, the bereaved had to contact each person, typically by phone, to inform them about the death and give an overview of the events that led to their death. Now, Facebook enables the bereaved to announce a death to a large audience of family and friends rather than having to make individual calls, easing the burden of painful one-by-one disclosures. However, finding out about a loved one's death by reading about it on Facebook may be shocking and unsettling to some.

Another advantage of announcing a death on Facebook is that it is possible to obtain support rapidly, as response times to posts on Facebook are typically very quick (McEwen & Scheaffer, 2013), often occurring within minutes. This may be especially important in the days and weeks following the loved one's death. As one woman expressed it, "Grieving left me exhausted and averse to spending time with friends... Facebook allowed me to stay connected when I was too heartbroken to do much else" (Hawkins-Gaar, 2019, p. 3). Additionally, the bereaved can reread posts at any time, especially when they are in the need of emotional fortitude.

Yet another major advantage of expressing grief on Facebook is that it promotes connection between grieving individuals, and thus provides the opportunity to become part of a network of support. Also, when they make a post, support providers can decide in advance exactly what they want to convey to the deceased person's family members or close friends. Many find in-person encounters uncomfortable because they don't know what to say or do. In addition, mourners can express their feelings on Facebook without physical displays of distress, such as crying. This is typically not the case if condolences are offered in person. At the same time, sharing one's condolences on Facebook may cause undue pressure for those who feel that they will be judged for what they write. Thus, mourners may make posts reflecting how their peers think they should feel, not how they actually feel (Giaxoglou, Doveling, & Pitsillides, 2017). Posting on a memorial site also makes it possible for friends of the deceased who did not know each other prior to the loss to support one another. It is not uncommon for these to develop into real-life friendships (Hobbs & Burke, 2017).

Facebook is also home to a variety of grief support groups, which can be especially beneficial for those who do not have in-person support in their local community, who feel like sharing grief feelings with close friends would be a burden, who experience challenges with transportation, or who would prefer a support group whose members are available 24/7. There are general grief support groups as well as those for a specific type of loss, such as the loss of a parent, a spouse or significant other, a child, a sibling, or pregnancy loss, such as stillbirth or miscarriage. Some are organized by a collective theme, such as for those who endorse a certain religion or who identify as LGBTQ+, or by the circumstances of the death, such as suicide, homicide, or substance abuse. In addition, Facebook also hosts grief-related events sponsored by organizations throughout the world, such as live support group meetings, workshops, seminars, courses, and programs. Facebook can play an especially important role in the healing process when the cause of death is stigmatized in our society. Those bereaved by suicide, for example, often describe feeling rejected and blamed by others. One woman whose son died by suicide said that she found the silence of others, both strangers and close friends alike, exceedingly difficult to bear. Parents in this situation have reported that the loving and supportive comments received on Facebook are a lifeline to them (Bailey, Bell, & Kennedy, 2015; Bell, Bailey, & Kennedy, 2015).

Expressing one's grief on Facebook is dramatically different from traditional mourning practices (e.g., attending a funeral or sending a condolence card) where the options for grieving the loss and connecting with other mourners are far more limited. Since traditional mourning provides few opportunities for engagement, the thoughts and images of the deceased may recede more quickly than they do for those who mourn the loss via Facebook. As Kasket (2012) emphasized, when more and more comments, photos, and videos are posted publicly, "the image of the deceased builds in complexity and becomes more multifaceted, more detailed, more vivid" (p. 67). In a sense, the person who died is physically deceased but virtually alive. In other words, the bereaved person can experience the presence within absence of their loved one through the remembrances shared on Facebook. This can be a source of enormous comfort to some mourners, giving them additional time to accept the reality of their loved one's death and to move forward (Kasket, 2012).

It should be emphasized that not all Facebook death notifications result in a supportive grieving community. For example, family members of the deceased may receive condolences that are not comforting and that, in fact, add to their distress (e.g., "At least your husband won't have to suffer anymore"). Family members and close friends of the deceased may also resent the emotional displays of grief made by distant friends and relatives (Sabra, 2017). As time passes, bereaved people may watch their family and friends withdraw from public expressions of grief. This can give the appearance that others have "moved on" and may leave the bereaved feeling isolated, "further compounding their grief experience" (Bell et al., 2015, p. 385).

Some responses made to Facebook death notifications do not consider the feelings of the deceased's family. Some people ask insensitive questions about how the person died. Others post inappropriate images, such as a photograph of the car crash that resulted in the death. Mourners may also offer unsolicited advice—advice that they may not be qualified to give—causing additional distress for the bereaved. In addition, the bereaved may be subjected to information, emotions, and experiences that they do not wish to encounter. One example is a family who lost a college-aged son. Shortly after his death, members of his fraternity posted recent photographs of him at a party where he appeared drunk. These images were extremely difficult for his parents to see, as they felt that they did not reflect well on their son's character. The deceased person's reputation may be tarnished by such posts, and there is no opportunity for the deceased to defend themselves. Misinformation about the deceased can spread quickly online and may never be remedied (Rossetto, Lannutti, & Strauman, 2015).

Family and close friends of the deceased may be also troubled by "emotional rubberneckers," individuals who were not acquainted with the deceased but nonetheless post comments on their Facebook page (e.g., "I did not know Lisa, [but] I want to send out condolences to her family and friends"; DeGroot, 2014, p. 82). DeGroot also described "grief tourists" who visit memorial sites regularly because "seeing other people's pain makes them feel better about their own lives." (p. 80). Some of the most malevolent visitors are the rest-in-peace or "RIP" trolls, who make malicious, inflammatory remarks on the Facebook memorial pages of the deceased for the deliberate purpose of upsetting and provoking the bereaved. An example of such a comment is "Your son was an alcoholic but did a good job of hiding it from you" (for a more detailed discussion of RIP trolls, and the destructive comments they make to provoke and upset the bereaved, see Craker & March, 2016).

Empirical Research

What types of empirical studies have examined the role that Facebook plays in the grieving process and what are the main conclusions that can be drawn from them? To address these questions, a literature search was conducted by entering "Facebook X Grief" into the PsycINFO and Google Scholar search engines in September of 2020. Articles were requested for a ten-year period beginning in 2010, and the search parameters were designed to locate qualitative and quantitative studies. A total of 36 studies were identified. Only three of these studies were carried out by psychologists. The others were conducted by investigators from many different disciplines including communication studies, applied linguistics, political science, anthropology, and journalism. The vast majority of investigators used content analysis to identify and describe posts made to the deceased person's profile, although some relied on interviews with Facebook users who had posted on the site of a family member or friend who had died.

These studies focused on a wide array of topics. For example, Willis and Ferrucci (2017) researched bereaved individuals' motivations for posting on a memorial wall. Pyng (2020) studied the extent to which posting on the wall of a deceased individual strengthened relationships among mourners. Bell et al. (2015) investigated the role that Facebook plays in the mourning process of those whose loved ones died by suicide.

The majority of these studies were designed specifically to determine whether bereaved individuals use Facebook as a way of continuing their relationship with the deceased. The studies were based on the model of grieving put forth by Klass, Silverman, and Nickman in their groundbreaking book, *Continuing Bonds: New Understandings of Grief* (2014). This concept of *continuing bonds* has revolutionized the way that researchers and practitioners understand the grieving process. Previously, it was widely held that in order to come to terms with a loved one's death, the griever must relinquish the relationship at an emotional level (see Wortman & Boerner, 2007). In addition, it was believed that once freed from the attachment, the bereaved individual could move forward in a healthy way. Klass and colleagues challenged this view by arguing persuasively that relationships do not end just because the loved one is not physically present. They asserted that most people continue to maintain a connection with the deceased, and that this often provides comfort and solace. Examples of what it means to maintain a continuing bond include talking to the deceased loved one each day or carrying out projects or plans that were important to the loved one. Thus, it is easy to see why Facebook, too, has become a relevant means for grievers to remain bonded with the deceased person even after their death.

A comprehensive review of studies on how grief is portrayed on Facebook is beyond the scope of this chapter. However, it is important to illustrate how these studies are typically conducted, and to describe the findings that have emerged from this body of work. Toward that end, a study carried out by Bouc, Han, and Pennington (2016) is reviewed here in some detail. This study was selected because, in addition to examining posts made to the deceased, the investigators assessed how the posts changed over time. Bouc et al. (2016) did a content analysis of ten profiles of deceased adolescents, resulting in over 2,500 messages contributed by over 750 users. Their research focused solely on messages written directly to the deceased, which they reported were by far the most prevalent of the posts that were sent. They reported that common expressions, such as "I love you" or "I can't believe you are gone," were the most frequent, appearing in 72.6% of the messages. The authors classified the remaining comments into three overarching themes: *Remembering the Deceased, Processing the Death,* and *Continuing the Connection.* (Some posts met the criteria for more than one category; therefore, the total of percentage of posts exceeds 100.)

Bouc et al.'s (2016) Remembering the Deceased category was reflected in the Facebook posts of 37.6% of the participants. Some friends of the deceased reminisced about the past, for example, "It was fun going to the football games with you," while others complemented the deceased, for example, "You were such a great guy." The authors report that memories focused entirely on the positive—painful or unpleasant memories were never expressed.

The Processing the Death category was reflected in 32.5% of the Facebook messages to the deceased. Messages were coded as evidence of Processing the Death when mourners indicated that they were having difficulty comprehending the loss or did not know how to cope with what had happened. The authors report that the primary way that bereaved individuals attempted to process the death was by expressing difficult emotions, such as guilt, despair, or confusion about what had happened. For example, one griever's post stated, "If I didn't ask you to go with me, you would still be here."

Nearly half (48.2%) of the remaining messages fell into the Continuing the Connection category. The authors identified three kinds of posts that, in their judgment, were indicative of a desire to maintain a connection with the deceased. One type of connection involved making requests of the deceased, such as "Please keep our family safe," or "Please help me pass my biology test tomorrow." A second type involved checking in with the deceased. For example, friends made comments like "I'm just stopping by to say hi," or "I'll come back to see you when my exams are over." A third type of post indicative of maintaining an ongoing bond involved updating the deceased about what is happening in the mourner's life. For example, one friend wrote, "Hey Bud! I am married!"

Bouc et al. (2016) is the only study that has examined how the messages changed over time. Messages were divided into four timeframes: Time 1: those that occurred during the first month following the death; Time 2: 2–6 months postloss; Time 3: 7–12 months postloss; and Time 4: 1–2 years postloss. The authors reported that Facebook posts categorized as Remembering the Deceased showed a dramatic drop between Time 1 and

Time 2 and then gradually declined. Posts reflecting memories of the deceased occurred in nearly one-third of all messages throughout the second year of the loss. The frequency of messages categorized as Processing the Death showed a significant drop between one and six months. The frequency of these messages remained fairly consistent thereafter, occurring in more than a quarter of all messages throughout the second year of the loss.

Messages reflecting the Continuing the Connection theme showed an opposite pattern from the other themes—a significant increase in frequency over time—with nearly half of those posting doing so throughout the second year of the loss. In fact, checking in with the deceased increased markedly, so that by Time 4, it was the most mentioned of all categories, except for common expressions such as "I love you" or "I miss you." Bouc et al. (2016) concluded that their results provide strong evidence for the importance of maintaining a continuing connection with the person who died. Thus, highlighting the use of Facebook as a way that bereaved individuals are likely to benefit from experiencing the presence within absence of their deceased loved one.

Taken together, all of the categories of responses that Bouc et al. (2016) identified—maintaining a connection to the deceased, sharing memories of the person who died, and attempting to process the loss—serve as examples of meaning reconstruction and sense making in those who made memorial posts (see also DeGroot, 2012; Pennington, 2017). This clearly demonstrates that finding meaning in their loved one's death is a motivating force in the memorial posts.

Many other investigators have conducted studies on the Facebook posts of bereaved individuals (e.g., Church, 2013; DeGroot, 2012; Getty et al., 2011; Irwin, 2015; Kasket, 2012; Kern, Forman, & Gil-Egui, 2013; Pennington, 2017; Pyng, 2020). Although these studies focused on different populations and used different coding categories, their findings are consistent with Bouc et al. (2016) in that they demonstrated that Facebook posts made after a person has died are intended to maintain the relationship with the deceased, not to mourn its ending. For example, DeGroot (2012) reported that many respondents felt guilty about their actions prior to the death. They wished to express these feelings to the deceased and implicitly receive forgiveness before they could move forward with their lives. Similar results were obtained by Pyng (2020), who reported that many bereaved individuals made posts with the goal of "finishing their unfinished business." For example, one bereaved individual in his study failed to save a drowning friend. Pyng (2020) reported that this respondent expressed sorrow and regret to the deceased.

In virtually all of the studies that have addressed the idea of maintaining a continuing bond, they found that the vast majority of posts were written directly to deceased individuals as if they were alive (e.g., Church, 2013; Kasket, 2012; Kern et al., 2013; Rossetto et al., 2015). For example,

Irwin (2015) conducted a content analysis of 12 Facebook pages of deceased individuals under the age of 35 and examined a total of 1,270 posts made by 579 individuals. Consistent with her predictions, one overarching theme emerged throughout all 12 of the Facebook memorial pages she studied: the belief among bereaved individuals that the deceased loved one continues to be present in their daily lives—that, in essence, they were experiencing the deceased person's presence in spite of their absence. On the basis of her findings, Irwin (2015) maintained that making posts on a memorial page "serves a vital function for those who are left behind and who find comfort in the continuing connection they can have" (p. 143).

Recommendations for Future Research

To fully understand the ramifications of these findings, several questions must be addressed. The first is to investigate why the vast majority of Facebook users in these studies make such posts directly to the deceased, and why they continue to do so for as long as two years after the death. Possible areas to research include: How does making memorial posts to the deceased affect the process of grieving? Does writing such posts facilitate integration of the loss into one's overall life narrative? If so, how does this occur? Do such posts help the bereaved to make sense of what happened? Does creating an online narrative facilitate finding meaning in what has happened? Do mourners who use Facebook to communicate with the deceased become more resilient over time and/or show greater levels of post-traumatic growth than those who do not?

As noted previously, Bouc et al. (2016) found that some bereaved individuals seemed to be struggling with their grief, including experiencing feelings of guilt, pain, sadness, and confusion. DeGroot (2012) found that many people felt guilty about how they treated the deceased in the past. These individuals felt that they must express these feelings to the deceased and implicitly receive forgiveness before they could move forward with their lives. Similar results were obtained by Pyng (2020), who reported that many bereaved individuals made posts with the goal of taking care of unfinished business between them and the deceased. One individual in his study failed to save a drowning friend. Pyng (2020) indicated that this person expressed sorrow and regret to the deceased. Findings like these prompt follow-up questions such as: Are individuals with high levels of grief symptomatology more likely to make memorial posts? Do they find it comforting and/or healing to do so? Does posting on the Facebook page of their deceased loved one lower their distress with regard to their grief symptoms?

Moreover, many of the researchers cited in this chapter have maintained that mourners in their study are invested in their relationships with the deceased and took steps to keep the relationship alive. This raises the question of how online connections affect a respondent's offline relationships. Do those who post comments to the deceased become more indifferent, more isolated, or more withdrawn from their offline friends? Or is the opposite true? Is there something about engaging with the deceased and other mourners via Facebook that enables the one posting to become more compassionate, caring, and involved with others?

None of these critically important questions can be addressed through content analysis of Facebook text, the methodology utilized in almost all of the studies included in this chapter. Instead, it is critically important to interview individuals who have lost a loved one and who intend to make posts on that person's wall to understand better their subjective experience. It is also important to collect quantitative data, perhaps pre/post scores from scales that assess various forms of bereavement distress (e.g., complicated grief, post-traumatic stress disorder, depression), meaning making, resiliency, and post-traumatic growth, to objectively determine whether various types of posting moderates and or mediates bereavement outcome. Additionally, longitudinal studies are necessary to examine respondents over time to determine how the process unfolds and how long posts continue to be made. These are only some of the questions that will demand our attention in the coming years. Research conducted to date has only scratched the surface. Given the widespread acceptance of and engagement with social media thus far, it is clear that Facebook will continue to affect the grieving process in the future in ways we are only beginning to appreciate. Bereavement professionals would benefit from learning more about the ways their clients may use Facebook to maintain a continuing connection with their deceased friend, and ultimately come to terms with their loss.

Note

1 The author would like to acknowledge Jessica Gregory for the many important contributions she has made to this chapter.

References

Bailey, L., Bell, J., & Kennedy, D. (2015). Continuing social presence of the dead: Exploring suicide bereavement through online memorialization. *New Review of Hypermedia and Multimedia, 21*(1–2), 72–86, 10.1080/13614568.2014.983554

Bell, J., Bailey, L., & Kennedy, D. (2015). "We do it to keep him alive": Bereaved individuals' experiences of online suicide memorials and continuing bonds. *Mortality, 20*(4), 375–389.

Bouc, A., Han, S., & Pennington, N. (2016). "Why are they commenting on his page?": Using Facebook profile pages to continue connections with the deceased. *Computers in Human Behavior, 62,* 635–643.

Church, S.H. (2013). Digital gravescapes: Digital memorializing on Facebook. *The Information Society, 29,* 184–189.

Craker, N., & March, E. (2016). The dark side of Facebook®: The Dark Tetrad, negative social potency, and trolling behaviours. *Personality and Individual Differences, 102*, 79–84.

DeGroot, J.M. (2012). Maintaining relational continuity with the deceased on Facebook. *Omega: Journal of Death and Dying, 65*(3), 195–212.

DeGroot, J.M. (2014). "For whom the bell tolls": Emotional rubbernecking in Facebook memorial groups. *Death Studies, 38*, 79–84. 10.1080/07481187.2012. 725450

Facebook. (n.d.). *Company info: Our history*. Retrieved March 20, 2021, https:// about.fb.com/company-info/

Facebook Help Center. (n.d.). *What will happen to my Facebook account if I pass away?* Retrieved March 20, 2021, from https://www.facebook.com/help/ 103897939701143?helpref=faq_content

Facebook Help Center. (n.d.). *Request to memorialize or remove an account.* Retrieved March 20, 2021, from https://www.facebook.com/help/ 1111566045566400/request-to-memorialize-or-remove-an-account

Getty, E., Cobb, J., Gabeler, M., Nelson, C., Weng, E., & Hancock, J. (2011). I said your name in an empty room: Grieving and continuing bonds on Facebook. In *Proceedings of the SIGCHI Conference on Human Factors in Computing Systems* (pp. 997–1000). ACM. 10.1145/1978942.1979091

Giaxoglou, K., Doveling, K., & Pitsillides, S. (2017). Networked emotions: Interdisciplinary perspectives on sharing loss online. *Journal of Broadcasting & Electronic Media, 61*(7), 1–10.

Hawkins-Gaar, K. (2019, January 16). *The unexpected best use of Facebook.* Retrieved from https://www.vox.com/first-person/2019/1/16/18183686/facebook-social-media-grief-grieving-widow

Hobbs, W.R., & Burke, M.K. (2017). Connective recovery in social networks after the death of a friend. *Nature Human Behaviour, 1*(5), 1–6. *1:0092.*

Irwin, M.D. (2015). Mourning 2.0: Continuing bonds between the living and the dead on Facebook. *Omega: Journal of Death and Dying, 72*(2), 119–150.

Kasket, E. (2012). Continuing bonds in the age of social networking: Facebook as a modern-day medium. *Bereavement Care, 31*(2), 62–69.

Kern, R., Forman, A.E., & Gil-Egui, G. (2013). R.I.P.: Remain in perpetuity. Facebook memorial pages. *Telematics and Informatics, 30*(1), 2–10.

Klass, D., Silverman, P.R., & Nickman, S. L. (Eds.). (2014). *Continuing bonds: New understandings of grief*. Washington, DC: Taylor & Francis

Lambert, A., Nansen, B., & Arnold, M. (2018). Algorithmic memorial videos: Contextualising automated curation. *Memory Studies, 11*(2), 156–171.

Lincoln, S., & Robards, B. (2017). Editing the project of the self: Sustained Facebook use and growing up online. *Journal of Youth Studies, 20*(4), 518–531.

Macrotrends. (2021). Facebook net worth 2009-2020 | FB. Retrieved from https:// www.macrotrends.net/stocks/charts/FB/facebook/net-worth

McEwen, R.N., & Scheaffer, K. (2013). Virtual mourning and memory construction on Facebook: Here are the terms of use. *Bulletin of Science, Technology & Society, 33*(3-4), 64–75.

Pennington, N. (2017). Tie strength and time: Mourning and social networking sites. *Journal of Broadcasting & Electronic Media, 61*(1), 11–23.

Perrin, A., & Anderson, M. (2019, April 10). *Share of U.S. adults using social media, including Facebook, is mostly unchanged since 2018.* Retrieved from https://www.pewresearch.org/fact-tank/2019/04/10/share-of-u-s-adults-using-social-media-including-facebook-is-mostly-unchanged-since-2018/

Pyng, T.H. (2020). "You are dead, but you are not": Social medium (Facebook) is the message in grieving and continuing bonds. *Informasi, 50*(2), 97–110. 10. 21831/informasi.v50i2.18462. ISSN (p) 0126-0650; ISSN (e) 2502-3837

Richter, F. (2021, February 4). *Facebook keeps on growing.* Retrieved from https://www.statista.com/chart/10047/facebooks-monthly-active-users/#:~:text=By%20the%20end%20of%202004,PayPal%20co%2Dfounder%20Peter%20Thiel.&text=By%20the%20end%20of%202020,grown%20to%202.8%20billion%20users

Rossetto, K.R., Lannutti, P.J., & Strauman, E.C. (2015). Death on Facebook: Examining the roles of social media communication for the bereaved. *Journal of Social and Personal Relationships, 32*(7), 974–994.

Sabra, J.B. (2017). "I hate when they do that!" Netiquette in mourning and memorialization among Danish Facebook users. *Journal of Broadcasting & Electronic Media 61*(1), 24–40.

Sandberg, S. (2019, April 9). *Making it easier to honor a loved one on Facebook after they pass away.* Facebook. Retrieved from https://about.fb.com/news/2019/04/updates-to-memorialization/

Statista. (2021). *Average daily time spent on selected social networks by users in the United States from 2014 to 2021.* Retrieved from https://www.statista.com/statistics/324290/us-users-daily-facebook-minutes/

Wiederhold, B. (2017). Collective grieving in the digital age. *Cyberpsychology, Behavior and Social Networking, 20*(10), 585–586.

Willis, E., & Ferrucci, P. (2017). Mourning and grief on Facebook: An examination of motivations for interacting with the deceased. *OMEGA: Journal of Death and Dying, 76*(2), 122–140.

Wortman, C.B., & Boerner, K. (2007). Beyond the myths of coping with loss: Prevailing assumptions versus scientific evidence. In H.S. Friedman & R.C. Silver (Eds.), *Foundations of health psychology.* New York: Oxford University Press, pp. 285–324.

14 Complicated Spiritual Grief: Wrestling with Faith in the Wake of Loss

Laurie A. Burke

For many years, even while their three children were little, Elise and her husband, Jed, had been active leaders in their small, non-denominational church. Their family was considered a model to other congregants, primarily because their marriage and parenting reflected stability and solidity. Over the years, as well as experiencing consistent growth in their personal faith, their family also enjoyed deepening relationships with those in their fellowship. At least that was the case before Jed was involved in a car fatality while on his way home from a work conference. To say that Elise took his death hard would be an understatement. Given what we know about what makes some people struggle more profoundly than others with their loss (e.g., being female, losing a partner, losing someone suddenly, unexpectedly to a traumatic death, having frequent contact prior to the death; see Burke & Neimeyer, 2013*), an astute clinician might recognize these and other risk factors and might have predicted that Elise would experience complicated grief following the loss of her best friend and husband, and struggle to make a life without him as a single parent. What might have been less predictable was the spiritual struggle that ensued, especially once Jed's absence became less surreal to Elise over time. Somewhere around the second anniversary of Jed's death, Elise's simmering disappointment toward God began to boil over into full-blown anger. It's not that she thought that she should be spared hard things. What bothered Elise was the sense that God had abandoned her. Prior to the death, she knew God's plans for her life—a life spent serving her husband and family. Now, that plan no longer made sense. She felt confused, betrayed, and lost. When it came to her spiritual community, Elise referred to much of the support she received as "cold comfort." "Seriously? Do they really think I don't already know those Bible verses they are quoting? Do they really expect me to smile and act like my heart's not ripped out of my chest? Most of all, what they want me to do is pretend that I'm ok because that's easier for them—that way they don't have to wonder how they'd respond if they were in my shoes. It's incredibly sad and disheartening that they can only support me if I act 'spiritual' and say what they want me to. Fact is, they aren't there for me. Despite how spiritual they think they are, they can't even sit with me in my pain."*

DOI: 10.4324/9781003105077-18

Introduction

For many bereaved individuals, faith, religion, and spirituality prove supportive and comforting following the loss of a loved one. For others who are grieving, the opposite holds true. *Complicated spiritual grief* (CSG) is a spiritual crisis following the loss of a loved one in relation to God and/or the mourner's spiritual community. CSG has been shown to exacerbate the bereavement experience. To assess CSG in bereaved adults, a simple-to-use, multidimensional measure of spiritual crisis following loss called the Inventory of Complicated Spiritual Grief 2.0 (ICSG 2.0; Burke, Crunk, Neimeyer, & Bai, 2019) was developed, validated, and is now being used in both clinical and research settings.

However, upon further examination, participants' narratives used to develop the scale revealed a potential area of inquiry beyond just that of CSG. We know that grieving adults commonly maintain an ongoing attachment with and seek the presence of their deceased loved one (Steffen & Coyle, 2012), often as part of the meaning-making process in bereavement (Steffen & Coyle, 2011). Thus, if death and the survivor's subsequent grief can compromise one's spiritual connection with God and others, what difficulties might exist for grievers who contemplate connecting in some way with their deceased loved one? Or how might one's ability to interact with their deceased loved be affected by experiencing CSG when their spiritual struggle surrounds their uncertainty about the deceased's place or contentment in the afterlife? This chapter highlights spiritual struggle following loss, generally, and explores it in light of maintaining an ongoing connection with the deceased, specifically.

Complicated Spiritual Grief

Complicated spiritual grief occurs when a spiritually inclined survivor experiences a crisis of faith following the death of a loved one. According to Burke and Neimeyer (2014), CSG can be spiritually disabling to the griever as she or he attempts but is unable to reconstruct a sense of spiritual stability following a significant death and when his or her relationship to God and/or the faith community has been undermined by the loss.

More research is needed to understand the prevalence of CSG in the bereaved population, however, a recent study showed rates as high as 43% (Burke, Neimeyer, Young, Piazza Bonin, & Davis, 2014). Such findings congruently depict the faith struggle of bereaved individuals in other studies. Examples include parents who reported feeling spiritually devastated by the lack of answers needed to make spiritual sense of the death of their child (Lichtenthal, Currier, Neimeyer, & Keesee, 2010), church congregants who endorsed feeling angry toward and experienced an increased sense of distance from both their faith community and God (Burke & Neimeyer, 2014), and homicide survivors whose anger toward

God at the violent way in which their loved one died was coupled with their inability to trust that God's promise to take care of them would be realized in the face of their excruciating anguish (Burke, Neimeyer, McDevitt-Murphy, Ippolito, & Roberts, 2011). Hill and Pargament (2008) argued that it was exactly this type of rock-bottom spiritual plunge that had the potential to make or break a believer's faith.

Complicated Spiritual Grief and Bereavement Distress

In terms of human distress, grief is commonly experienced and often emotionally disruptive. Studies report that adults respond to loss by exhibiting reactions that span the continuum from resilient to complicated (Galatzer-Levy & Bonanno, 2012) and that their efforts to cope are equally varied (Crunk, Burke, Neimeyer, Robinson, & Bai, 2019). In terms of coping, spiritually inclined adults frequently turn to their faith following major life crises (Hill & Pargament, 2008), especially the loss of a loved one (Wortmann & Park, 2008). Although many bereaved individuals find solace in turning to their faith, contemporary studies show that this is not the case for all spiritually inclined grievers (e.g., Burke et al., 2011). In fact, what tends to be equally as common as experiencing a sense of solace is that some grievers find that they experience strong, difficult sentiments (e.g., anger, distrust) toward God, especially when circumstances surrounding the death and/or their excruciating grief are juxtaposed with their previously held spiritual beliefs, practices, or experiences (Burke et al., 2011).

Burke and Neimeyer's (2014) findings revealed that a crisis of faith is seen when a spiritually inclined griever is faced with the notion that the God with whom they have to date shared a caring, comforting connection now appears to have abandoned them, is punishing them, or, perhaps worse yet, appears distant, silent, and disinterested in their pain. Similar sentiments are reportedly experienced by grievers in relation to their spiritual community as well. Burke and Neimeyer termed this phenomenon when it occurs during bereavement *complicated spiritual grief* (CSG), and operationalized CSG as "the collapse or erosion of the bereaved individual's sense of relationship to God, which is often accompanied by discord with and/or a distancing from his or her faith community" (Burke et al., 2019, p. 1).

To recognize the psychological significance of CSG, we need only to look at its relation to other forms of bereavement distress. Burke and her colleagues have studied CSG contemporaneously and prospectively with a variety of samples of bereaved adults and in each case have found a positive association between CSG and poor bereavement outcome. Specifically, spiritually inclined grievers with high levels of anticipatory grief (Burke et al., 2015), complicated grief (CG; a protracted, debilitating, often life-threatening response to loss; Burke & Neimeyer, 2014; Burke,

Neimeyer, Bottomley, & Smigelsky, 2017; Burke et al., 2011; Prigerson & Jacobs, 2001), depression, or post-traumatic stress disorder (PTSD; Burke et al., 2011) also tended to have high levels of CSG.

In terms of how CSG tends to surface across time, longitudinal bereavement studies (e.g., Burke et al., 2011) have shown that spiritually inclined survivors who experience CG symptoms are more likely to go on to develop CSG symptoms than their counterparts who do not experience CG. Similarly, losing a loved one to a violent death (e.g., suicide, homicide, fatal accident) puts spiritually inclined grievers at greater risk of experiencing CSG than grievers whose loss stemmed from a natural death (e.g., lengthy illness; Burke & Neimeyer, 2014). Stated differently, both survivors of violent death loss (Burke & Neimeyer, 2014) and those who struggle in terms of their lost relationship with the deceased are more prone to struggle spiritually in relation to God and/or their spiritual community (Burke et al., 2011).

Burke et al. (2014) developed and validated a measure of CSG, called the Inventory of Complicated Spiritual Grief (ICSG). Prior to this, CSG had been measured using scales that were not grief specific, such as the Brief RCOPE (Pargament, Smith, Koenig, & Perez, 1998), which measures both positive and negative religious coping. Using subsequent qualitative data (Burke, Neimeyer, Young, et al., 2014), the ICSG was revised and updated to the current version, the ICSG 2.0 (Table 14.1; Burke, et al., 2019), which is represented by the following three subscales: *Estrangement from Spiritual Community*, *Insecurity with God*, and *Disruption in Religious Practices* (Burke et al., 2019).

Examples of Complicated Spiritual Grief

Complicated spiritual grief occurs when a griever's spiritual system of coping is compromised, resulting in relational distress both vertically and horizontally—in terms of their relationship with God and their relationship with their spiritual community, respectively. Burke, Neimeyer, Young, et al. (2014) qualitatively examined the narrative data of 84 grievers and a five-person focus group. Their findings revealed 17 CSG themes that when compiled showed, at least in these samples, that CSG was predominantly characterized in grievers by resentment and doubt toward God, dissatisfaction with the spiritual support received, and substantial changes in their spiritual beliefs and behaviors following the loss. To accurately illustrate what is meant by spiritual struggle following loss, the best examples come from the lived experiences of grievers who have experienced CSG. To derive these data, study participants were asked a series of four questions surrounding the griever's loss experience to assess their feelings and thoughts about God and their spiritual community and to ask whether their relationships with God and their spiritual community had been challenged or strengthened as a result of

Table 14.1 Inventory of Complicated Spiritual Grief—2.0 (ICSG 2.0)

Important points to read before completing this questionnaire:

- During bereavement, many people experience struggles, concerns, or doubts regarding spiritual or religious issues.
- The purpose of this scale is to understand how you have been coping spiritually since your loss.
- On the list of items below there are no right or wrong answers. The best answer is the one that most accurately reflects your experience. If a statement does not apply to you or your situation, simply mark N/A (not applicable).
- When items refer to your "spiritual community," please allow that to represent whatever *spiritual community* means to you. It's meant to include all spiritually inclined individuals in your social network, for instance, fellow believers, members of your church, spiritually like-minded friends or family, etc.
- Please read each statement with the loss you are currently grieving in mind.
- We want you to respond based on how you *actually* feel, not how you believe you *should* feel.
- Please think about your loss of _____, and then read each statement carefully.
- Choose the answer that best describes how you have been feeling *about your loss* during the **past month** including today.

Since the death of _____	Not at all true/ NA	A little true	Somewhat true	Mostly true	Very definitely true
1. People in my spiritual community don't want me to express my grief much or at all.	0	1	2	3	4
2. I feel it is unfair that God took [LOVED ONE].	0	1	2	3	4
3. My spiritual community appears to care more about their own comfort than my pain.	0	1	2	3	4
4. I struggle with accepting how a good God allows bad things to happen.	0	1	2	3	4
5. My spiritual community places unrealistic expectations on my grieving process (e.g., suggesting I should "get over it").	0	1	2	3	4
6. I feel angry at God.	0	1	2	3	4

(Continued)

Table 14.1 (Continued)

	0	1	2	3	4
7. My grief responses often contradict my spiritual community's spiritual beliefs.					
8. I sometimes feel disappointed by God.	0	1	2	3	4
9. I find that spiritual/religious activities (e.g., prayer, worship, Bible reading) are no longer fulfilling.	0	1	2	3	4
10. People in my spiritual community act as if [LOVED ONE]'s death didn't happen.	0	1	2	3	4
11. It is challenging to find a spiritual leader to discuss difficult spiritual issues with.	0	1	2	3	4
12. I sometimes feel like God is punishing me.	0	1	2	3	4
13. I'm confused as to why God would let this happen.	0	1	2	3	4
14. My spiritual community criticizes my anger toward God.	0	1	2	3	4
15. I am a faithful believer, so I don't understand why God didn't protect me.	0	1	2	3	4
16. My spiritual community thinks I've been grieving for too long.	0	1	2	3	4
17. Since my loss, my spiritual beliefs are overshadowed by the beliefs of my spiritual community.	0	1	2	3	4
18. Sharing my spiritual struggle with my spiritual community seems to complicate our relationship.	0	1	2	3	4
19. I sometimes feel abandoned by God.	0	1	2	3	4
20. My doubts about my spiritual beliefs trouble me.	0	1	2	3	4
21. I have lost my desire to worship.	0	1	2	3	4
22. I no longer feel safe and protected by God, knowing that anything can happen to anyone.	0	1	2	3	4
23. My spiritual community might reject me because of the way that my loss has re-shaped my spiritual beliefs.	0	1	2	3	4
24. I feel like I have been robbed of the future God had planned for me.	0	1	2	3	4
25. I go out of my way to avoid spiritual/religious activities (e.g., prayer, worship, Bible reading).	0	1	2	3	4
26. I have walked away from my faith.	0	1	2	3	4

	0	1	2	3	4
27. I find it difficult to pray.	0	1	2	3	4
28. I have withdrawn from my spiritual community.	0	1	2	3	4

OPEN-ENDED ITEMS

If your spiritual struggle has been experienced in ways not covered by the items above, please add your statements below:

	0	1	2	3	4
1. _____	0	1	2	3	4
2. _____	0	1	2	3	4
3. _____	0	1	2	3	4
4. _____	0	1	2	3	4
5. _____					

Notes:

The ICSG 2.0 is placed in the public domain to encourage its use in clinical assessment and research. No formal permission is therefore required for its reproduction and use by others, beyond appropriate citation of the present article.

Scoring Instructions:

A total ICSG 2.0 score can be calculated by summing all 28 items and dividing that sum by 28.

Subscales by item #

(calculated by summing the items and dividing by the number of items in parentheses):

Estrangement from Spiritual Community (9): 1, 3, 5, 7, 10, 16, 17, 18, 23

Insecurity with God (13): 2, 4, 6, 8, 11, 12, 13, 14, 15, 19, 20, 22, 24

Disruption in Religious Practices (6): 9, 21, 25, 26, 27, 28

the loss. Elise's crisis of faith and struggle with her spiritual community following her loss is not an uncommon experience. Below are selected narratives from research participants showing other examples of CSG:

In Relation to God

When given the opportunity, spiritually inclined grievers were forthright in terms of sharing their feelings of insecurity in their relationship with God following devastating loss:

> "I am crushed. How could you (God) let him die? Why didn't you save him?"

> "I felt angry ... that God was abusing me [through her death]. I felt confused. Why would the God that I love and honor allow this to happen to me? I felt lost (depressed) and began to hurt myself [because] it was the only way to take the pain away."

> "Is God still a healer? If Jesus died on the cross for us to be made whole, free from sin, loss, and disease, [then] why did my dad die when he believed that he was healed?"

In Relation to the Griever's Spiritual Community

Survivors in our sample unequivocally reported experiencing a sense of estrangement and lack of support following their loss, which seemed to not only increase their distress but also compromised their relationships with other believers:

> "The majority of those in my spiritual community haven't the foggiest notion of what it feels like to lose a loved one to homicide. The only ones who were of any comfort were the individuals who had experienced the same horror. I tired of the others' clichés such as 'God makes no mistakes,' so I avoided them."

> "I felt abandon, No one knew how to deal with my pain, and I was angry because they didn't try to help."

> "I was very angry. I felt judged by my close friend who was also a pastor at my previous church. Like I was crazy or something for being so angry and having feelings that I didn't understand."

> "Most that I was in contact with before the loss seemed to have all the answers, but after my son's death they had none. But instead of saying that, they just abandoned me and my family. We were left alone with our grief. Eventually we left that particular place of worship and found a new place."

"I … worry about my granddaughter …she saw her mother murdered. I can't talk to the spiritual community about this. I don't feel that they really care."

"I thought I could rely on them, but they grew tired of trying to console me and took advantage of my vulnerability. They said they would be there for me, but I didn't realize there was a time limit."

"I felt that I was wronged by those in the spiritual community, because I was told to 'live right' and God would bless me. I knew that struggles would happen but not something as senseless as my baby dying. I felt a struggle between my faith and my feelings of anger, sadness, and terror."

Substantial Changes in Grievers' Spiritual Beliefs and Behaviors

Unsurprisingly, the emotional distress felt by mourners with CSG was exhibited in abandonment or modification of their actions and long-held spiritual beliefs:

"My loss challenged my relationship with my particular denomination. I lost faith in their 'way of life.' I no longer see the need to participate in the rituals or rules that this community holds as truths of godliness and holiness."

"I cut all ties with the spiritual community I had at the time of [deceased]'s death … and sought a megachurch where I was anonymous and everyone thought of me as a regular person not a crime victim."

"I became a bench member rather than an active member, and I now attend church [about half as often as I used to]."

"I am very troubled [and] very confused. [I'm] not sure what to believe in or trust on."

Sensing God's Absence

For some Christians, to acknowledge an inability to sense God's nearness in the midst of life's greatest storms is tantamount to heresy. In fact, oft-quoted Bible verses assure the believer that God will definitely show up when needed and that his mere presence will bring comfort when he does:

"I long for the presence of God, to feel him near. By presence I mean a strong sense of peace [that I right now don't have]."

"I felt that God was not there. At times I wondered if there was a God."

Afterlife Concerns

The example below of emotional distress surrounding the *not knowing* how or where the deceased loved is one represents countless other examples expressed by grievers using similar words across many multiple study participants:

> "Will I see [deceased] again? Did he/she go to heaven?"

Spirituality as Both Solace and Struggle

Finally, consistent with other studies (Burke & Neimeyer, 2014; Burke et al., 2011) we found that grievers can simultaneously experience their faith as a source of both strength and strife:

> "I felt conflicted about God, I felt that God had allowed the capriciousness of life to invade our world. I wondered aloud if our entire family and our belief system were merely a cosmic joke. I questioned God as to why he permitted such a painful and horrendous act when he had the power to stop it. This was particularly troublesome because [my loved one] was trying so hard to stay out of trouble and avoid bad contacts. We, as a family, were so hopeful. All those hopes were dashed by one bullet from a murderous young man's gun. On the other hand, I knew from past experience that the only way I could get through this trauma with any degree of sanity was by leaning on God, relying on His strength and the peace that only he can give in times of dire stress. Therefore, while I cried in anger and disappointment, I prayed to Him for strength and comfort."

> "I felt forsaken by God, yet as I cried out to God in my grief, I was also deeply comforted by Him (even though this was really hard to go through)."

> "I despised God for taking away the person I loved most in the world. Yet, when I would finish screaming at Him, I felt more acceptance from Him than I would have ever anticipated."

Discussion

Complicated spiritual grief is a crisis of faith that occurs during bereavement that is characterized by disharmony and relational distance between the griever and his or her deity and/or faith community. CSG has been associated with other forms of bereavement distress, including CG, PTSD, and depression, and is more prevalent in survivors of violent death loss.

Given how traumatic the death of a loved one can be, and knowing that some grievers struggle with their loss more so than do others, and because of the relation between high levels of grief distress and CSG, it raises the question of whether CSG might affect other aspects of the bereavement experience for those who are spiritually inclined, specifically when it comes to ongoing interactions with the deceased. For instance, one might speculate that if a griever struggles in terms of his or her relationship with God and/or faith community that this might affect his or her ability to interact with their deceased loved one, as well. Perhaps much in the same way that for some people with CSG God seems distant and unapproachable—not present during their especially troubling time of loss—that the connection with the one who died, likewise, might seem difficult to establish or that the deceased's presence might be hard to find and/or feel. Moreover, inasmuch as it is common for grievers to express anger at their deceased loved one for leaving them prematurely by dying (Root, 2011), it seems reasonable that that type of discord might, in turn, preclude the survivor's inclination to initiate an ongoing connection with the deceased during bereavement.

Conversely, it might be just as true that when bereaved individuals experience CSG and their relationship with God and/or their faith community is compromised that they, in fact, might be *more* not less inclined to try to connect with the person that they lost. Perhaps establishing and maintaining an ongoing connection with the deceased is a means of spiritual coping, especially when their other spiritual relationships have been undermined by loss and grief. On the other hand, when survivors feel concerned about the whereabouts of their loved one (e.g., heaven, hell, or otherwise), or wonder whether they are okay, safe, or content in the afterlife, does this make them less likely to attempt to reach out to the deceased or seek their presence? More extensive research is needed to explore bereavement experiences such as these that are more nuanced with regard to the intersection of spiritual struggle in bereavement and maintaining an ongoing attachment with the deceased. Elise's experience highlights this need and also the type of support that might be most helpful when someone experiences CSG:

> When the pain of grief and spiritual struggle became more than she could bear and began to negatively affect a number of areas of her life, Elise sought assistance from a psychologist specializing in traumatic death loss. Fortunately, the therapeutic relationship that was forged allowed honest expression of the wide array of emotions she was experiencing, both with regard to her spiritual community and with God. Whereas for a long time she was unable to pray, read the Bible, or attend church, Elise's work in therapy and her own reconstruction of her spiritual beliefs and needs aided in repairing and healing some of her spiritual wounds. Slowly, she created what

she referred to as a "new relationship" with God and found a congregation that better suited who she was now, several years after the death. In addition, she took great comfort in feeling Jed's presence in specific ways at specific times, such as during her daily walks on the beach near their home. "He comes to me in the clouds, with a new cloud formation every day. I know it sounds crazy, but I know it's him. It's like God has reopened the clouds of connection between us. And all I know is that it brings me great comfort."

References

Burke, L.A., Clark, K.A., Ali, K.S., Gibson, B.W., Smigelsky, M.A., & Neimeyer, R.A. (2015). Risk factors for anticipatory grief in family members of terminally ill veterans receiving palliative care services. *Journal of Social Work in End-of-Life & Palliative Care, 11*(3-4), 244–266. doi: 10.1080/15524256.2015.1110071

Burke, L.A., Crunk, A.E., Neimeyer, R.A., & Bai, H. (2019). Inventory of Complicated Spiritual Grief 2.0 (ICSG 2.0): Validation of a revised measure of spiritual distress in bereavement. *Death Studies*, 1–17. doi: 10.1080/07481187. 2019.1627031

Burke, L.A., & Neimeyer, R.A. (2013). Prospective risk factors for complicated grief: A review of the empirical literature. In M.S. Stroebe, H. Schut, J. van der Bout, & P. Boelen (Eds.), *Complicated grief: Scientific foundations for health-care professionals*. New York: Routledge, pp. 145–161.

Burke, L.A., & Neimeyer, R.A. (2014). Complicated spiritual grief I: Relation to complicated grief symptomatology following violent death bereavement. *Death Studies, 38*, 259–267. doi: 10.1080/07481187.2013.829372

Burke, L.A., Neimeyer, R.A., Bottomley, J.S., & Smigelsky, M.A. (2017). Prospective risk factors for intense grief in family members of Veterans who died of terminal illness. *Illness, Crisis, & Loss, 27*(3), 147–171. doi: 10.1177/1054137317699580

Burke, L.A., Neimeyer, R.A., Holland, J.M., Dennard, S., Oliver, L., & Shear, K.M. (2014). Inventory of Complicated Spiritual Grief scale: Development and initial validation of a new measure. *Death Studies, 38*, 239–250. doi: 10.1080/07481187.2013.810098

Burke, L.A., Neimeyer, R.A., McDevitt-Murphy, M.E., Ippolito, M.R., & Roberts, J.M. (2011). In the wake of homicide: Spiritual crisis and bereavement distress in an African American sample. *International Journal for Psychology of Religion, 21*, 1–19. doi: 10.1080/10508619.2011.60741

Burke, L.A., Neimeyer, R.A., Young, M.J., Piazza Bonin, B., & Davis, N.L. (2014). Complicated spiritual grief II: A deductive inquiry following the loss of a loved one. *Death Studies, 38*, 268–281. doi: 10.1080/07481187.2013.829373

Crunk, A.E., Burke, L.A., Neimeyer, R.A., Robinson, E.H., & Bai, H. (2019). The *Coping Assessment for Bereavement and Loss Experiences* (CABLE): Development and initial validation. *Death Studies, 45*(9), 1–15.

Galatzer-Levy, I.R., & Bonanno, G.A. (2012). Beyond normality in the study of bereavement: Heterogeneity in depression outcomes following loss in older adults. *Social Science & Medicine (1982), 74*(12), 1987–1994. 10.1016/j.socscimed.2012. 02.022

Hill, P.C., & Pargament, K.I. (2008). Advances in the conceptualization and measurement of religion and spirituality: Implications for physical and mental health research. *Psychology of Religion and Spirituality, 1,* 3–17.

Lichtenthal, W.G., Currier, J.M., Neimeyer, R.A., & Keesee, N.J. (2010). Sense and significance: A mixed methods examination of meaning making after the loss of one's child. *Journal of Clinical Psychology, 66*(7), 791–812.

Pargament, K., Smith, B., Koenig, H., & Perez, L. (1998). Patterns of positive and negative religious coping with major life stressors. *Journal for the Scientific Study of Religion, 37,* 710–724.

Prigerson, H.G., & Jacobs, S.C. (2001). Traumatic grief as a distinct disorder. In M.S. Stroebe, R.O. Hansson, W. Stroebe, & H. Schut (Eds.), *Handbook of bereavement research.* Washington, DC: American Psychological Association, pp. 613–645.

Root, B.L. (2011). *Bereaved individuals' feelings of anger toward deceased family members: A mixed methods approach* (Doctoral dissertation, Case Western Reserve University).

Steffen, E., & Coyle, A. (2011) Sense of presence experiences and meaning making in bereavement: A qualitative analysis. *Death Studies, 35*(7), 579–609.

Steffen, E., & Coyle, A. (2012). "Sense of presence" experiences in bereavement and their relationship to mental health: A critical examination of a continuing controversy. In *Mental health and anomalous experience. Psychology research progress.* Hauppauge, NY: Nova Science Publishers, pp. 33–56.

Wortmann, J.H., & Park, C.L. (2008). Religion and spirituality in adjustment following bereavement: An integrative review. *Death Studies, 32,* 703–736.

15 Psychic Mediums for the Bereaved: Exploring Their Procedures and Contemplating the Use of Their Services

Camille B. Wortman[1]

Introduction

Following the death of a loved one, some individuals choose to consult with a psychic medium. Mediumship can be defined as the alleged ability to communicate with people who are deceased. Although many people use the words "medium" and "psychic" interchangeably, there are notable differences between the two. Mediums claim to be intermediaries between the living and the dead (Beischel et al., 2014–2015); conversely, psychics assert that they can read peoples' minds and predict the future (Kelly & Arcangel, 2011). This chapter emphasizes the work of mediums because they purport to put bereaved people in touch with their deceased loved ones whereas psychics do not. The terminology is confusing because at times both mediums and psychics are referred to as *psychic mediums*. Throughout the chapter, the words "psychic mediums" and "mediums" are meant to highlight the work of those who are believed to be communicating with people who are deceased.

Although there are no systematic studies regarding the percentage of bereaved individuals who seek the services of a medium, therapists who work with the bereaved report that this is a common occurrence (Beischel et al., 2014–2015). Consequently, grief therapists are highly likely to encounter clients who want to see a medium or have already done so. Thus, grief therapists may be asked to offer an opinion about the value of seeing a medium and may request assistance in locating one. Similarly, clients who have consulted with a medium may confide this to their therapist, hoping that the therapist will support their decision. In fact, in the Beischel et al. study, 29 participants (59%) told their mental health professional (MHP) about their reading.

It is important, therefore, for therapists to understand why bereaved individuals choose to see a medium and how they are likely to be affected by such an encounter. This chapter begins by addressing the following questions: How prevalent is the belief that mediums can communicate with the dead? What percentage of bereaved individuals seek out their services? What reservations do people have about the legitimacy of mediums' claims?

DOI: 10.4324/9781003105077-19

This is followed by a discussion of the types of individuals who are most likely to have a reading done by a medium. (A *reading* is the meeting during which a medium conveys information that allegedly comes from the deceased. The individual or group of people participating in a reading is often referred to as *sitters*.) Next, the author addresses the types of messages typically received in a reading. This is followed by a review of the scientific research on the perceived benefits of consulting a medium. Drawing from the research, the author summarizes the implications for best practice. The chapter concludes with recommendations for future research.

Case Study

Readers of this chapter have a right to know whether the author holds favorable or unfavorable attitudes toward mediums. When Dr. Wortman started working with bereaved individuals over 40 years ago, she had no strong feelings one way or another about mediums. However, she occasionally encountered a bereaved person who sought the services of a medium. For example, she worked with a woman named Joan whose college-aged son, David, was murdered on his way home from soccer practice. Joan sought therapy immediately after David was killed and continued seeing a therapist for more than a year. She said that she liked her therapist but did not find the sessions very helpful in coming to terms with her son's death. Five years after David's death, Joan was struggling, and her pain was still raw. Joan explained that because she was feeling so despondent, she decided to go to a medium in hopes of speaking with David. She contacted her therapist, who encouraged Joan to do so.

Dr. Wortman noticed a change in Joan's voice one day during a phone call. For the first time, she sounded different. There was a slight up note when Joan spoke that had not been present previously. She said, "Dr. Wortman, I went to a medium. I can't wait to tell you about it." Joan told Dr. Wortman that at the beginning of the session, the medium said that David wanted to see his wallet. Only Joan knew that she had been carrying her son's wallet in her purse since the day he had died. The medium also reported that David had a tattoo on his foot with two wings and that his favorite food was sauerkraut, both of which were true. What impressed Joan the most is something that occurred at the end of the reading. The medium told her that David wanted to share one more thing. He said, "Don't worry, Mom. You'll always be my number one girl." Joan said that her son would always say this to her before he went out on a date. It is Dr. Wortman's belief that this encounter jumpstarted Joan's healing and helped her begin to move forward with her life.

Belief in Psychics and Mediums

To the author's knowledge, there are only a handful of formal opinion polls that have examined the frequency of beliefs in psychics or mediums in recent years. A 2009 Pew Research Poll (Many Americans mix multiple faiths, 2009) showed that 15% of the respondents consulted a fortune teller or psychic. In a poll conducted eight years later, the Pew Research Center found that 41% of all American adults believe in psychics (Gecewicz, 2018).

In a 2017 YouGov poll, 10% of Americans responded that they had been to a psychic or medium multiple times, 12% had gone once, and 10% indicated that they "would like to in the future." The poll also captured skepticism of psychics and mediums, with 62% responding "no, and I have no intention of doing so." Interestingly, 21% of all of the respondents indicated that they believed that "there are individuals with the ability to contact the dead" (Bame, 2017). Similarly, a 2016 Canadian study by the Angus Reid Institute (Soloducha, 2018) reported that 36% of the participants believed that it is possible to communicate with the dead. Taken together, these polls demonstrate that a portion of our population believe that there is an ability for those who are living to receive messages from our loved ones who are not.

These figures also suggest that there is a demand for the services of psychics and mediums. Perhaps one reason for this is the intense interest in mediums in the media, many of whom have gained international fame. One example is Theresa Caputo. Her reality television program, *Long Island Medium*, is currently in its 15th season. Caputo is a three-time *New York Times* bestselling author and has a waiting list that is more than two years long. Another famous celebrity psychic medium is James Van Praagh, who has produced and starred in several prime-time television shows, including *Living with the Dead*. He has also written several *New York Times* bestsellers. Both Caputo and Van Praagh tour the United States, working with live audiences. Americans are fascinated by the idea that it is possible to contact the dead, which likely is why these mediums have been so phenomenally successful. In fact, a September 2018 Market Report on Psychic Services in the United States estimated a total industry revenue of $2.2 billion in 2018 and predicted continued growth in the future.

In their advertisements, psychic mediums claim that they can help people discover what they want out of life, assist them in making important life decisions, or put them in touch with a loved one who has died. However, unlike many other service professions throughout the United States, there are no industry guidelines that psychic mediums must follow to substantiate these claims. For example, there are "no standardized education requirements" for psychics or mediums (HG.org, n.d.), and virtually anyone can set up a training program. Many are started by celebrity mediums, such as James Van Praagh's School of Mystical Arts. On his website, Van Praagh claims that his school offers "one of the most in-depth and well-regarded psychic and mediumship certification programs available today" when, in fact, no agreed-upon criteria for certification exist.

On many occasions, psychic mediums have been subjected to harsh criticism. For example, they have been described as driven by financial motives above all else (Osborne & Bacon, 2015). In addition, Olson (2019) stated that some psychics mediums have "outlandish business practices," which have hurt the profession as a whole (p. 2). He indicated that some psychics and mediums do not charge a preset amount, but rather a fee based on each minute spent talking with the client. For example, if the psychic medium charges $5.99 per minute, this amounts to $359.40 per hour. Some psychic mediums charge as much as $15.00 per minute ($900 per hour). It is unlikely that any client could anticipate the overall cost of such a reading in advance. Olson (2019) also called out unscrupulous psychic mediums who are skilled at keeping callers on the line. To illustrate how predatory some psychic mediums can be, Olson (2019) drew the following analogy: "Imagine consulting a lawyer online who offered his first name only ... and asked for your credit card in order to charge you by the minute with no agreed-upon time limitation" (p. 3).

Another criticism often raised about mediums is that they willingly provide advice about issues for which they have no expertise, such as health. For example, psychic mediums might be asked whether the client should seek a particular treatment for a chronic health condition (Macdonald, 2021). Even worse, most mediums have not received training in disciplines that are directly relevant to their work, such as grief, trauma, or mental health. Osborne and Bacon (2015) have emphasized that this is very problematic, since in many cases, sitters are emotionally vulnerable and tend to be trusting of mediums. This sets the stage for sitters to experience psychological harm at the hands of mediums who may have little understanding of the grieving process. According to Osborne and Bacon (2015), it is imperative that mediums have some basic knowledge of mental health and other psychological issues known to influence grieving, which seems especially important given their claims of being able to connect the griever with their deceased loved one. In fact, they advised mediums to keep a list of MHPs who have had some training in mediumship or, at the very least, that they themselves are open-minded about the important role that MHP plays in the grieving process.

Who Is Most Likely to Seek the Services of a Medium and Why?

Despite the importance of these questions, the author is not aware of any rigorous empirical studies that have addressed them. However, the findings from three qualitative bereavement studies on the topic are relevant.

Each is based on a small number of observations (Walliss, 2001; Walter, 2008) and/or interviews with sitters (Baugher, 2013), mediums (Walliss, 2001), or bereavement counselors (Walter, 2008). Both Walliss (2001) and Walter (2008) reported that parents who lose a child are especially likely to seek the service of a medium. In addition, both authors found that individuals are more likely to contact a medium if the loss occurred under violent circumstances, such as murder or suicide. Walter (2008) identified another group of grievers who are likely to visit a medium: people who had a troubled relationship with the deceased. These bereaved individuals tended to contact a medium in an effort to repair the relationship by asking for the deceased for forgiveness.

In her work with bereaved parents, Dr. Wortman learned that there are several reasons why bereaved individuals seek out the services of a medium. First, consulting a medium eases what many see as the most excruciating part of grief—that their loved one is gone forever. Many bereaved individuals comment that they would give anything if they could have one more day, or even one more hour with their loved one. Wolterstorff (1987) stated that the hardest thing about his son's death was the *neverness* of it. He explained how heart-wrenching it was that they would never have dinner together, and he would never go to his son's soccer games. Mr. Wolterstorff said that he could deal with the prospect of waiting one year, even five years, to see his son, but emphasized that the recognition that he would never see his son again was unbearable. Another man expressed similar feelings when he said, "You think their dying is the worst thing imaginable. Then they stay dead" (personal communication, July 6, 2014).

A second reason why bereaved individuals may meet with a medium is because they have deep concern about whether their loved one still exists in some form. As one father said, "The main question I struggled with after Jake died was where he was. Was he gone forever or existing in some other reality? Was he safe, comfortable? Was he calling out to me and his mother wondering where we were?" (personal communication, November 6, 2015).

Third, bereaved individuals may seek out a medium because they are preoccupied with whether and how much their loved one suffered. This is most likely to occur in cases where a child died, when the death occurred under violent circumstances, or there was harm to the body. As one father explained it, "I have nightmares about how my son struggled with his killer" (personal communication, January 6, 2017). The bereaved may also experience other troubling thoughts, such as: "Did my daughter know she was going to die?," "Did she see it coming?," or "Did she experience intense fear or terror?" (personal communication, March 18, 2018).

A fourth reason, mentioned above, is that people seek mediums in an effort to ameliorate feelings of remorse and to ask for forgiveness from the deceased. Bereaved parents, in particular, are likely to struggle with powerful feelings of guilt. As Rosof (1994) expressed it, "Your job as a parent was to protect your child, and you could not" (p. 15).

Additionally, the bereaved may reach out to a medium because they have been unable to obtain support from those in their social network. This is especially likely to occur among parents who have lost a child. Feigelman, Jordan, McIntosh, and Feigelman (2012) conducted a study of bereaved parents, most of whom had lost a child to suicide. They examined comments made by the parents and found three recurrent themes. First, parents experienced a wall of silence, where other people studiously avoided all discussions about their deceased child. Second, parents reported that others seemed uncaring, and rarely asked about the survivors' well-being. Third, virtually all parents received advice from others that they found unhelpful. The authors maintained that, for the most part, others could not appreciate that the ramifications of the death of a child can last for a lifetime. Parents were deeply hurt by such statements as "Why are you still going to that support group?" or "Isn't it time you moved on?" (p. 53). Such comments tend to leave the bereaved person feeling that no one understands what they are going through.

In her work with bereaved parents, Dr. Wortman encountered other bereaved individuals who, like Joan, experienced dramatic shifts in their well-being and peace of mind following a reading with a medium. She noted that this marked shift in perspective typically occurred in a single session. The man mentioned earlier who was tortured by thoughts about his son made the following comment after one meeting with a psychic medium,

> All of my questions were laid to rest when I connected with Jake. Now I know that he is happy and well cared for. This has put my mind at ease and enabled me to put my attention to other things, like my marriage, my job, and my relationship with my surviving son. (personal communication, November 6, 2014)

His remarks are consistent with Baugher's (2013) statement that, following a reading, many people experience instantaneous relief of unremitting pain.

Types of Messages Received

Research has shown that there is a striking parallel between why people go to a medium and the content of the messages that are received. Beischel et al. (2014–2015) and Walliss (2001) found that in every reading they examined, there were messages indicating that the loved one still exists (e.g., "I'm OK here.") In almost all cases, the deceased reported that they did not suffer at the time of death. It was common for the deceased to indicate a continuing connection with their loved one, such as "I'm still here for you" or "I'm watching over you." Sometimes the deceased made statements that were very specific, such as "I'm glad you decided to take the new job." There were many cases in which the deceased offered advice to the bereaved. Comments like "You have grieved enough" or "It's time to start dating again" occurred frequently. According to Wallis, such advice was meant to encourage the bereaved to move on. The most frequent type of message that mediums tended to pass along involved sending love to bereaved individuals (e.g., "I will always love you;" p. 134). These statements were ubiquitous and were sometimes offered several times in a reading. Messages of forgiveness were also extremely common, with the deceased making comments such as "There is no way you could have prevented my death."

Taken as a whole, these comments seemed to imply that the deceased continued to observe and participate in the life of the bereaved. Thus, our review of the literature indicated that, for the most part, the messages that mediums give to the bereaved are designed to alleviate their concerns and give them peace of mind. As Beischel et al. (2014–2015) have stated, mediums recognize what the bereaved want to hear and cater to this.

Scientific Studies Pertaining to Mediums

There is a large body of research involving mediumship, most of which focuses on bereaved adults who have lost a spouse. Virtually all of these studies have focused on the accuracy of mediums' statements about deceased persons (e.g., Beischel et al., 2014–2015; Kelly & Arcangel, 2011; Rock, 2014). This chapter does not address the question of whether mediums can communicate with the deceased; rather, it focuses solely on the following question: Do bereaved individuals believe they have been helped by mediums? If so, how does the experience help them to cope more effectively with their loss? To date, only two empirical studies have addressed these questions, and both have serious methodological shortcomings. Notwithstanding their limitations, each of these studies provides powerful evidence that mediums can play a vital role in helping the bereaved. Each will be discussed in turn.

In 2012, Feigelman et al. (2012) conducted a survey of parents whose child had died. They collected data from a convenience sample of 575 parents of children of all ages, making their study the largest-ever sample of bereaved parents. Parents were recruited largely through support groups, including the American Foundation of Suicide Prevention and The Compassionate Friends. Of the 575 cases, 80% of the children died by suicide. Other causes of death were drug overdoses, automobile accidents, homicide, and natural deaths (e.g., cancer, heart disease). The vast majority of children who died were male.

A major goal of the Feigelman et al. (2012) study was to determine where parents turned for help in dealing with their child's death. They identified six sources that were most frequently utilized by the respondents:

support groups for survivors of suicide, general bereavement support groups, grief counselors, MHPs (e.g., psychologists, psychiatrists, social workers), clergy persons, and psychics. The authors report that only 20% of the bereaved parents did not utilize any type of help. Twenty-three percent used one resource only, 26% used two, and 31% used three or more resources. Support groups (suicide and general bereavement groups) were the most frequently used resource, followed by MHPs and bereavement counselors. The number of respondents who went to psychics was considerably lower—approximately 25% of respondents visited a psychic sometime during the first seven years following their loss, and approximately 30% of those did so during the first two years.

Next, the investigators (Feigelman et al., 2012) examined which bereavement resources were rated as most and least helpful. Support groups for survivors of suicide was the highest rated of all the resources, with 43.8% of bereaved parents rating them as "very helpful." The second highest was psychics (34.6%). General bereavement groups were rated third (31.6%), followed by grief counselors (27%), and MHPs (25.7%). Members of the clergy received the lowest rating of all the sources studied (21.5%). It is interesting to note that psychics were rated almost 9% higher than MHPs. (Because participants were recruited largely through support groups, results regarding how frequently support groups were utilized, and how beneficial they were, might be artificially inflated.)

Feigelman et al. (2012) also assessed the percentage of respondents who rated sources as of "little or no help." For bereaved parents who consulted psychics, the percentage viewing that source as of "little or no help" was quite small (24%). This was lower than any other source of help except for support groups for survivors of suicide (22.2%). Fully one-third of the respondents rated MHPs as of "little or no help." In fact, they were rated as "of little or no help" more frequently than any of the other sources of help that were studied. Based on these findings, Feigelman et al. (2012) concluded that "the help that bereaved experience from psychics is likely to remain an enduring feature in the bereavement resource landscape" (p. 145).

In addition, Feigelman et al. (2012) found that the percentage of bereaved parents who sought out psychics was influenced by the cause of death. They reported that over half of the bereaved parents whose child died of a drug overdose turned to a psychic, compared to 31% for all other bereaved parents. Feigelman et al. (2012) highlighted that the parent/child relationship is often strained when a child struggles with an addiction. The authors pointed out that

> psychics often play a special role in helping to heal [their relationship] ... Psychics frequently offer comforting reassurance that the child continues on in another plane, that they are well and healed, and that the child wishes the parents to heal and continue on with their lives. (pp. 145–146)

To the author's knowledge, there is only one peer-reviewed journal article that has examined the perceived effectiveness of mediums. Beischel et al. (2014–2015) conducted a pilot study to address the following question: Do bereaved individuals regard their experience with a medium as helpful in ameliorating their grief? As noted previously, the study has many methodological shortcomings. To recruit participants, the investigators sent an email to mediums[2] describing the study. The mediums were asked to forward a message to people on their email lists inviting them to complete an anonymous survey. Specifically, the investigators requested that the mediums select "an accurate representation of different kinds of people from those on their mailing list," and not handpick only those who had a good or healing experience. A total of 83 participants completed the survey. Over 90% (*n* = 75) of the respondents were female and their mean age was 52. The mean time between the loved one's death and the participant receiving a reading was three years. Using a scale ranging from "none" (0) to "very high" (4), the participants were asked to provide retrospective ratings of their grief prior to and following their reading with a medium. The researchers reported that respondents' before-and-after ratings showed a sizeable drop in grief: from 3.13 ("somewhat high") to 1.96 ("somewhat low").

A subset of the respondents (*n* = 29) worked with a MHP in addition to a medium. These individuals were asked to rate their level of grief before and after their work with the MHP, using the same five-point grief scale. Ratings went from 3.69 (with 4 being "very high") to 2.93 ("somewhat high"). These results suggested that respondents were helped more by mediums than by MHPs. As the authors themselves pointed out, this study had many methodological shortcomings. Participants were not randomly chosen; instead, the pool of participants was hand-selected by the mediums. Ratings of grief were retrospective. Grief was assessed using a single item rather than a grief scale with demonstrated validity and reliability. The sample size was quite small (*n* = 83), this is especially the case for those who worked with a MHP as well as a medium (*n* = 29). The authors emphasized that because of these weaknesses, the findings should be regarded as preliminary.

Best Clinical Practices

According to Beischel et al. (2014–2015), the interests of the client are best served when MHPs and mediums work together. In an excellent discussion of this topic, these authors emphasize that collaboration between MHPs and mediums will require additional instruction for both. Specifically, they maintain that it is critical for MHPs to receive training about mediums and the role they can play in helping those who are mourning. Without such education, MHPs may respond harshly to clients who reveal that they have visited a medium or plan to do so.

To date, no studies have examined how therapists react to clients who raise the subject of mediums. However, Taylor (2005) conducted a qualitative study of bereaved people who reported that they sensed the presence of the deceased and brought it up with their therapist. According to Taylor, participants reported that they were satisfied with their counselor's response to this revelation in only 4 of the 21 counseling experiences. The researcher regarded these findings as "… surprising and shocking… Participants all described feeling unaccepted, abnormal, not understood, unable to connect to counselors, and they had received no empathy" (p. 60). This is a single study of a small number or mourners, the findings of which may not generalize to the larger population of bereaved adults. Nonetheless, the results have important implications. If MHPs react this harshly to clients who report sensing the presence of the deceased, how will they respond to clients who have visited a medium?

Taylor's (2005) study implied that, if not explored carefully in treatment, the issue of presence within absence may compromise or even jeopardize the client/therapist relationship. This type of risk is also evident when clients mention psychic mediums. As one therapist emphasized,

> If a bereaved person wants to consult with a psychic, it's not my place to dissuade them or scoff at their need. It is my place, and my duty, to talk with them about what they hope to gain from the consultation and how they'll cope with what they might hear. It's also my responsibility to psychologically process it with them afterwards. (Pearlman, Wortman, Feuer, Farber, & Rando, 2014, p. 224)

Bidwell Smith (2015), an author and therapist specializing in grief, has provided specific guidance in her online article about how to support those who plan to visit a medium. She advised the bereaved to "review your current state of grief" before visiting a psychic medium. She recommended that those who are "still deep" in their grief to "seek individual counseling in order to find more solid ground before seeing a medium." Bidwell Smith also advised that following a reading, the bereaved "write your initial thoughts and impressions down as soon as possible." She added, "It's helpful to review the process later from a more grounded state." A similar opinion was expressed by Baugher (2013), who recommended that MHPs elicit a detailed account of the sitting from the client. Specifically, Baugher (2013) counseled MHPs to ask their clients to identify which aspects of the reading were helpful and which were not. He suggested that in discussing the reading with the client, the MHP should explore whether the sitting affected issues pertaining to grief resolution, such as yearning, intrusive thoughts, and guilt.

For those clients who have indicated a desire to see a medium, Rando's (2014) opinion is that it is the therapist's obligation to help them with the process of locating one. Rando recommended that therapists draw on information from previous and current clients, as well as other therapists, to compile a list of mediums for referrals. Therapists who are not comfortable engaging in conversations about psychic mediums with their clients may want to consider referring them to a colleague who is willing to do so.

Summary

Most grief experts would agree that it is not uncommon for the bereaved to seek the services of a medium. In all likelihood, those who visit a medium do so because they are experiencing distress as a result of their loved one's death. Further, many grief experts would likely endorse the view that a good session with a medium can facilitate the healing process, while a bad session can result in psychological harm. As psychic medium Morning Star (n.d.) expressed it like this,

> One session with a qualified, reputable medium has the potential to do more for your peace of mind than years of grief counseling. Sadly, one session with an unqualified medium can cause you extreme angst at the worst possible time of your life and may increase your sorrow.

Given a medium's potential to have a positive impact on the bereaved, one would expect to find a number of rigorous quantitative studies assessing whether this is indeed the case. Surprisingly, not one methodologically rigorous, quantitative study has appeared in the scientific literature. The two studies described previously, Feigelman et al. (2012) and Beischel et al. (2014–2015), have produced findings suggesting that mediums can be effective in helping the bereaved come to terms with their loss and move forward with their lives. Moreover, respondents in both studies reportedly rated mediums as more helpful than MHPs. These findings are noteworthy when one considers the investment of time and money in seeking help from a medium as compared to a therapist. The author is not aware of any studies assessing the average number of times a bereaved person consults a medium versus that of an MHP. Yet it is reasonable to assume that most people consult a medium on one or two occasions whereas it is not uncommon for people to see a counselor for months, or even years, especially following a traumatic death loss.

The author maintains that the bereaved are likely to benefit from a reading if they need reassurance that their loved one exists in some form, that their loved one did not suffer, and that the deceased forgives them for perceived transgressions. While a single visit to a medium may provide answers to these questions and even bring a level of comfort to the mourner, there are many other bereavement-related issues that cannot be addressed in a single sitting. For example, a woman who lost a spouse may benefit from a discussion of the secondary losses she is experiencing, such as the loss of a caring presence day-by-day, a co-parent, and a sexual partner. A therapist may also be able to assist her in helping other family members deal with their grief. For example, she may benefit from her therapist's support in helping her son to navigate his first year in high school.

The information reviewed in this chapter indicates that both MHPs and mediums have a role to play in helping people process their grief. Some of the respondents in the study conducted by Beischel et al. (2014–2015) maintained that clients would benefit most if they could receive both of these treatments together. One respondent noted that these treatment modalities complement one another. As she expressed it, "The medium reached my heart, the social worker my mind" (p. 188).

Recommendations for Future Research

It would not be difficult to conduct rigorous empirical studies on the effectiveness of mediums. In each of the studies reviewed previously, respondents made a retrospective rating of the effectiveness of mediums, and the dependent variables were limited to one question: grief (Beischel et al., 2014–2015), or two questions: "little or no help" or "very helpful" (Feigelman et al., 2012). A prospective, longitudinal design assessing respondents prior to a session with a medium, and at various intervals thereafter, would be ideal. Collection of data could include reliable and valid assessments of grief, as well as other important constructs reflecting mental health (e.g., depression, anxiety, PTSD) and grief processing (e.g., yearning, intrusive thoughts, guilt). It would also be important to assess positive emotions, as well as the griever's level of functioning in important life roles.

Conclusion

When Joan, like many people who have lost a loved one (Feigelman et al., 2012), decided she needed help, she initially went to a therapist. But this had little impact on the resolution of her grief. In sharp contrast, her life began to change for the better after a single session with a medium. The support and encouragement of Joan's therapist played a key role in her decision to seek out a medium. Therapists are almost certain to encounter bereaved clients who have consulted a medium in the past, plan to in the future, have mixed feelings but are contemplating it, or are experiencing emotional turmoil because having a reading is altogether undesirable but they feel pressure from others to consider it. These clients will be best served if their therapist puts aside any preconceived notions they have about mediums and takes an open-minded approach. It is clear that more research is needed before this type of treatment can be embraced and widely recommended for use with grieving adults. Nonetheless, it is essential that we do so, because, as Feigelman et al. (2012) remind us, the use of psychics or mediums is not going away.

Notes

1 The author would like to acknowledge Jessica Gregory for the many important contributions she has made to this chapter.
2 Mediums were recruited from the Forever Family Foundation, Inc. (FFF) According to their website, the FFF's mission is to "educate the public about the evidence for life after physical death."

References

Bame, Y. (2017). "How common are psychic moments? 1 in 3 American feel that they have experienced one." *Today.yougov.com*. Retrieved May 12, 2021, from https://today.yougov.com/topics/entertainment/articles-reports/2017/10/31/1-3-americans-feel-they-have-experienced-psychic-m

Baugher, B. (2013). Psychics: Do they help or hinder the bereaved people? In S. Kreitler & H. Shanun-Klein (Eds.), *Studies of grief and bereavement: Psychology of emotions, motivations and actions*. New York: Nova.

Beischel, J., Mosher, C., & Boccuzzi, M. (2014–2015). The possible effects on bereavement of assisted after-death communication during readings with psychic mediums: A continuing bonds perspective. *Omega: Journal of Death and Dying, 70*(2), 169–194. doi: 10.2190/OM.70.2.b

Bidwell Smith, C. (2015). "5 things to do before visiting a psychic medium." *Modern Loss*. Retrieved May 12, 2021, from https://modernloss.com/5-things-to-do-before-visiting-a-psychic-medium/

Feigelman, W., Jordan, J.R., McIntosh, J.L., & Feigelman, B. (2012). *Devastating losses: How parents cope with the death of a child to suicide and drugs*. New York: Springer.

Forever Family Foundation. (n.d.). *Medium evaluation certification process*. Retrieved April 19, 2021, from https://www.foreverfamilyfoundation.org/pages/medium-evaluation-certification-process

Gecewicz, C. (2018). "New Age" beliefs common among both religious and nonreligious Americans. *Fact Tank: News in the Numbers*. Retrieved April 25, 2021, from https://www.pewresearch.org/fact-tank/2018/10/01/new-age-beliefs-common-among-both-religious-and-nonreligious-americans/

HG.org. (n.d.). Are there any laws that regulate psychics? HG.org. Retrieved April 25, 2021, from https://www.hg.org/legal-articles/are-there-any-laws-that-regulate-psychics-31845

Kelly, E.W., & Arcangel, D. (2011). An investigation of mediums who claim to give information about deceased persons. *Journal of Nervous and Mental Disease, 199*(1), 11–17. 10.1097/NMD.0b013e31820439da

Macdonald, F. (2021, January 15). What, if anything, can psychics tell us about all of this? *The New York Times*. https://www.nytimes.com/2021/01/15/style/did-you-predict-this.html

Many Americans mix multiple faiths. (2009). *Pew Research Center*. Retrieved April 25, 2021, from https://www.pewforum.org/2009/12/09/many-americans-mix-multiple-faiths/

Morning Star, Mollie. (n.d.). *Consumer advocacy*. Retrieved April 19, 2021, from http://www.molliemorningstar.com/consumer-advocacy

Olson, B. (2019). It's time for change in the psychic medium industry: A request for assistance. https://bestpsychicmediums.com/it's-time-change-psychic-medium-industry%20%E2%80%93%20-request-your-assistance

Osborne, G., & Bacon, A.M. (2015). The working life of a medium: A qualitative examination of mediumship as a support service for the bereaved. *Mental Health, Religion & Culture, 18*(4), 286–298.

Pearlman, L.A., Wortman, C.B., Feuer, C., Farber, C., & Rando, T. (2014). *Treating traumatic bereavement: A practitioner's guide.*

Rock, A.J. (Ed.). (2014). *The survival hypothesis: Essays on mediumship.* Jefferson, NC: McFarland.

Rosof, B.D. (1994). *The worst loss: How families heal from the death of a child.* New York: Henry Holt and Company.

Soloducha, A. (2018). My afternoon with a psychic was anything but predictable. *CBC.* Retrieved April 25, 2021, from https://www.cbc.ca/news/canada/saskatchewan/psychic-reading-in-your-shoes-1.4932741

Taylor, S.F. (2005). Between the idea and the reality: A study of the counseling experiences of the bereaved people who sense the presence of the deceased. *Counselling and Psychotherapy Research, 5*(1), 53–61.

Walliss, J. (2001). Continuing bonds: Relationships between the living and the dead within contemporary spiritualism. *Mortality, 6*, 127–145.

Walter, T. (2008). Mourners and mediums. *Bereavement Care, 27*(3), 47–50. doi: 10.1080/02682620808657727

Wolterstorff, N. (1987). *Lament for a son.* Grand Rapids, MI: Wm. B. Eerdmans Publishing.

Section IV
Existential Experiences

16 Restorative Connection with the Deceased: A Panel Interview with Grievers

Laurie A. Burke

The focus of this book has been to explore the numerous ways in which bereaved adults attempt to maintain an ongoing connection with their deceased loved ones. Grievers appear to maintain a continuing bond or sense the presence of the person who died in a variety of ways, many of which include aspects of their belief system or occurrences and connections associated with an ethereal world (e.g., through religion, spirituality, unsolicited encounters with the deceased). However, this book's relatively comprehensive approach to this topic would be incomplete without the inclusion of the lived experiences of bereaved individuals. This chapter reflects narratives from a panel of grievers who participated in a small conference on this topic, and who were recruited from the author's private practice in Portland, OR, where her area of specialty is working with bereaved adults. In response to a series of questions from the facilitator/author (LAB), each panelist was invited to share their experiences of solicited and unsolicited encounters with their deceased loved one, followed by questions from the audience.

After a brief welcome, the facilitator addressed the panelists, explaining the nature of their participation:

> You are each here because you have experienced some type of encounter or interaction with the person you lost. Some of these encounters are ones you solicited or sought out or hoped for, and other encounters are ones that came to you unbidden. Often times, these types of interactions, whether bidden or unbidden, can be particularly comforting or come just when you needed them most. But, for some people, these types of interactions can be unsettling, or raise questions about the afterlife or the well-being of the deceased.

After sharing panel members' biographical information with the audience, the facilitator invited each griever to introduce their deceased loved one (i.e., they briefly described what he/she was like, e.g., caring, smart, the life of the party) and, if willing, to briefly share their own beliefs about the afterlife, followed by sharing their encounter

DOI: 10.4324/9781003105077-21

experience(s). As well as providing prompting, the facilitator asked follow-up questions of each griever.

The first panelist, Rebecca, was 33 years old and was grieving the loss of her 66-year-old mother to suicide as a result of anti-freeze poisoning. Her mother had long struggled with chronic depression, which contributed greatly to her decision to end her life two years earlier. Rebecca was unable to participate as an in-person panelist; thus, her interview with LAB, which had been videotaped several weeks prior, was shared with the audience via video instead.

LAB: Rebecca, thank you so much for your willingness to share with us your experiences. Before we hear about those, would you be willing to describe your worldview or belief system, especially with regard to the afterlife?

Rebecca: I was raised Catholic but never practiced. I guess I would consider myself spiritual in adulthood. But, for my mom's sake, she had such a hard time being on this earth, it's hard to imagine her being here spiritually or emotionally. She spoke so much in the past about not wanting to be here. It's very comforting to me to think that she could exist happily in an afterlife.

LAB: And yet, she came to you, even though it doesn't fit into your or her worldview. Could you say more?

Rebecca: Six months after she passed away, I was having a series of anxiety attacks. I remember sitting on the bed with my husband next to me. Then I started experiencing for about 10 or 15 minutes having a very vivid sense of feeling something rubbing my back in a big circular motion, just like my mom used to do when we were young, even into adulthood when there was something bothering us. If we were upset, if we were crying, we'd sit on the edge of the bed and she'd rub our backs and listen to us. As soon as I felt that, it was this overwhelming sense of peace and comfort and support. Even though I don't believe in the afterlife, I had an overwhelming feeling that it was my mom. And that helped calm me down and helped me kind of reorient and come out of whatever I was experiencing.

LAB: Even though your husband was there and was doing the same—trying his best to comfort you—your mom, in essence, came to you and was able to do that in a way that he perhaps couldn't?

Rebecca: Yeah, and it definitely was not solicited. It's not something that as nice and as comforting as it would be to have those experiences with my mom after she passed away; it's not something I've ever asked for or solicited. It was incredibly comforting.

LAB: And were you very clear that this was your mom?

Rebecca: Without a doubt. I didn't hear voices or anything like that, but I had this overwhelming sense of feeling or hearing kind of internally that things were going to be alright. It really struck a chord with me for what we would experience from her in comfort when we were growing up.

LAB: So, even though her death was so troubling to you, she was able to come back to you in your time of need and really help you.

Rebecca: Yes, and I wish that was something I could solicit, to be honest.

LAB: What do you make of this, when you try to make sense of it? I mean, it doesn't fit your worldview about what happens after death.

Rebecca: I don't have a good explanation for it. I think the rational part of my brain says that it was my body self-soothing and doing what I needed to do to get out of the anxiety attack. The less rational side of me wants to say "Maybe there is an afterlife. Maybe this was her reaching back." But, I don't think I can believe that so it's sorta in a juxtaposition to what I believe. But I take it for what it was at the time—something super comforting for me—and I'm very grateful that I got to experience it.

LAB: But I hear a tug of war there, trying to make sense of it. Like saying, "This doesn't fit into what I know, what I believe, but there's part of me that wants to fit it in somewhere."

Rebecca: Coming from an agnostic worldview, I think there's a lot we can learn and understand about the world and I also think there's a lot that we can't. I'm ok with not understanding the things I don't understand. For me, this encounter falls into one of those. Whether that's the realm of spirituality for me, I've yet to figure that out. I don't need to have a box for everything and this is one of those things I'm not going to try to find a box for.

LAB: Why do you think she would have come to you right then?

Rebecca: In the panic of what was going on for me, I had a very overwhelming sense of doom. Even though it was not actually a near-death experience, it felt like one. One of the very strong positive qualities of my mom was that she was a caregiver. That defined who she was. I don't think I'll ever understand it. But if there's a part of her that has remained spiritually, then it's not surprising that she'd be able to sense when one of her kids needed her the most. And that, for me, was definitely one of my low points in recovering from her passing.

Layered on top of the suicide, Rebecca had had a near-lifelong complicated relationship with her mother that had worsened steadily in the final
five years of her mother's life. Her mom's mental illness, her requests to
have Rebecca assist her in suiciding, all of it had overshadowed the *other*
mother that Rebecca had also known—the caring, loving, supportive
mom. Though completely unsolicited by her, Rebecca's openness to not
second guessing her unexplainable encounter with her deceased mom
allowed her to continue to benefit from her mother's caregiving qualities
posthumously in ways that greatly facilitated her grieving process.

Erica, age 55, was our second panelist. She lost her 22-year-old son,
Griffin, 4½ years prior, when he died suddenly of an undetected heart
defect while jogging late at night. Erica first came to see me for individual
grief therapy approximately 17 months after Griffin's death at the strong
urging of family members who were concerned about her *stuckness*. In the
several years that we worked together, Erica shared countless examples of
the ways in which Griffin came to her, which served for her as a means of
understanding her grief and provided meaning to the life she had been
forced to live without him.

LAB: Erica, we're so glad you could join us and we're eager to hear
        from you. Before we get started, first, please tell us a little bit
        about your beliefs about what happened to Griffin after he died,
        where you believe he is.
Erica: I've been a quaker my whole life. For 30 years, my husband and I
        have been leaders of a quaker meeting. But after losing Griffin so
        suddenly like that, I think my beliefs changed a little bit. I found
        myself reading a lot of books about the afterlife and people
        having afterlife experiences. I was craving having a knowledge
        about what happened to Griffin. The last time I saw him lying
        there on the table [in the morgue], I found myself saying "I
        believe, I believe, I believe. He's in heaven, he's in heaven."
LAB: You have had a lot of encounters with Griffin, but you've
        selected a few to share here that you have found particularly
        meaningful.
Erica: Yes well, early on in therapy, because so much of my memory of
        Griffin was his death day, as my therapist, you were trying to
        help me to remember that while, yes, that the day he died was
        significant, that I also had 22 years of memories with him—he
        was fun, funny, and creative. I often take notes in therapy, and I
        remember that when you said that I jotted down "Goofy, silly
        Griffin." You continued yacking away (laughs with the audience)
        and I all of a sudden felt so strongly that Griffin was sitting right
        next to me on the loveseat. Then, he started making these
        ridiculously silly faces while also looking intently at you with all
        this non-verbal ridiculousness like he was getting so much out of

what you were saying. I totally sensed this happening right there next to me and I was so afraid to look over where I sensed he was because I thought he might go away, because nothing like this had ever happened to me. Because this was happening, I totally tuned you out and didn't say anything until I emailed you later about it. (Laughs)

LAB: (Laughs) I love that story! So, tell us, what do you make of that, that he came to you during our therapy session when you were trying to take in and process some serious information?

Erica: (Laughs) I think he was saying, "Lighten up, Mom!" (Laughs again)

LAB: (Laughs) What a great experience. Anything about your grief process that you associate with some meaning about his showing up and being there with you as you mourned his death? I know you have really struggled over these years to kind of work through it and find some peace.

Erica: Yeah, it was really comforting because I have just struggled so much with the death and the overpowering emotion of him being gone. So, I do pull on that, to try to recall that experience to help when the pain comes back, which it does.

LAB: You've also had other experiences of encounters with Griffin?

Erica: Yes, he died on Sept. 10th, so one month on the 10th I was really missing him, so I texted "I really miss you" to his old cell phone number. Immediately, the new owner of the number replied, "Who?" At first, I ignored it. But after several more texts saying, "Who is this?" I decided to tell this poor soul my whole story. It could have gone either way, but it turned out very well and I feel like Griffin had a hand in that. Turns out, it was this woman's birthday, and, like me, she also likes to hike, is an artist and an art teacher. And, not only does she also have a daughter named Graci just like I do but her Graci had just learned that she has a heart issue, just like Griffin. At Christmas time, I received a text from "Griffin." Of course, it was this woman. She was texting to wish me a Merry Christmas and to say that she had created this amazing frame out of sticks that she had found while hiking, with an inscription that said: "Forever Separated, Never Apart." She had watched all of his movies [that he created in college], and we started to connect even more. It has really been a remarkable connection.

LAB: How does that feel to you that Griffin's phone number has now created an amazing connection for you? How do you make sense of that?

Erica: I tend to cling to anything that connects me to Griffin. All of those things, I take meaning from if at all possible.

LAB: You have said in the past that letting go of the pain of grief feels like you have to let go of Griffin. Do you feel like these sorts of connections and the way he sort of appears to you, do you feel like these encounters help supplant that need to hold onto the pain and trauma part of this?

Erica: My rationale brain knows I need to let go of the pain, but these connection things definitely help.

As Erica alluded, Griffin seemed to present himself to her through other people, through animals, while she was hiking, in her dreams and thought life on numerous occasions. And, what Erica emphatically took from these encounters has been a profound sense of meaning about his life, his death, and her ability to maintain a continuing bond with her son.

Next in our group of panelists was Rebekah. Rebekah, is the 26-year-old daughter of Steve, a 30-year military veteran, who died two years prior at age 57 from a self-inflicted gunshot wound to the head. Rebekah, who was newly married and had given birth to the couple's first child shortly before her father's unexpected and traumatic death, had shared a very close relationship with her father in both childhood and adulthood. Like Erica, she has had a number of encounters with her dad since his death, but here she shares some that came to her in her sleep.

LAB: Welcome, Rebekah. First, could you share a little about your perspective about what happened after your dad died? Where did he go?

Rebekah: My family is Jewish but not very religious. I definitely feel spiritual. I was always under the impression that we'd be reincarnated after death but was always open to the idea that if people don't want to be reincarnated then they're not. If you want to just die and have nothing happen, then that's an option for you. I don't really have very rigid ideas about what the afterlife looks like or whether it exists for everybody.

LAB: Thank you for sharing that with us. Can you also share some of the encounters you've had with your dad since he passed away?

Rebekah: Immediately following his death, I found myself talking to him a lot. And, I got to this point where I wasn't sure if he was hearing me and felt like it was pointless and stupid that I was talking to him. About two weeks after his death, I had a dream. He walked into the room I was in and he was a young man. We locked gazes for a very, very long time. Even in my dream, I felt I was having an encounter with him. I felt if I said something, he'd go away. Finally, he told me to just keep talking to him. And then he winked at me, which was very characteristic of my dad, and then went away. That felt very important to me because it was right at the time when I felt ridiculous for trying to continue this type of relationship with him. It felt like he came to tell me that it was not ridiculous, that he was still listening in some capacity.

LAB: I'm curious, what did that mean to you that he came to you at that time?

Rebekah: It felt extremely comforting. I remember I woke up that morning and it was like I didn't feel gut wrenched. That whole first month after he died just nothing felt real. After that dream, I felt very ok with the fact that everything felt totally awry in my life. It felt ok that he was dead. That morning I felt very comforted.

LAB: You're now almost two years post loss. Has the meaning of that dream changed for you overtime?

Rebekah: It has. I think right after he died maybe he didn't know how to navigate being dead. Like it was new for all of us. So, maybe it was important for him to let us know that he was there and still listening. But maybe now since so much time has passed he feels more comfortable being further away, in a sense, and maybe I feel more comfortable with him being further away. So, I think it was very representative of that time but I don't tap back into that dream. It feels a little less relevant now.

LAB: Why might he have come to you in that way, right at that time?

Rebekah: I had had a baby three weeks before he died, so in my waking time I feel like there was no appropriate time for me to be inviting him to come to me and I think my dad would be very respectful of that. So in my dreams is the only time he could encounter me. So, I think that's why he chose a dream to manifest himself to me.

I also feel like it was important that he came to me as a young person. Whenever I dream of him and he's 57 and gray with a beard, and when I have those dreams I know that's just me imaging him, but when he shows up young I know that's him visiting me.

LAB: Any other encounters with your dad you'd like to share?

Rebekah: After he suicided, I've had times when I imagined my own suicide. In some of those dark moments, I have felt his overwhelming presence just trying to comfort me. So, I felt he had a moment with me and shared with me that I wouldn't benefit from [suicide]—he hadn't benefited from that. That was extremely, extremely, extremely comforting for me. And, it wasn't like there were words exchanged. It was just an overwhelming feeling of his energy being present.

As many other grievers also attest, Rebekah's post-death interactions with her father served to provide her with much-needed reassurance and comfort—much like a soothing balm for her troubled soul—a form of inexplicable peace in the wake of a loss she never would have chosen.

Our final panelist, Elaine, is the daughter-in-law of Jo, who is an 85-year-old woman whose husband, Jim, died of lung cancer two years before. Jo began seeing me for individual grief therapy at the suggestion of Elaine who drove her mother-in-law to each session and managed her care. As an integral part of Jim's and Jo's lives, it was from this role of caregiving support that Jim seemed to *come to* Elaine, almost as a way to ensure that Jo's needs continued to be met after his death.

LAB: We appreciate you being here, Elaine. Before we hear more about your encounters with Jim, could you tell us a little bit about your beliefs about where he is now?

Elaine: I'm a very strong practicing Catholic, and I firmly believe in an afterlife, and God and a Higher Being.

LAB: Thank you for sharing that. I invited you here, Elaine, because you have had encounters with Jim in which he communicates with you his wishes for how Jo should be cared for. Could you share some of those experiences with us?

Elaine: Something to know about Jim—Jim wants Jo taken care of. Several times since Jim has died, I have suddenly started to feel ill. Each time this happened, I knew something was wrong with my mother-in-law. When I have called or gone to see her, sure enough, she would be emotionally or physically not well. This pattern started to occur less and less over time, but one time recently, I told my husband "Your dad is talking to me again. I feel that ill, dark cloud." This past September, Jo went through a very deep, dark time. I got a phone call from her at 9:30 at night and it was that same intuitive sense—I knew something was definitely wrong. She ended up in the hospital and that's when [we initiated grief therapy]. Jim's visits have been less and less now, and I don't hear from Jim as much now that Jo is working on her grief and navigating her stuff.

LAB: So, you're saying that Jo's struggle with processing her grief feelings affected her both emotionally and physically, and each time you'd learn of this through Jim? And, not only would you feel uneasy and unsettled but you also knew it was a message about Jo that Jim wanted you to hear?

Elaine: Yes, exactly. However, I feel that Jim is more distant now. I don't feel that pall now that Jo's in a much better emotional place. I think Jim is more content now, feeling better about Jo, so he's not needing to nudge me as much.

LAB: What is the meaning you associate with him coming to you in this way—because you didn't solicit this, right, Elaine? You didn't sign up for this, right?

Elaine: I did not sign up for this. This is not what I wanted for my life, not in any way shape or form. I don't know why me, not Jim's own kids, but I'm open to it. I have for some reason been placed as *it* in this family by Jim.

Like many grievers, Elaine experienced the presence of the deceased as a being whose purpose was to bring peace—arriving as a caring, compassionate other to a survivor who was seemingly in need of comfort and care. However, unlike the other panelists, Elaine's encounter with her deceased loved one was specifically meant to guide her in the care of someone else. Whether in a lifelike dream, an audible laugh, a felt caress, or some other form of connection, and, seemingly, regardless of the nature of why they show up, it appears to be the *sense* of the deceased, their palpable presence, however they present themselves, that binds these grievers' experiences together.

For the final segment of the panel, we invited the audience to ask questions of the panel or to share their own or their clients' experiences related to this topic. Below are a few examples of the panel and audience discussion.

Member of the Audience: What's it like to hear the other panelists share encounter experiences similar to your own?

Panel responses:

Erica: I always think it's helpful to hear from others. I feel tremendous comfort. I know these people get me like no one else does.

Rebekah: I think that it's extremely validating because it's one of those things that's just up in the air. Am I crazy or is this really happening? So, to hear that it happens to other people is helpful.

Member of the Audience: What about with people who have not experienced a loss, do you share these experiences?

Panel responses:

Erica: I just tend to talk about it with everyone all the time. [Laughs] I just have to talk about it, even though it's risky. I need to. I never used

	to make connections like this, but I need to make connection with him. I view it every time as a comforting gift from my son.
Rebekah:	I feel a certain level of responsibility that I have to tell people to demystify it or to make it seem less like quackery.
Elaine:	I mostly share with my father-in-law's adult children so they understand the meaning of why I take care of their mother the way I do.
Member of the Audience:	This question is for Elaine: I'm wondering, given that Jim has four other adult kids, don't you feel angry that he put this on you, that he chose you not one of them?
Elaine:	I do feel angry. I sometimes feel very angry. I've been trying to work through my anger using my faith, and I'm making some progress. But I also welcome the opportunity, as hard and as inconvenient as it can be at times, to serve Jim and my mother-in-law in this way.
LAB:	So, what I hear you saying, Elaine, is that even though this was unsolicited by you, and in one sense it's an honor that Jim chose you, it also comes with a burden and it's a burden you are choosing to bear. I appreciate your honesty. It's worth circling back to say that not all of these encounters are these wonderful, mystical, magical experiences. Sometimes, they can be a little bit troubling, or disturbing, and/or full of responsibility.

The four women who comprised our panel and their representative stories of encounters with their deceased loved ones illustrate a small but important example of what is meant when a griever claims to have sensed the presence of their loved one after their death. With these examples, clinicians, clergy, and other helpers, both professional and lay persons, who serve those who are mourning might be better equipped to grasp not just the how and what of these encounters but the potential and specific meaning and importance that they hold for the survivor. Equally as beneficial is our increased understanding with regard to the felt connection and the sense of comfort inherent in these types of post-death interactions.

17 To Seek or Not Seek Contact with the Deceased through a Medium: A Panel Interview with Grievers

Laurie A. Burke

Introduction

A medium is a person who regularly communicates with deceased persons and has been commissioned to do so in order to facilitate connection between the decedent and the survivor. Consulting a medium following the death of a loved one is surprisingly prevalent (Beischel, Mosher, & Boccuzzi, 2015). Mediums are frequently called upon to provide an answer to a specific question that weighs heavily on the minds of many grievers, namely, whether their deceased loved one is okay. The limited empirical research suggests that mediums are generally perceived as helpful, or at least not unhelpful (Walter, 2007). Without making an evaluative judgment, this chapter provides an overview of the role of mediums in the grieving process by highlighting the experiences of several grievers who considered using the services of a medium.

Panel of Grievers

The panelists showcased in this chapter participated in a small conference focusing on the topic of this book. These grievers were recruited from the author's private practice in Portland, OR, where her area of specialty is working with bereaved adults. Prompted by a series of questions from the facilitator/author (LAB), each panelist was invited to share their thoughts and experiences regarding the use of a medium in connecting with their deceased loved one.

After the panelists' interviews, the audience was invited to ask questions of the panelists. Portions of the panelists' interviews have been transcribed below. Following a brief welcome, the facilitator addressed the panelists by first describing the nature of their participation:

> You are each here because you've considered and/or have chosen to seek the services of a medium in order to make contact with your deceased loved one. For some grievers, a session in which connection with their loved one is facilitated by a medium is comforting and reassuring.

DOI: 10.4324/9781003105077-22

For other grievers, these types of interactions can be unsettling because they can challenge one's worldview by raising questions about the afterlife or the well-being of the deceased.

After sharing panel members' biographical information with the audience, the facilitator invited each griever to introduce their deceased loved one (i.e., briefly describe what he/she was like, e.g., easygoing, strict but loving, always helping others); and, if willing, to briefly share their own beliefs or worldview—spiritual, secular, or otherwise—related to the afterlife, followed by sharing their sentiments regarding the use of mediums. The facilitator asked the same basic questions of each panelist, followed by questions specific to each griever's experience. In general, an attempt was made to understand the personal rationale (i.e., for or against) the griever's decision to use or not use a medium to connect with their deceased person, and also the pros and cons that emerged during that decision-making process. More specifically, if the cons outweighed the pros for the panelist and they decided not to connect with their loved one through a medium, we wanted to learn how they felt once that decision was made and how it feels for them today. Conversely, if the pros outweighed the cons for the panelist and they decided to connect with their loved one through a medium, we asked them to tell us not only what that experience was like in terms of restoring connection with their loved one, but also the meaning it held for them both then and now. Panelists who saw a medium were asked to describe how the interactions they had with the medium made them feel, if they thought it would be helpful for them to connect with their loved one in this way again, and whether they would encourage others to seek the services of a medium. Finally, we asked all panelists if they had told other people, other than this audience, about their decision to seek or not seek the services of a medium. If they had chosen not to share it with others, we asked why they felt compelled to withhold the information. If they had shared, they were asked to describe how it felt for them to discuss this experience with others.

Kristen

Our panel consisted of four female grievers. The first panelist, Kristen, was 40 years old and her long-term partner, Ryan, used a gun to take his life almost 2½ years prior to the interview. At the time of his death, the couple had been together for three years, had a happy relationship, and were planning a future together that included Kristen's two middle-school-aged children.

LAB: So, Kristen, I'm curious about what your thoughts were before Ryan died, what you thought happened when people die. Did you have any kind of faith tradition or any ideas that spoke to that?

Kristen: Yes, I grew up evangelical Christian, in a very faith-filled home. A real black and white idea of heaven and hell—you went to heaven if you accepted Jesus as your savior and you went to hell if you did not. As I went to college, that evolved for me, allowing for more openness. I lost my ideas about hell, but even as I've grown up into adult life, that's evolved into more agnosticism. I just embrace the mystery. I don't know. I don't think that I know anything. I have a real gut or heart sense of what I want and hope to be true—that the stuff that your soul is made of continues, but I don't have any certainty about that.

LAB: Sounds like things evolved for you over time. Can you extend that journey for us and take us on the path that led you to a medium?

Kristen: I have a friend with empathic gifts, and she told me about her friend who is a medium. I had never considered that—I thought it was strange. She told me this woman was grounded and loving and kind. I was coming out of my second Christmas without Ryan and was in a really low place, having a lot of self-pity, low energy, and I was like, "Sure! Let's do it! Let's try." We went together to see the medium, and I just kind of went in with a lot of openheartedness, saying, "I'm not sure if Ryan's spirit is out there and wanting to connect with me, but maybe."

LAB: In terms of readiness (see Neimeyer & Rynearson, Chapter 9), it sounds like you were not only at a low point but also really ready to engage with your loved one in an intentional way.

Kristen: Yes, and on the other side of that hour with the medium, there was a really marked change in me. If healing is a spiral, I felt like I had jumped up three spirals. Not something I can really explain or pinpoint, not like a lightbulb moment, just I knew I was pretty changed.

LAB: Can you set this up for us? What it was like to be present with the medium? Was it really a cold reading (see Wortman, Chapter 15)? Did you give her any idea why you were there?

Kristen: She invited us to record the session. When she turned to me, she immediately recognized that I was there for a loss, though I hadn't told her that. And, except for maybe a few things, there weren't many things where I was like, "Oh, there's no way she could have known that." I did feel like Ryan's energy was there, like she was channeling his energy. I was skeptical if that was actually him or her picking up on what I needed. But it was really powerful, and it felt like he was encouraging me. That connection was really powerful.

The eight-minute excerpt of the recording of the interaction between Ryan, the medium, and Kristen was played for the audience. The tape picks up where, after a brief pause to listen again to Ryan, the medium continues speaking:

Medium: I feel a sense of reassurance from him about his role here. That, what a gift it was to be able to spend time with you and to connect in that way with you. And, that it was ok that he left. I feel that my words are inadequate but that you understand what I'm saying.

Kristen: Yes

Medium: He really feels like he was a magical person. Like the energy just came off of him. He would light up any room he entered, literally, with his energy. And, he was really positive, right? And, you have that quality, too, and that's why he is attracted to you, and you him.

Kristen: (now sobbing) Yes.

Medium: (after long pause) Is there a necklace? And, does it sit right here near your heart?

Kristen: Yes.

Medium: Not up here or down here, but right here (she points to her chest)? For some reason, that's important, where it sits on your body. (pause) Yes, because it feels to me like he's wrapping his energy around you right at the heart, when you wear that. Or, you don't even need to wear it, that it's like basically a doorway for you to connect with him. And, I do feel like he is sorry to have left you. It was his time to go but he is sorry that he left—just what it means to leave, the difficulty, the missing. However, this seems like it was part of your contract with each other. I do feel as though he's with you—your time together is not totally done. You're both doing your thing, but there's this residual kind of lovely connection there. I don't feel it should keep you from moving on with your life, but what I'm seeing is this connection. Don't let that keep you from experiencing—it will enhance what you're experiencing.

After allowing a moment for the audience to return their attention to the panel, the facilitator followed up by asking Kristen specific questions regarding her session with the medium.

LAB: What was that like for you, Kristen, to connect with Ryan in this way and to hear the things the medium said?

Kristen: She was speaking to the heart of my connection with him that was severed by his death. So, to feel that that was reattached in some way and that there was positive energy around that was encouraging for me. It just felt like it was building me back up, in the moment. Since then, I've felt more strength in my own capacity to live my life without him. I can tuck away the things he gave me and remember them—that contract she talked about—being able to process that and going back to the heart of what we had. That has been very meaningful to me.

LAB: And, you've been back to see her, correct?

Kristen: Yes, I went back on the second anniversary of his passing. That second reading, she actually focused in on the day of his death. She spoke of him wanting me to know that he wasn't in his right mind that day (though she had not known that he suicided), he had a lot of pain he was dealing with, residual from his childhood. That was really amazing.

LAB: Outside this audience today, have you shared with anyone else these experiences?

Kristen: No, I don't. I have a small handful of close friends and my parents and brother, and they are all really open. But it feels intensely personal, too risky to share. I had an evening with our best friends and shared about it. But I pretty much lost that friendship after that.

Kristen's interview illustrates the key points that made her experience in seeking a medium meaningful for her. First, although it likely was not something she would have considered apart from her friend's suggestion, she felt a need—she found herself at a low point in her grief journey, facing the second Christmas without Ryan. Secondly, there was a readiness, an openness to maintain the bond she had shared with him in life. In meeting with the medium, it seems she was not disappointed. The "contract" between them became a highlight of Ryan's outreach to her through the medium. Despite her initial skepticism, Kristen endorsed feeling Ryan's energy, and stated that, overall, the experience was powerful, encouraging, and satisfying enough that she returned for a follow-up visit on the second anniversary of his date of death.

Lizzie

Lizzie was our second panelist. At the time of the interview, Lizzie was 33 years old. She was grieving the loss of Kyle, her partner of 3½ years, who hung himself 2½ years prior. Although Kyle's final months were marked by significant psychological distress, the majority of their three-plus-year relationship had been exceptionally enjoyable for both of them.

LAB: (to the audience) Kristen and Lizzie were introduced through me, as I sometimes do with patients with similar losses. By all accounts, they have become fast friends, right Lizzie?

208 Laurie A. Burke

Lizzie: Yeah, not only do we live blocks away from each other, and Kyle and Ryan's memorial services were held at the same place, but both of our partners were very similar too—both were left-handed and definitely both very charismatic—the light of any room they entered.

LAB: Lizzie, can you introduce Kyle to us?

Lizzie: He was inappropriate with his humor, but he was so charming and disarming and everyone loved him. He loved me so much. He was so passionate about anything he got into, borderline obsessive, he always had to have something fulfilling him. So smart but didn't give himself enough credit. He really had a tough time, especially toward the end.

LAB: Your background, your belief system, tell us something about that.

Lizzie: My family was not religious in any way. But preteen/teenage years, I attended a non-denominational Christian church, and Young Life (a Christian outreach for adolescents and teens). But it was much more of a social world, and I never really had a strong belief in God or the afterlife or heaven and hell. Still like that.

LAB: I'm interested in what it was like for you when Kristen came and suggested that you, too, see a medium to make connection with Kyle.

Lizzie: It actually caused a lot of conflict for me. The afterlife being something I do not believe in. Kyle and I talked about not being religious in any way, and that, after passing, your remains could become part of a tree, and talked about pursuing that when we passed. So, for me, we become earth, that's where our energy goes. That brings me a lot of resolve knowing that my energy will be earth, grass, or a tree that could provide shade for someone. Otherwise, it makes me feel very uneasy because Kyle clearly was very distressed in his last days and I have a hard time believing that just because he passed that he's "in a better place." I don't know that. I can't believe that, and what if he's not? That's such a terrible feeling for me. But I also feel a lot of guilt for not reaching out. What if he wants to reach me? But still, I'm more fearful of a medium than anything, because I don't know what's out there. But, it's not to say that I won't or don't find comfort in some things. The day he passed, I was giving my police statement on my porch, and I looked up and there was the biggest, most colorful rainbow in the sky. Even my friend said, "I can't believe there's a f---ing rainbow!" And, I knew it was Kyle, showing up, being really inappropriate and flashy, very "Look at me!" (laughs along with the audience).

LAB: That rainbow theme has followed you, hasn't it?

Lizzie: Yes, he has showed up in the form of a rainbow in times when I was really low or needed to make a hard decision. And, even today, the conference Wi-Fi password is "rainbow," which feels comforting on what I knew would be a really hard day.

LAB: So, he has shown up to you in the form of nature, in line with your shared beliefs. You also said that the thought of a medium bringing Kyle into the room might be unsettling to you.

Lizzie: Yes, that it could be. I don't know that he's passed on somewhere and everything is great, hunky dory, and he's glad he did what he did. I can't believe that that would be the case. And, I still have some feelings of anger inside me and I don't want to be put in connection with him only to not have a positive experience. What if he's not ok? I just feel better that he's earth.

LAB: Almost, like he might be still struggling, like taking his own life didn't really change that.

Lizzie: Yeah, and I don't want him watching over me all the time. I've done a lot of really hard work on my grief. I've started a new career. I'm really fulfilled and never thought I could be again. But I don't want him to look down and say "Look, she's ok. What I did was fine."

LAB: Almost like his death was justified?

Lizzie: Yeah, because it's not—it not ok.

LAB: What's it been like for you two, Lizzie and Kristen, to share such disparate experiences?

Lizzie: I think it's great. I think it's wonderful that anyone finds anything that helps them feel better. While I may not believe it, I don't know what's out there.

Kristen: As one of Lizzie's best friends, I would never push anything on her that causes her fear.

LAB: Kristen, did you ever try to alleviate Lizzie's fears?

Kristen: She asked some cursory questions, but she's never heard the medium recording. I would not push that, even though she does know that it's been a positive experience for me.

The friendship between Lizzie and Kristen meant that they shared in each other's experiences, but it did not ensure that those experiences would be experienced the same or stem from the same foundational worldview. Lizzie felt uncomfortable with the uncertainty of facing the many questions that might come up if she engaged the serves of a medium—whether the work of a medium is actually real, whether Kyle was okay or not, and whether his existence in an afterlife state meant that his dying was vindicated. Instead, Lizzie's belief that Kyle was now a part of the earth fell in line with her previously held construct that no life after this one exists. But rather than this being a negative experience, she received encouragement and comfort just as Kristen had through a medium, except that Lizzie's came when Kyle showed up repeatedly in the form of a rainbow.

Debbie

Next in our group of panelists was Debbie, a 65-year-old newly retired woman who lost her husband, Gary, 18 months beforehand following a lengthy battle with metastatic melanoma. The couple had been married nearly 25 years, and they were each other's best friend. Although Gary's cancer cycled in and out of remission across nearly two decades and, eventually, he developed a terminal brain tumor, as his caregiver, the loss of Gary felt sudden and unexpected to Debbie.

LAB: Thank you for being here, Debbie. Before we start, can you share a little bit about your beliefs about where Gary is?

Debbie: I was raised a Methodist and so was Gary, but as adults we drifted away from church. In 2002, when his melanoma had metastasized to his lungs, we found a church we liked and started going. When he was, once again, "cured," we knew we had been blessed. That really reaffirmed that there is a God, and a heaven or someplace we go when we die.

LAB: So, tell us about how you decided to go to a medium. Because, as your therapist, this was not something you and I talked about beforehand. It was something you kinda came in after the fact and told me about a little sheepishly. (smiles)

Debbie: Yeah, I didn't want you to think I was cheating on you! (laughs along with the audience) But, before Gary died, I would watch those TV programs [about mediums] (see Wortman, Chapter 15), and Gary, who was very skeptical, would say "You believe in that stuff?" But I have girlfriends who have lost their spouses and they've gone to a medium and, with one, it was pretty freaky how accurate it was. So, it was something in the back of my head. I mean, I was looking for signs. I really wanted signs, but I wasn't finding anything. I had a little bit of guilt. By the time he went on hospice, Gary trusted me to do the right thing. To me, the right thing was to make him better.

LAB: Sounds like the decision to see a medium was partly to do with taking care of some unfinished business. Before we share with the audience the recording of your session with the medium, I wanted to note that you did not tell her anything about why you were there, correct?

Debbie: Correct, I gave her only my first name.

LAB: And, what's so interesting to me is that probably the first third of your session with her did not even involve Gary. Immediately after starting, your deceased mom showed up, front and center. After a lengthy interaction with her that included some much-needed healing for you, your dad showed up. Then, it was your mom and dad together, and they began joking and talking, using the words and phrases they always did, including dissing your brother a bit, as they also often did. (audience laughs) After a few more relatives and even a deceased animal, Gary eventually showed up. Later in the session, he said that your mom had to talk him into it because he wasn't sure about it. You've told me previously that you found these experiences to be genuine but that what felt particularly authentic was that Gary went straight into talking about his own death.

Debbie: Yes. The first thing he said was, "We were blindsided. We got knocked off our feet." And, that's exactly what happened, especially when we heard it was an inoperable brain tumor.

LAB: Debbie, now seems like an appropriate time to share with the audience a clip of your session with the medium. Let's listen.

An audiotaped excerpt of Debbie's session with the medium was shared with the audience, focusing on what Gary seemed to want Debbie to know about his perception of his final days.

Medium: He's saying that, "We thought it was under control. We were treading water, holding on, but then it came from another angle." (pause) He says, "We knew the inevitable, but we weren't ready for the end. We thought we were on it, we were handling it, but it was so much more than we knew." He says, "He's sorry it was so hard on you." "Truth be told," he says, "he's not sure he could handle it if the tables were turned."

As well as contending with the idea of his own death, through the medium, Gary mentioned how hard it was for him to feel and witness his own physical decline, specifically in feeling "unkept," which Debbie reported as being characteristic of the "put-together" guy he was.

Medium: It's impressive that he wants us to know that he kept trying, trying to manage things for as long as he could, too. And, I keep hearing (brief pause) that his brain wasn't working properly—that he wasn't able to be him, it wasn't really him. (pause) And, there was apparently some depression, too.

	But it's all gone. So, any of the worry, any of the angst, it's all gone.
Later in the recording:	He's going back to what happened, talking about his treatment, and saying that there was a sense that you guys had this under control, under wraps, like, "We can do this, we'll be ok." And, not just because you guys are fighters, but because you guys got some positive feedback. (pause) And Debbie, I'm picking up on something about maybe [the medical team] missed something, like they weren't on it? He's giving me the impression that some things could have been handled better. Did we wonder if they missed something?
Debbie:	I think they were on it, but I know I wasn't in tune with what was going on.
Medium:	He wants you to know that he understands that it was just so much more than we knew. (pause) Oh, and he says, "Always. I will always love you. And I'm not going anywhere." (Debbie and the medium laugh) In closing, the medium encouraged Debbie to continue talking with Gary because he said he hears her and wants her to continue.
LAB:	Debbie, what more might you add? What does this experience mean to you now?
Debbie:	Going to the medium, having my mom, my dad, Gary, and others come to me brought me comfort and joy. Not sure how they find each other up there, but it was good that they did because it lets me know that when I do die that they'll be waiting for me. It was also comforting because she said there are other ways in which Gary is trying to communicate with me, too.

The notion of seeking the services of a medium was neither new nor foreign to Debbie. So, when the right time presented itself, she was both open and ready to engage. Fortunately, Debbie's experience with a medium brought with it detailed information and highly characteristic interactions with not only Gary but also other significant family members, all of which Debbie found to be incredibly accurate, right down to the sentiments and particulars. Debbie was able to learn during her session how Gary viewed his own dying experience, including his rightly alluding to the fact that Debbie was in denial prior to his imminent demise. In all of this, and especially in learning that Gary enjoyed this type of two-way communication, Debbie found the experience of working with a medium reassuring and comforting.

Rebekah

Our final panelist is Rebekah, the 26-year-old daughter of Steve, who was a career Veteran with 30 years of service in the US Air Force. Steve struggled emotionally in his final years of life and had died two years earlier at the age of 57 from a self-inflicted gunshot wound to the head.

LAB: Rebekah, you participated in another panel earlier today (see Chapter 16), during which you told us that in terms of your worldview you were raised Jewish but that you are more spiritual than religious. You also indicated that you believed in reincarnation, but that you also believe that people are only reincarnated if it's something they themselves want. You stated that your views about the afterlife are not hard and fast, and you really aren't sure it's the same for everyone. I'm curious, with that in mind, can you tell us how you came to seek the services of a medium?

Rebekah: I went to this metaphysical gathering. I didn't know if I was actually going to have a reading done, I just showed up. I felt a little overwhelmed when I walked into the room because there were all these mediums and tarot [card] readers, and I thought, "Oh god, who do I sit down with?" I was afraid of choosing the wrong person, but I ended up sitting down with this lady. She asked me to say my name three times, so I did. She took a long pause and then asked what kind of a reading did I want? I asked, "Well, what's on the table?" The options she gave were things like career decisions, relationship issues, a loved one who died. So, I said, "Let's do that." Then, she instructed me to say the name of the person I wanted to contact three times, which I did. After a long pause, she said that she just wanted to make sure that she had the right person. She told me that he had been helping a lot of people since he was gone. Then she asked me if I wanted to ask him some questions. I said that I wanted to know if he was far away. To this, the medium responded, "He doesn't know what you mean by that, because he says he's not bound by space and time anymore." I was still unsure if she was talking to my dad or not at this point, but I kept listening. She said that she saw him sitting on a couch at my house. And, I said, "We don't have a couch." Nevertheless, she said he was sitting on a couch. Then, I asked her if he is able to see my son grow up. And, without pausing, she said, "Beansprout."

I thought that was interesting because we call my son string bean all the time. At that point, I was thinking "Ok, ok, maybe this is my dad."

I asked her to ask him if he was afraid, scared after he died? She said he was surprised. Surprised that he was dead. Which seemed ironic since it was a suicide. But he was very drunk when he died, so maybe he was surprised. That meant a lot, her saying he was surprised. He said it was very big on the other side and he was really taken aback by that. She said that a lot of times when someone has experienced a traumatic death that they are ripped from the body quicker so it's more abrupt and comes as more of a shock to the soul that they are in this huge abyss. That was interesting to me that she said that because I hadn't told her how my dad died. My dad was a very private person and I knew that if wanted to tell her, he would tell her. He didn't end up telling her and neither did I, but she surmised that it was traumatic. I asked her if he felt like we had helped him before he died. She said, "He says he doesn't know what you mean by that." I felt disappointed because I felt Dad definitely would know what I meant.

She then said, "He's getting ready to say something, but he's going tell it to you because it's not for me to hear." That's totally characteristic, given he's such a private person. So, I closed my eyes and immediately felt an overwhelming presence of my dad sitting next to me, totally undisguisable from reality. I started tearing up a lot. She asked, "Do you feel him hugging you?" I did. I felt his arms around me, my face in between his hands. It felt exactly like reality. And, what was so striking to me is I could not have manifested that on my own because there is no way I could remember how it felt to have my dad hug me because it's been so long. But to actually feel that exact same feeling, I can't tell you how striking that was for me. We sat there for a long, long, long time. I didn't want to move or say anything because I didn't want it to end. I heard my son in the other room and then my dad said, "That's your boy." At that moment, I remembered that I used to think how much my dad is missing out not seeing my son grow up, but then I realized that I was actually the one who was missing out on seeing the two of them together. But now I think maybe there's a way for the two of them to still stay connected.

At that point, my dad said he had to go, and he laid down and was absorbed back into the floor. My eyes were still closed, and I didn't want to open them because my body felt enormous. Eventually, I got up and walked away. I didn't even know who that medium was or really anything about her, but it changed a lot of things for me. For one, before this, I wasn't sure that my dad was anywhere around. But now, I am quite certain of that. I also feel quite certain that he's watching our lives to some degree and if we choose to entertain that we can. So, the idea of a continuing relationship after death was so abstract for me before, but now, I have a better sense of how I might be able to do that. It was extremely reassuring, and I felt I got a lot out of it.

LAB: So, for you it was very much a facilitated connection, where you don't feel you could have done that without the help of the medium.

Rebekah: I couldn't even imagine it—it felt very organic.

LAB: And, it sounds like you had kind of an out-of-body experience.

Rebekah: Yes, and she told me I was doing really well. A lot of people really get scared when they feel untethered like that, but she said that she would help me recollect my energy. As she said that, I felt like my body was being filled up like a pitcher of water. It was so, so, so bizarre.

LAB: Have you had a chance to tell anyone else about this experience?

Rebekah: I've told my husband, my family, and a few close friends. And, I wanted to text you immediately (laughs with the audience) but I waited to get home and just sent you a long email.

LAB: (laughs) Globally, what did that experience mean to you?

Rebekah: I think it means that, in terms of after-death relationships, it's all on the table. As living people, we can engage as much as we want. The ball is in our court.

LAB: It seems like this was a comforting, reassuring experience for you.

Rebekah: It was. It only cost $20 because of the setting, but I would have paid $1,000. I felt extremely, extremely fortunate to have gotten so much out of it.

Rebekah's experience in seeking the services of a medium seemed to be quite striking and memorable for her—in many ways it took her by surprise. Like the other panelists who connected with their deceased loved one through a medium, Rebekah found the experience to be comforting, worthwhile, and encouraging. But, for her, rather than the interactions with her dad primarily expressed verbally through the medium, she felt his presence in very real ways. He sat beside her, hugged her, and held her face in his hands, exactly as he had done so many times before in life. Now, in death, he was seemingly reaching back to do the same. For Rebekah, his doing so provided more than just a much-needed hug. Her medium-facilitated encounter with her dad answered gnawing questions. It confirmed that he was near, he was looking over her family, and that she could not only reestablish a relationship with him but also continue to connect with him.

Audience Participation

Following these interviews, the audience was invited to ask questions of the panelists and/or comment on what they had learned from them. Below are examples of that discussion:

Member of the Audience:	What, if any, difference do you find in your relationship with your deceased person since considering meeting with a medium?
Lizzie:	I don't think it has changed. I still have struggled with the idea that we can just connect with our loved ones whenever we want, and I struggle with the guilt of not connecting with him.
Kristen:	I've not had a lot of other encounters, except a dream or two, so I feel like my Ryan is really far away. Those really brief moments where he drew close were important, but they haven't opened up a portal to me. I could go back and open up that again, but not by myself.
Debbie:	I feel like Gary is always with me. The medium said to keep a look out because he was going to be communicating with me, and he does in lots of ways.

Numerous audience members thanked the panel for their bravery and vulnerability in sharing.

Lizzie:	I think that's why we are all here, to hopefully help. Despite someone's beliefs, if it is helpful then people should be encouraged to seek it out. I think it's sad and silly that people feel they need to be sheepish about this. (turning to Kristen) I know even you didn't want to tell Dr. Burke that you saw a medium—I outed you (both women laugh). When you first told me, I immediately wanted to tell Dr. Burke about it—my reservations, questions, and conflict with it.

Member of the Audience:　I want to thank all the clinicians here for taking this seriously. As someone who saw a medium shortly after my son died, I know the importance of being able to share these experiences without judgment.

Discussion

In tandem with the sentiments of the audience members' comments, the grievers who were willing to share their journey of contemplation regarding whether or not to attempt reconnection with their deceased love one via a medium are to be commended for their bravery. But, so are the audience members who were willing to listen supportively with the goal of understanding and learning how to use the panelists' narratives to help other grievers. These four panelists likely represent many other mourners who, because of the strong inherent desire to maintain an ongoing bond with their deceased loved one, and because of their equally substantial sense of separation distress at being apart, act on these longings in a variety of ways and use an array of resources, including mediums. Although there is much more to learn about the lived experiences of grievers who contemplate using a medium, of particular interest is that, in this small sample, all of the panelists, both those who sought the services of a medium and those who did not, initially felt skeptical about the idea of doing so. They also all felt cautious about sharing their experiences with others, including their grief therapist. Through this, clinicians, clergy, and all those who assist bereaved individuals might glean a better understanding of the emotionally sensitive nature of even the idea of contacting a deceased loved through a medium, which, in turn, might encourage us in developing better skills and techniques for supporting the bereaved person in their subjective decision-making process on this topic.

References

Beischel, J., Mosher, C., & Boccuzzi, M. (2015). The possible effects on bereavement of assisted after-death communication during readings with psychic mediums: A continuing bonds perspective. *Omega: Journal of Death and Dying, 70*(2), 169–194. doi: 10.2190/OM.70.2.b

Walter, T. (2007). Mourners and mediums. *Theology, 110*(854), 92–100.

Presence within Absence: Summary Discussion

Laurie A. Burke

Introduction

The theme of this book (*presence within absence* following loss), the sections (faith perspectives, clinical implications, research considerations, and existential experiences) and the individual chapters themselves all ultimately point in one direction—in service of the grieving individual. What the reader might glean from any one segment or another of this book is all designed to be received with service of the survivor in mind. Thus, this summary chapter acknowledges the implied contribution and importance of the book as a whole as a way to alert the reader to the role of faith/spirituality/healing traditions, research findings, and the lived experiences of grievers themselves in the bereavement process and care of the mourner.

Brief History of Bereavement Care

Faith Traditions and Healing Practices

Meaning-making plays a critical role in the bereavement experience for humans (Neimeyer, 2020). For spiritually inclined grievers, spiritual sensemaking (Baumeister, 1991) is fundamental to the potential ability to formulate an understanding of not only why their loved one died (e.g., God decided it was their time) but also where they now are (e.g., reincarnated, in heaven) and, for some survivors, how they *should* live in the wake of the permanent absence of their significant person who died (Park & Edmondson, 2011).

The five oldest faith traditions (i.e., Judaism, Christianity, Islam, Hinduism, and Buddhism) all have as part of their foundation a focus on meaning-making regarding the life and death of humans (see Chapters 1, 2, 4, 5, 6, and 7). The work of shamans focuses on the energies encompassing the body, mind, and soul of the griever, enabling a restorative perceiving of the pain of the loss within the revised nature of the relationship through death (see Chapter 3). Thus, these and other belief

DOI: 10.4324/9781003105077-23

systems and healing practices have long provided direction and care during bereavement, including specific guidelines on how the body should be attended to after death and what, if any, contact is possible with the deceased in the afterlife. As many bereaved individuals tap into their belief systems and use their own worldview as a guiding light in the dark days following loss, shaman, clergy, and others in the healing profession continue to play an essential role in providing much-needed comfort, care, compassion, and counsel.

Psychotherapy

In offering a similarly brief synopsis of bereavement care from a traditional psychotherapeutic perspective, we first look to Freud (1917) whose psychoanalytical model of grieving incorporated a three-pronged theory of: (1) acceptance of the death, (2) withdrawal of attachment to and identification with the deceased, and (3), moving on and forming new attachments as the main clinical goals of the bereavement process. Subsumed in this theory is the notion that psychological health is attained once the bereaved person severs ties with their deceased loved one, enabling the survivor to subsequently open her/his heart to new love (e.g., a new romantic relationship, birthing another child). The implied context is that remaining connected with the deceased potentially hinders the bereavement process and stymies the ongoing mental wellness of the bereaved.

Conversely, with regard to the posthumous relationship between the mourner and the person they loved and lost, contemporary theories of healthy bereavement processes include factors such as the importance of making meaning of the death, loss, and ongoing life for the bereaved, and preserving not severing the attachment between the bereaved and deceased persons (Hagman, 2001). Placing value on an ongoing attachment of this kind, says Hagman, can aid in the survivor's reconstruction of meaning that was deconstructed through death. Thus, the concept of maintaining a continuing bond with a deceased loved one has challenged earlier theories on how mourners adapt to loss, suggesting that successful adjustment to bereavement often includes an ongoing attachment to the deceased (e.g., Field, 2008). An overview of these and other concepts found in this book are outlined further below.

Presence within Absence Following Loss

Empirical Foundation of Presence within Absence

Steffen and Kamp provide an invaluable, empirically based introduction on presence-within-absence experiences (see Chapter 12). We learn from them that the experience of a griever sensing the presence of their deceased loved one is common and can be experienced as a physical or psychological awareness of the deceased that often includes a meaning-making component. The particular worldview of the griever frequently comes into play as the presence within absence of the deceased person is experienced and sometimes includes the survivor's afterlife beliefs, often strengthening or challenging them (see also Chapter 14). Their research also elucidates that these experiences feel real to the griever and usually are a source of comfort (see also Chapter 16). Additionally, they report that grievers with differing demographic backgrounds and a wide range of kinds of losses tend to have these experiences, but it remains unclear if they are experienced more often by those with higher levels of bereavement distress. Moreover, it is not uncommon for the mourner to report that their presence-within-absence experience of the deceased shares similarities with how the deceased person was in life (e.g., caring), and, in some cases, the deceased provides guidance or even direct assistance with a current need (e.g., helping the griever know how to solve a home-repair problem). But the authors also found that problematic relationships between the griever and the deceased prior to death are sometimes borne out in the sensory experience of the deceased following death, often in the form of a fixation that can create a level of *stuckness* in the survivor's bereavement process (see also Chapter 11). Overall, however, their findings revealed that the deceased's presence within absence is usually experienced by the bereaved as benevolent and welcomed.

The Desire to Reconnect

With these understandings about presence within absence as our backdrop, there are a variety of things that clinicians, clergy, and other providers of care to the bereaved would do well to know and a variety of reasons why they need to know them. To start, there appears to be a desire by many grievers to experience the presence of their deceased loved one (Kamp et al., 2020). Anecdotally, this author (L. Burke) can report the frequent occurrence of mourners receiving grief therapy who ask, "Why doesn't [my deceased loved one] come to me in my dreams when it happens to other people I know?" It seems that even if they themselves have had another type of presence-within-absence experience (e.g., sensing their deceased person's hand on their shoulder), grievers long to have additional presence-within-absence experiences as well. In some cases, the griever seeks out and attempts to initiate contact with the person they lost (e.g., through a medium; see Chapter 17). In other cases, the deceased loved one seemingly comes to and interacts with the griever in an unbidden manner (see Chapter 16). However, generally speaking, regardless of who initiates contact—the griever, the deceased person, or a medium on behalf of the deceased—the interaction is usually experienced by the griever as comforting, reassuring, and positive. Unfortunately, though, this is not always the case. Although most grievers have a desire to maintain an ongoing connection with their deceased loved one (Kamp et al., 2020) some tend to be selective in how those interactions occur. For instance, not every mourner feels comfortable initiating the interaction, say, for instance, with a medium, sometimes out of fear that doing so might not produce positive outcomes (see Chapter 17) or in other cases because it is viewed as unnecessary or undesired. One therapy patient recently expressed her sentiments this way,

> When I was a kid, my mom used to take me to classes with psychic healers. But, as an adult, I know that I don't need a medium to connect with my [deceased] dad. He's a part of me all the time. The most cathartic connection is self-manufactured—I trust my own ability to stay connected with him. (personal communication with L. Burke, May 25, 2021)

The Role of Belief

It appears that the worldview of the survivor also often plays a role in how presence within absence is experienced by the griever. Beliefs about where the dead person now resides following death vary widely from mourner to mourner. For instance, if a griever believes that the person who died has now become earth, they might have a harder time imagining that a presence-within-absence interaction naturally could occur because such a thing lies outside the realm of their understanding of how the universe works. Thus, belief in some sort of afterlife might be the key to a griever's ability to entertain the notion that it is possible to have an on-going connection with those who have died (see Chapter 16); though, some grievers also report that their long-held, no-afterlife construct has been challenged by an unbidden afterlife encounter with their deceased loved one (see Rebecca's account in Chapter 16). For some grievers, spiritual distress following loss can prevent them from not only main-taining healthy interactions with their spiritual community and their deity but also may compromise or altogether inhibit their ability to have an ongoing relationship with their deceased loved one or to recognize and appreciate a sense of presence within absence as some grievers seemingly do (see Chapter 14).

Clinical Considerations Surrounding Presence within Absence

Many bereaved individuals seeking assistance with their grief tend to be sheepish when it comes to discussing their presence-within-absence experi-ences with their bereavement-care providers, whether it be with regard to their consideration of seeing a medium (see Chapter 17) or that they have had some other kind of visitation from their deceased loved one (see Chapter 16).

The chapters in the clinical section, which highlight the role, treatment, and challenges faced by those working with bereaved individuals, illuminate and expound more on what has been outlined above.

The Restorative Role of Presence within Absence

For instance, in Chapter 8, through a narrative of spousal loss, we learn that the idea of presence within absence often has at its core a sponta-neous and restorative purpose that can assist in the healing of the grie-ver's primary sense of psychological distress. The author (E. Rynearson) asserts that this restorative process includes adaptive principles that are neurobiological, neuro-psychological, and neuro-developmental in nature. In terms of the neurobiological element, he asserts that a re-organization can occur through the bereavement process where the de-ceased's presence within absence serves to provide a sense of equilibrium for the griever much like the brain does when there has been the ampu-tation of a body part. The neuro-psychological element is witnessed in the grief process when the dying and living representation of the deceased person, which feels *amputated* through death, is experienced through the *phantom* phenomenon of presence within absence, which allows the narrative memory of the deceased to be reorganized across time. Additionally, from a neuro-developmental perspective, this presence-within-absence connection between the griever and their deceased loved one often includes transitional objects belonging to the deceased, con-versations with the deceased, a sense of their presence, and/or engagement with the deceased that is facilitated by clinicians (e.g., psychotherapists, shaman, clergy) using a variety of techniques to facilitate the presence-within-absence phenomenon.

Presence within Absence and Bereavement Distress

The authors of Chapter 9 (R. Neimeyer and E. Rynearson) provide an understanding of what clinicians might expect to see when working with grievers—what the grief process looks like when it serves the mourner well and when it does not. Through use of an interview-style dialogue between them, the authors outline the potential risk factors of a protracted, debil-itating, often life-threatening reaction to loss (frequently referred to as *complicated grief*) and provide guidance on how to assess for psychological distress following loss. Specifically, through use of a case vignette, they offer recommendations on how to help survivors who are struggling to process the event story of the death due to unhelpful rumination through facilitation of a restorative retelling of the death and suggest creative ways to assist and support grievers in reestablishing connection with the de-ceased through a sense of their presence within absence.

Distinctive Applications of Presence within Absence

In a unique exploration of an unusual but seemingly highly effective form of grief treatment, the author of Chapter 10 (C. Van Dyke) introduces us to the Wind Telephone—a privately owned telephone booth located in rural Japan that has provided much-needed space and comfort initially to local survivors of unimaginable tragic loss (the massive tsunami on March 11, 2011), and later to mourners from around the world. Bereaved visitors to the humble phone booth came in an effort to seek out the presence within absence of their deceased loved one. Dr. Van Dyke highlights not only the experiences of the grievers in terms of why they might benefit from this kind of therapeutic practice but also contrasts it with more traditional forms of grief therapy that are facilitated by a psychotherapist, by asking intriguing questions of benefit to any clinician seeking to work with bereft adults. Also explored is the role of verbal speech and its significance for those who visit the Wind Telephone, including how speaking out loud to a dead loved one, despite knowing that they are not physically present to hear it, often refines the survivor's private thoughts and heartfelt sentiments in a manner that enhances the presence of the loved one despite their absence.

When Presence within Absence Stymies Effectual Grief Treatment

This book's clinical section concludes with Chapter 11, in which the authors (Drs. E. Rynearson & J. Ruark) use a case vignette of a patient who has struggled greatly in terms of her own psychological distress and in her ability to engage wholeheartedly and benefit from grief therapy. The authors not only provide a challenging inquiry into how often and what percentage of the bereaved population struggles in this way, but, more specifically, they also describe and illustrate how conflictual relationships between the griever and the deceased prior to death can create a fixation with grief that prevents the survivor from altering or releasing the presence within absence of the deceased after the death. Like the clinical interaction between authors in Chapter 9, in this chapter, Dr. Rynearson consults Dr. Ruark on a challenging clinical case involving relational and other traumas, and, together, they discuss, explore, and ultimately come to terms with the limits of both the client's and the clinician's ability to heal intractable grief that is experienced in the context of debilitating internalization of presence within absence of the deceased.

Clinical Applications

Clinicians have the opportunity and privilege of playing a vital role in assisting bereaved clients in navigating what it might mean for them to continue to relate to their loved one after death. The too-numerous-to-mention list of how such presence-within-absence assistance could occur in the context of a therapy session includes such things as encouraging the bereaved person to:

- View their presence-within-absence experiences as normal and common (Datson & Marwit, 1997).
- Investigate what maintaining a continuing bond might look like for them (e.g., wearing the deceased's favorite t-shirt to bed, seeking their advice, connecting through a medium, writing letter to the deceased).
- Share ways in which their deceased loved one comes to them or interacts with them (e.g., in the form of an animal or bird, a visual image, a general knowing or sense of their presence; Steffen & Coyle, 2012).
- Accept that not every bereaved person has presence-within-absence experiences, despite their desire to or that others do, and that this is normal (Daggett, 2005).
- Process intrusive or unwanted presence-within-absence experiences and understand that they may be resultant of unfinished business with the person who died (e.g., Parker, 2005).
- Discuss the social challenges of sharing their presence-within-absence experiences with others outside of therapy (e.g., Bennett & Bennett, 2000).

Even this limited list shows that providing care to the bereaved goes beyond merely attending to their emotional needs in an effort to obtain psychological equilibrium following loss. Most grievers experience heartache in the absence of their lost loved one. Many mourners not only long to be reunited with their deceased person in an afterlife but also express strong desire to have them be present in their current, ongoing life as well. Research findings indicate that the therapeutic alliance is strengthened when those working with grievers who have had presence-within-absence experiences are attentive, interested, non-judgmental, supportive, accepting, and reassuring (e.g., Chan, 2005; Sanger, 2009; Steffen & Coyle, 2011).

In Service of Grievers

The final two chapters of this book provide a unique glimpse into the presence-within-absence theme of this book through interviews with two separate panels of grievers who convened at a small conference to graciously share their experiences. The first panel consisted of four women who shared their unbidden encounters with their deceased loved ones, all of whom had different deaths, and likewise, varied ways of interacting with their surviving loved one (see Chapter 16). Finally, in Chapter 17, a four-member panel of women explained their interest in and decision-making processes surrounding if and why they considered seeking the services of a medium to connect posthumously with their dead loved one. The culmination of this book in these two closing chapters is crowned with the narrated, lived experiences of grievers themselves.

Conclusion

It is imperative for anyone working with bereaved individuals to recognize that many grievers have a strong, natural desire to remain connected to the person they lost. The word *bereaved* means "to be robbed of" (Merriam-Webster.com, 2021). For those experiencing the oft-intense feelings of separation distress that comes when someone they love has been taken from them, especially when it occurs suddenly, unexpectedly, and traumatically, they frequently look for ways to regain the physical and emotional closeness that has been lost through death (Mikulincer & Shaver, 2008). Clinicians, clergy, shaman, and other professionals helping grievers with their losses are privileged to assist in lessening the distress that comes from the deceased's palpable absence. Thus, bereavement-care providers stand to benefit from taking the composite of the sections and chapters in this book into consideration as they ponder how they themselves view the topic of presence within absence with an eye to supporting survivors.

References

Baumeister, R.F. (1991). *Meanings of life*. New York: Guilford Press.

Bennett, G., & Bennett, K.M. (2000). The presence of the dead: An empirical study. *Mortality*, 5, 139–157.

Bereft. Merriam Webster Dictionary. Retrieved on May 13, 2021, from https://www.merriam-webster.com/dictionary/bereft

Chan, C.L., Chow, A.Y., Ho, S.M., Tsui, Y.K., Tin, A.F., Koo, B.W., & Koo, E.W. (2005). The experience of Chinese bereaved persons: A preliminary study of meaning making and continuing bonds. *Death Studies*, 29(10), 923–947.

Daggett, L.M. (2005). Continued encounters: The experience of after-death communication. *Journal of Holistic Nursing*, 23, 191–207.

Datson, S.L., & Marwit, S.J. (1997). Personality constructs and perceived presence of deceased loved ones. *Death Studies*, 21, 131–146.

Field, N.P. (2008). Whether to relinquish or maintain a bond with the deceased. In M. S. Stroebe, R.O. Hansson, H. Schut, & W. Stroebe (Eds.), *Handbook of bereavement research and practice: Advances in theory and intervention*. Washington, DC: American Psychological Association, pp. 113–132.

Freud, S. (1917). Mourning and melancholia. In J. Strachey (Ed.), *The standard edition of the complete psychological works of Sigmund Freud*. London: Hogarth Press, Vol. XIV, pp. 252–268.

Hagman, G. (2001). Beyond decarthexis: Toward a new psychoanalytic understanding and treatment of mourning. In R.A. Neimeyer (Ed.), *Meaning reconstruction and the experience of loss*. Washington, DC: American Psychological Association, pp. 13–31.

Kamp, K.S., Steffen, E.M., Alderson-Day, B., Allen, P., Austad, A., Hayes, J., ..., Sabucedo, P. (2020). Sensory and quasi-sensory experiences of the deceased in bereavement: An interdisciplinary and integrative review. *Schizophrenia Bulletin*, *46*(6), 1367–1381. doi: https://doi.org/10.1093/schbul/sbaa113

Mikulincer, M., & Shaver, P.R. (2008). An attachment perspective on bereavement. In M.S. Stroebe, R.O. Hansson, H. Schut, & W. Stroebe (Eds.), *Handbook of bereavement research and practice: Advances in theory and intervention*. American Psychological Association. pp. 87–112. https://doi.org/10.1037/14498-005

Neimeyer, R.A. (2020). What's new in meaning reconstruction? Advancing grief theory and practice. *Grief Matters: The Australian Journal of Grief and Bereavement, 23*(1), 4–9.

Park, C.L., & Edmondson, D. (2011). *Religion as a quest for meaning.* Paper presented at the 4th Annual Herzlyia Symposium on Personality and Social Psychology: The Social Psychology of Meaning, Mortality, and Choice, Herzliya, Israel.

Parker, J.S. (2005). Extraordinary experiences of the bereaved and adaptive outcomes of grief. *Omega: Journal of Death and Dying, 51,* 257–258.

Sanger, M. (2009). When clients sense the presence of loved ones who have died. *Omega: Journal of Death & Dying, 59,* 69–89.

Steffen, E., & Coyle, A. (2011). Sense of presence experiences and meaning making in bereavement: A qualitative analysis. *Death Studies, 35,* 579–609.

Steffen, E., & Coyle, A. (2012). "Sense of presence" experiences in bereavement and their relationship to mental health: A critical examination of a continuing controversy. In C. Murray (Ed.), *Mental health and anomalous experience.* Hauppauge, NY: Nova Science Publishers, pp. 33–56.

Index

Note: Page numbers in **Bold** refer to tables; page numbers followed by 'n' refer to notes.

Printed in the United States
by Baker & Taylor Publisher Services